MW00885211

12 Months of Leadership Insights

A Compendium of Leadership Lessons from 40 Leaders

"The best leaders are the best note takers, best askers and the best learners."

Tom Peters

Be humble, Be teachable and Always keep learning

"Leaders are more powerful role models when they learn than when they teach."

Rosabeth Moss Kantor

Richard Dool, DMgt.

Contributions by:

Stephen Dool
Gregory Dool
Rachel Beardsley

Published by Richard Dool
ISBN: 9781706691570

Manufactured in the United States of America.

DEDICATION

This book is dedicated to the study of leadership. It is a rich, complex, dynamic and sometimes maddening endeavor. We are living in an unprecedented leadership laboratory due to remarkable access and reach driven by technology. We can witness great, good, average, poor and even toxic leaders in action and try to learn from them all.

We also can reach back in history and learn from leaders past. Even though there are contextual and situational differences, some leadership insights are timeless.

For current leaders, hopefully this book will offer you insights which you can deploy to extend your leadership brand, enhance your leadership practices or extend your leadership network. We hope you will reflect on the shared insights and use them productively.

For aspiring leaders, this can be a rich source of insights, some of which you can deploy to begin your leadership journey. Read them, internalize them and put them into action in a manner that is personalized and authentic.

For leadership scholars, I have tried to present the shared insights by honoring the works of various leadership authors and sources, while also offering insights to infuse leadership practice.

Richard Dool

HOW TO UTILIZE OUR BOOK

We intended this compendium of leadership insights as a resource that can be used over and over and with an array of intentions. We hope you find it a valuable asset in building your leadership brand or enhancing your leadership practices. We also hope you can use the collected insights to develop the next generation of leaders in your organizations.

You can certainly read this in the traditional front to back process. You may also consider:

- Starting with your birth month and read the insights of the leaders who share your month.
- Select leaders who interest you and read them individually.
- Scan the 'Key Takeaways' and dive deeper into the insights of the leaders that get your initial attention.
- Select leaders based on backgrounds. For example, the political leaders like Hamilton, Jefferson, Lincoln and Churchill. Or, current business leaders including Dyson, Gates or Ma.
- You can dive into diversity and select leaders like Martin Luther King, Golda Meir, Amy Duckworth, or Nelson Mandela.
- You can start with the Ten common themes and then go back and explore individual leaders based on themes that resonate with you.

We encourage you to use the book and the collected insights with the intention of deploying the lessons in your professional context. We hope you 'read it today, and use it tomorrow' to your leadership advantage.

TABLE OF CONTENTS

CONTEXT

The Speed of Now

"We live in a white water world"

Steven Covey

*"Turbulence is occurring at a blistering pace,
leaving many businesses unprepared and vulnerable
to the chaos it brings."*

Kotler & Caslione (2009)

We live in what Stephen Covey calls a "white water world, a world of interconnections, fast pacing, constant change and systemic impatience" (Covey Leadership Center, n.d.).

Leaders today face a macro-environment filled with an unprecedented level of active "stressors" (e.g. technological advancement, increased globalization, nomadic workforce, economic shifts, increased competition, increase in overall pace, increased diversity) (Hamel (1998), Bienhocker (1999), Voelpel, 2003). It is being routinely argued that the rate of change is increasing (Axtell, Wall, Stride & Pepper, 2012). Previous generations of leaders could at least count on a reasonably stable world, where change unfolded at a much slower pace. These days, the past is increasingly less predictive, the future is almost unimaginable, and the present seems to exists for about a nano-second. (Green, 2011).

Kotler & Casilone, in "Chaotics" (2009) argued for the need to manage differently in what Alan Greenspan has referred to as the "Age of

Turbulence." They noted; "Change is new status quo, leaving managers without firm ground from which to gaze at the onrushing future as markets, technologies, governments, consumers and products undergo constant change with blinding rapidity" (p. 1). The overall pace of this environment creates a constant feeling of being rushed and having to be "on" for longer periods. Many of the challenges organizational leaders face today are the same as in past decades, but the pace and complexity of changes are of a magnitude never before experienced (Beckard & Pritchard, 1992).

This era has its own acronym..."VUCA" (volatile, uncertain, complex and ambiguous) world. The acronym was coined by the U.S. Army in the 1990s to describe the post-Cold War world: volatile, uncertain, complex and ambiguous. The idea of VUCA has since been embraced by leaders in all sectors of society to describe the nature of the world in which they operate: the accelerating rate of change (volatility), the lack of predictability (uncertainty), the interconnectedness, of cause-and-effect forces (complexity) and the strong potential for misreads (ambiguity) (Gruwez, 2017).

"Disruption is as great as we have ever seen it," says Joe DePinto, CEO of 7-Eleven. "We are seeing all aspects of VUCA." "There is no question that we are in a VUCA environment," says Bob Leduc, president of Pratt & Whitney, the $15.1 billion aircraft systems manufacturer. "When you think about our business, we've got a very complicated landscape. We have technology moving; we have commercial and military customers redefining what their business models are and what they value now versus what they previously did. So basically, the whole landscape is moving on us in many different directions. Because of that, we actually need to have an organization that can move quickly." (Forsythe, Kuhla & Rice, 2018).

Today's leaders have to manage a highly diverse and multi-generational workforce with differing values, interests, and needs that can often conflict. Not too long ago, leaders basically had to figure out what to do and then tell people what, when, where, and how to do it.

Today's managers and leaders face a whole new set of expectations in the way they motivate the people they work with or who follow them. People not only don't want to be managed, in most cases, they simply won't be managed. Today's employees want to be led. They want to participate and engage in every aspect of their job. Creating a two-way relationship is critical (Green, 2011). There is a war for talent and the leader who can forge meaningful engagement with members of his/her staff will have an advantage. Given the 'nomadic' nature of the workforce and the demand for talent, leaders who can attract, recruit, development and retain talent longer will have a competitive advantage.

From a customer perspective, today's leaders face great expectations and less certainty than ever. "Good enough" doesn't even come close anymore. Customers have unprecedented reach and access, more choices, less tolerance, more self-interest, and a dramatically different definition of satisfaction and loyalty.

We are in the era of "now." We are surrounded by "instant" access and response. Examples abound from texting, self-service checkouts, online bill paying and debit systems. Time is a prized asset and is clearly worth more to an array of both internal and external stakeholders (Green, 2011). There is an impatience in both management and its various stakeholders and a constant demand for results. This has created a 24x7 mindset, blurring professional and personal time in a myriad of ways.

Because of this systemic impatience leaders are also under intense scrutiny from a variety of stakeholders including: customers, suppliers, employees, regulators, community activists and governance officials. Lombardi once dubbed this "The Spotlight Era" (1996). It is now even more so with the rise of social media. Leaders are expected to deliver results at the speed of now. As an example, according to a recent Equilar study, the median tenure for CEOs at S&P 500 companies was 5.0 years at the end of 2017, this is down a full year since 2013 (Harvard, 2018).

Leader as Learner

"Leaders should be visible, accessible and approachable and never stop learning"

Richard Branson

"I am still learning."

Michelangelo at age 87

This 'speed of now' environment has also created the demand that leaders be able to continuously adjust. Mikkelsen & Jarche (2015) noted:

> Reinvention and relevance in the 21st century instead draw on our ability to adjust our way of thinking, learning, doing and being. Leaders must get comfortable with living in a state of continually *becoming*, a perpetual beta mode. Leaders that stay on top of society's changes do so by being receptive and able to learn. In a time where the half-life of any skill is about five years, leaders bear a responsibility to renew their perspective in order to secure the relevance of their organizations.

They added: "Sustainable competitive advantage depends on having people that know how to build relationships, seek information, make sense of observations and share ideas through an intelligent use of new technologies."

Green (2011) offers these leadership learning skill sets necessary for today's "guide and inspire" environment:

Continual learning and unlearning

There are almost no jobs left that will remain the same over time, which means that the demands of leaders are continually evolving. The great ones are constantly learning and developing themselves. They're internally driven to constantly get better, knowing full well that they will not, and should not, be perfect.

Broadening their perspectives, seek continuous feedback

Today's leaders need to be highly observant and flexible. They need to consider multiple perspectives to create general guidelines that help to make sense of what's going on around them. They're open to receiving information from conflicting sources, and can distill complexity. The seek out what they need to hear versus what they want to hear. They create both formal and informal networks of sources. Specific, direct, and candid with others, today's leaders expose their agendas and use good listening skills to really hear what others have to say, rather than simply planning their next response.

Learn don't blame

Today's leaders should consider current issues from the perspective of making things better versus blaming or worrying. Their thinking balances the ability to visualize what might or could be with an effective day-to-day approach to getting the right things done. They must seamlessly move between the strategic and operational, effective in both perspectives, continuously probing for new knowledge.

Developing self-awareness

Great leadership comes from within. Today's leaders constantly strive to become more aware of their own intentions as well as their impact on others. They also have the ability to admit mistakes and learn from them. They know that a lot of what got them to their role won't carry them to continuing success.

Thinking strategically and globally

When dealing with today's issues, leaders need to operate from a broad, long-term perspective balanced with the intense pressures of producing short-term results. They need to understand and appreciate the current state as well as see possibilities. Leaders need to seek out insights, perspectives and experiences from an ever shifting array of stakeholders. They need to constantly seek out new knowledge. They need to consider whole new ways of communicating and connecting. As our world becomes increasingly smaller, leaders need to appreciate, learn from and leverage diversity. They also need to become more innovative and proactive, anticipating problems and opportunities as well as entirely new markets and products. This requires a constant focus on seeking information, learning from an array of sources, connecting seemingly unconnected dots and "seeing" through the eyes of others.

This demands that leaders ask, listen, learn, adapt and act.

INTRODUCTION

Welcome to ***12 Months of Leadership Insights,*** our compendium of the leadership insights of 40 leaders. We selected three leaders for each month based on their birth month and added in four *bonus* leaders. Our selected leaders are from an array of backgrounds, positions and eras. We went as far back as the United States Revolution with Hamilton and Jefferson to current leaders like Bezos, Ma, and Nooyi. We have political figures like Lincoln and Churchill, civil rights leaders like Martin Luther King, Jr and Cesar Chávez, business icons including Branson, Welch, and Gates, as well as leaders from other cultures like Toyoda, Mandela, Gandhi, Wiesel and Meir. We also added in authors and inventors to include more holistic insights on leadership.

We added in four *Bonus* leaders as well to add more depth and diversity to the shared leadership insights. These are more recent or current leaders (*Blakely, Duckworth, Rometty and Rice*).

Each leader is presented with a picture, short biography, selected quotation and some of their leadership insights, either in their own words or those of researchers.

We hope this eclectic array of selected leaders offers a wide and engaging perspective on the practice of leadership and some of the underlying principles. We hope leaders today can gain from the insights of our selected leaders to enhance their effectiveness in this 21st century chaotic environment (the speed of now).

Our Selected Leaders

January Leaders:	Alexander Hamilton, Martin Luther King, Jr. and Jeff Bezos
February Leaders:	Abraham Lincoln, Thomas Edison and Sakichi Toyoda *Bonus addition: Sara Blakely*
March Leaders:	Albert Einstein, Dr. Seuss and Cesar Chávez *Bonus addition: Tammy Duckworth*
April Leaders:	Thomas Jefferson, Colin Powell and Maya Angelou
May Leaders:	Florence Nightingale, Golda Meir and James Dyson
June Leaders:	Vince Lombardi, Katharine Graham and Lewis B. Puller
July Leaders:	Nelson Mandela, John Glenn and Richard Branson *Bonus addition: Ginni Rometty*
August Leaders:	Mother Teresa, Warren Buffett and Fred Smith
September Leaders:	Jack Ma, Elie Wiesel and Malcolm Gladwell
October Leaders:	Theodore Roosevelt, Bill Gates, and Indra Nooyi
November Leaders:	Winston Churchill, Jack Welch and Indira Gandhi. *Bonus addition: Condoleezza Rice*
December Leaders:	Grace Hopper, Alex Ferguson and Walt Disney

JANUARY LEADERS

For January, we will learn from Alexander Hamilton, Martin Luther King, Jr. and Jeff Bezos.

Alexander Hamilton

(ca. January 11, 1755 – July 12, 1804)

"Those who stand for nothing fall for everything."

A list of Alexander Hamilton's professional accomplishments, even catalogued free of context, would be enough to warrant him a place in the ranks of America's most influential leaders. He is counted among the country's Founding Fathers, was a delegate to the 1787 Constitutional Convention, and became the first secretary of the US Treasury. He is credited with founding both the country's banking system and the Coast Guard, along with the more dubious distinction of establishing *The New York Post.* He was a lawyer and an author of the Federalist Papers (writing 51 of 85 essays) and was instrumental in establishing trade relations with Britain, no small feat in the post-Revolutionary War haze. He was also a Senior Officer in the US Army and an assemblyman in the New York State Legislature.

Although never elected President himself, Hamilton and his political maneuvering are inextricably linked to the heads of state who served during his lifetime. He was an aide-de-camp to George Washington during the Revolutionary War, often tasked with handling the then-General's written correspondence. He resigned before the war ended, but the relationship between both men would outlast the conflict when Hamilton took on his leadership role at the Treasury. During his presidency, John Adams recognized Hamilton's influence (despite a history of distrust) and appointed him a general during the run-up to a war with France in 1798 that was eventually avoided through peaceful negotiations. And his support for Thomas Jefferson during his Presidential campaign was impactful enough to play out as a significant factor in the extended rivalry between Hamilton and Aaron Burr, who would eventually kill Hamilton in a fateful and infamous duel in 1804.

But all of these achievements do little to illuminate how Hamilton's life informed his leadership abilities, beyond suggesting—as present-day biographers and historians have come to do—that he was often motivated by his own unrelenting, and occasionally blind, ambition. That certainly is a vital component toward understanding Alexander Hamilton the man, and, by extension, the leader.

Hamilton was born under relatively bleak circumstances on Nevis, an island in the West Indies. (His exact birthdate is the subject of some dispute, although it is commonly accepted to be January 11, 1755.) His parents never married, a source of shame at the time, and he took the last name of a man with whom his mother was only briefly involved. His education as a child was limited, but it's said that he took it upon himself to consume any available books voraciously. The story commonly goes that he was able to use his reading and writing skills as a ticket out of the Caribbean and to New York, where he would live out his adult life.

Alexander Hamilton—the definitive biography by Ron Chernow (2005) that also served as the inspiration for the wildly successful Broadway musical about his life—does much work to root Hamilton's rise in his implacable desire to make a name for himself despite his less-than-privileged upbringing. He married Elizabeth Schuyler, a wealthy New Yorker with substantially more social capital than he possessed. Throughout his life and various professional roles, Hamilton continued to rely on his prodigious writing skills honed during his youth. It's how he outlined his political ideology, but also how he eviscerated opponents who posed a threat to the legacy he was attempting to build for himself.

Certain pointed lines from his extensive body of written work endure. "A nation which can prefer disgrace to danger is prepared for a master, and deserves one," he wrote in a 1787 letter to T*he Daily Advertiser*, perhaps his most famous line of criticism. A gift for present day historians and those looking to glean more about this complicated man's life, the substantial written record Hamilton created often incited a small army of influential enemies while he was alive, setting in motion a lifelong, back-and-forth volley of insults on several different fronts.

John Adams, according to Hamilton, was an inept leader, possessing "a vanity without bounds, and a jealousy capable of discoloring every object." For his part, Adams referred to Hamilton as a "bastard brat of a Scottish peddler," and suggested, in much more colorful terms, that his relentless ambition comes from an overactive libido. (That remark, for what it's worth, may not have been entirely unfounded, as an extramarital affair with Maria Reynolds, a married 23 year-old woman, led to a blackmail scheme and the first major American political sex scandal on record.)

But perhaps no rivalry illustrates Hamilton's ambition as clearly as his intensely contentious relationship with Aaron Burr. By the time Burr challenged Hamilton to the duel that would end Hamilton's life on July 11, 1804, the two had spent years at one another's throats. Beginning when Hamilton's father-in-law, Philip Schuyler, lost a state senate election to Burr in 1791, Hamilton referred to Burr, publicly and privately, as corrupt, dangerous, and untrustworthy. He actively campaigned against his Vice Presidential bid in 1800 and his New York gubernatorial attempt in 1804. Burr lost both elections (although he would later become Vice President, serving under Jefferson at the time of the duel). Hamilton and Burr's dislike for one another only grew.

Hamilton issued a written statement that he was opposed to the practice of dueling, but he accepted Burr's challenge nevertheless to defend his own honor and clear the way for future political aspirations. Instead, he was fatally shot and died the following day. Hamilton left behind a financial debt, saddling Elizabeth with the burden of settling it while she simultaneously fought for the place of honor in the historical record she felt Hamilton deserved in the face of opponents who continued to discredit him for years after his death.

Leadership Insights and Hamilton

We begin with an icon of American history in Alexander Hamilton. His influence on U.S. history and the country's political system is still felt today. He was a visionary leader who also could navigate entirely new terrain at the birth of America in deep detail. He was a complex leader, not always exemplary, but ahead of his time to a large degree. He offers several interesting insights on leadership, especially considered in the context of his time.

Winder (2005) offered *"Five Major Characteristics of Leadership"* largely drawn from the writings and practices of Hamilton.

1. ***Creativity is paramount for a successful organization.***

   During the Revolutionary War and the subsequent development of the Constitution, creative minds left indelible impacts on our society. Thomas Jefferson (author of the Declaration of Independence), James Madison (principle author of the Constitution), Benjamin Franklin, and Alexander Hamilton are partly responsible for the development of principles that helped define this nation at a time when there were no templates for the creation of a 'modern' democracy.

   Insights for Leaders. An organization without ideas cannot move forward. Ideas are the stuff that makes us both what we are and what we will be. In any organization, it is an absolute necessity to have a core group of creative thinkers. Leaders must learn how to harness and direct creativity. This can be an incredible challenge. Creative persons are often referred to as "high maintenance" people because they are usually not only innovative and often progressive, but they also possess tremendous passion for their ideas and ideals. One of the major challenges of Washington's first administration was dealing with the constant quarrels between two of the great creative intellects of the day—Hamilton and Jefferson.

2. ***Humility is an important characteristic among leaders.***

Hamilton's Achilles' heel was his pride, which prevented him from acknowledging his own fallibility. Compromise was extremely difficult for him to accept. In the early years of their time spent working together, Washington was able to check Hamilton's hubris and helped him avoid some tactical mistakes. Without Washington's mentoring, Hamilton repeatedly let his pride—and in some cases his arrogance—paint him into dangerous corners. Ultimately, it was this lack of humility that led to his death in a duel at the hands of the equally prideful Aaron Burr.

Insights for Leaders. Pride and vanity are not prerequisites for leadership. Even the most brilliant leaders can benefit from seriously considering and, when appropriate, implementing the views of others. We all find ourselves in situations where we must take ownership of ideas, but we must also accept the fact that ideas created without critical review are often flawed. If our pride will not permit us to accept modification, we will likely find ourselves on a slippery slope toward failure.

3. ***Perseverance and patience are critical.***

After resigning as Secretary of the Treasury, Hamilton was given a commission and became the de facto commander of the army. He recognized the need for well-trained officers and drew up detailed plans for a military academy at West Point. But, there was strong sentiment against the creation of a large standing army at the time.

His peers were suspicious of Hamilton's motives in pressing for a strong defensive force instead of relying on an alliance of state militias. As a result, this great idea was not realized during Hamilton's tenure. Interestingly, it was Hamilton's frequent adversary, Thomas Jefferson, who eventually saw the merit in the plan and constructed the academy during his Presidency.

Insights for Leaders: Though it is important to exhibit humility, it can be equally important not to give up on a good idea. Transformative ideas are often overlooked simply because timing was wrong.

4. The Impact of Anger on Logic

There were times during Hamilton's career when anger generated by political battles led to questionable decision-making. When angered, he tended to make some of his poorest decisions. For example, he supported the Alien and Sedition Acts, which greatly curtailed individual liberties and resulted in imprisonment of those who spoke out against persons of authority—including journalists who criticized Hamilton's policies (often lobbing personal insults while doing so) and exposed his extramarital affair. In another instance, Hamilton's inability to resolve a conflict with fellow Federalist John Adams during Adams' term as President resulted in Hamilton supporting another presidential candidate. This split the Federalist vote and ultimately resulted in the election of the Republican candidate, Thomas Jefferson. Hamilton's behind the scenes efforts had, in effect, mortally wounded his own party.

Insights for Leaders. Anger and vindictive behavior are destructive if left unchecked. Effective leaders should know to never respond out of anger because their actions are more likely to be flawed, if not entirely wrong. Unfortunately, this is a far too common occurrence among persons in leadership roles.

Leaders should strive to possess cool heads in a tempest; angry outbursts rarely lead to a desirable end.

5. ***Ethics are important.***

Misbehavior among politicians is nothing new in the United States, or any other country, for that matter. It was actually very common among the Founding Fathers to conduct themselves in ways that history would rather gloss over. Hamilton had an affair with a married woman, and her husband later blackmailed Hamilton. Eventually, after Hamilton's indiscretions were made public, he was forced to acknowledge his activities. Although he may have mitigated some negative effects by admitting his affair, it was used by his political enemies repeatedly until his death.

Insights for Leaders. Leaders are often susceptible to the belief that power gives them the right to misbehave. In truth, persons in leadership roles are under constant scrutiny from others. Leaders set the ethical standard for their organization. Far too often we see otherwise great people become victims of their own undoing. Leaders must be aware of their actions in both their professional and personal lives and how they affect not only themselves, but the people who work with and for them. Especially today with the dramatically increased access the general public has to intimate details of everyone's lives via social media, 'private moments' for leaders are fewer and further in between; in some instances, it is as though they are always on stage.

Leidner (2017) offers his "Seven Steps to Revolutionary Leadership" largely drawn from the leadership principles and practices displayed by Hamilton. Many of these practices are as effective in modern day as they were in the time of the American Revolution. Some, in fact, are remarkable given often dramatically different culture and values of the times (e.g. respecting employees and the notion of mentoring).

- ***Prepare Yourself:*** Recognize your challenges, set personal goals, and never give up.
- ***Exemplify Moral Integrity:*** Be honest with your followers, admit your own weaknesses, and develop an environment of trust.
- ***Go Beyond Self-Interest:*** Define what is important, develop a plan for change, and demonstrate personal commitment.
- ***Establish Clear Goals:*** Define a challenging team goal, show everyone how to contribute, and provide meaningful guidance.
- ***Respect Your People:*** Treat them as individuals, intellectually challenge them, and honor their beliefs.
- ***Convey an Inspiring Vision:*** See the future, describe your vision, and turn followers into leaders.
- ***Be A Mentor*:** Be humble, keep learning, and share knowledge

"People sometimes attribute my success to my genius; all the genius I know anything about is hard work."

Key Takeaways

- Leaders invest in their people – seek their input, mentor and challenge them.
- Leaders need to foster ideas, prize creativity, and be open to others' inputs.
- Leaders need both humility and patience.
- Leaders must manage their emotions and stay in control.
- Leaders must be ethical and moral integrity exemplars and earn respect and trust.
- Leaders should be lifelong learners.

Martin Luther King, Jr.

(January 15, 1929 – April 4, 1968)

"The time is always right to do what is right."

Biography

By definition, the behavior of our heroes should be heroic, or at least heroic more often than it is not. But, there is no mandate that our heroes are also leaders, or vice versa. Leaders can be corrupt or selfish; heroes can act alone. Dr. Martin Luther King, Jr.—Baptist minister, icon of the American Civil Rights movement, champion of nonviolent resistance, and one of the most influential voices of the 20th century—is one of the rare figures whose leadership and heroism are inextricably linked.

Even as modern biographers, further removed from King's lifetime, concede to indiscretions in his private life—namely, reports that King cheated on his wife throughout their marriage—the portrait that endures is still one of a man who knowingly and willingly put his own life at risk for the greater good of the country and inspired others to do the same.

The persistently high stakes of King's work confronting systemic racism and widespread inequality in 1950s and '60s America are underscored by a list of facts that are astounding when considered separately, and even more jarring when read in succession: Over the course of his adult life, King was arrested 29 times, reportedly received hundreds of death threats, was stabbed in an attempted assassination in 1958, and had guns fired at his home, which was also bombed; later, an additional 12 sticks of unexploded dynamite uncovered by police on his front porch. All the while, King was surveilled, threatened or sabotaged by the FBI, the NSA, the CIA, select local police departments, and various government-appointed and publicly elected officials.

Despite the barrage of threats, King continued to make public appearances up until his assassination on April 4, 1968, a testament to his commitment to his cause and a symbol of courage for the legions of followers he amassed throughout his ascent.

King could have easily taken a less perilous path in his life. Had he elected to do so, he likely could have had a fruitful career in academia and could have feasibly taken a more conventional trajectory for a Baptist minister. A star pupil in his native Atlanta, he enrolled at Morehouse College when he was just 15 years old, eventually completing a Bachelor's degree in sociology before entering Pennsylvania's Crozer Theological Seminary and becoming a licensed preacher at age 19. He was awarded a PhD in systematic theology from Boston University in 1955.

That same year, though, he also embarked upon what was at the time his most high-profile social justice undertaking when he became the official spokesperson for the Montgomery Bus Boycott in Alabama. The Montgomery Boycott was a response to the segregation of city buses, fueled by similar protests across the South and the arrest of Rosa Parks. At the time, King was already working at the city's Dexter Avenue Baptist Church and serving on the executive committee of the National Association for the Advancement of Colored People (NAACP). But his work with the bus boycott—which lasted 381 days and culminated in a Supreme Court ruling in November 1956 that segregation on public transportation was unconstitutional—transformed King from an influential local leader to a nationally prominent figure.

Vitally, the boycott was proof positive that King could effectively call his followers to action. The Supreme Court ruling escalated the threat of violence against King, those who stood alongside him, and the black community at large. Gunmen shot at Montgomery buses and at King's home, African American bus riders were physically attacked, and, the following January, five black churches were bombed by the KKK, as was the house of a prominent white reverend who had publicly aligned himself with King. It was clear that King's work was just beginning, and that his supporters and followers would need to accept that their safety could be threatened as King's.

King's ascent within the Civil Rights Movement was swift. In 1957, he became president of the Southern Christian Leadership Conference (SCLC), which aimed to provide structure and leadership to the cause. King applied the nonviolent practices of Mahatma Gandhi to his own Christian ideals as a guiding belief system for his work. These principles were articulated in his *Letter from a Birmingham Jail,* a philosophical manifesto written in 1963 during King's campaign to support the integration efforts of activists in the Alabama city. The letter includes King's famous assertion that "injustice anywhere is a threat to justice everywhere."

King's "I Have a Dream" speech, his most well-known and galvanizing public action, also took place in 1963. Delivered from the steps of the Lincoln Memorial to over 250,000 protestors who marched on the US capital in support of Civil Rights, the speech is a masterclass in public discourse, underlining King's personal motivations and amplifying the ways in which they are universal. In doing so, King renewed and reinvigorated his supporters to continue fighting against persistent odds. The following year, at age 35, King became the youngest-ever recipient of the Nobel Peace Prize.

The Civil Rights Movement received two major victories in the period after the March on Washington and King's Nobel Prize win, when Congress passed the Civil Rights Act to end legal segregation in 1964 and the Voting Rights Act in 1965, which aimed to eliminate barriers that made it difficult or impossible for African Americans to participate in local and state elections. The latter is also closely connected to the voting rights march in Selma, Alabama led by King and other activists, during which they were assaulted by state troopers.

In the last years of his life, King was an outspoken critic of the Vietnam War, in line with his principles of peace. He also advocated for economic justice with the Poor People's Campaign, an ambitious effort to challenge, among other things, the systemic racism with which poverty is inherently intertwined. At the time of his assassination on April 4, 1968, King was in Memphis, Tennessee, to march in solidarity with striking sanitation workers.

After his death, King's wife, Coretta Scott King, herself an activist and intellectual, established the Martin Luther King, Jr. Center for Nonviolent Social Change to continue his work. King remains the only non-President with a national holiday in the United States, and only one of four non-Presidents with a memorial in the vicinity of the National Mall in Washington, DC.

Leadership Insights and King

Dr. King is one of the pivotal leaders in American history and a giant in the Civil Rights movement. He was a tireless and passionate advocate. In the span of 11 years starting in 1957, he spoke over 2,500 times at public events and traveled over six million miles. He was also a prolific writer, publishing articles and five books to spread his messages further. Dr. King was a masterful organizational leader, co-founding and leading the Southern Christian Leadership Conference. He also was co-pastor with his father of the Ebenezer Baptist Church.

We can gain insights into effective leadership practices by both his example and his words.

Smith (2016) shared these lessons on leadership from Dr. King:

1. ***See the bigger picture.***

   One trait that made Dr. King unique was his ability to see beyond the present situation. He had a vision and dream that was so much larger than the time in which he lived. Think about what your dream speech would be, and remain committed to your vision.

2. ***Live your beliefs.***

   Dr. King's beliefs drove his actions every day. Not everyone will fight for a national cause like he did, but you can rise to the occasion no matter the size of your initiative.

3. ***Be disruptive.***

   Dr. King's cause was fueled by his refusal to accept the status quo. By challenging yourself to step outside your comfort zone, you create opportunities for evolution and innovation.

4. ***Don't underestimate your employees.***

   Dr. King once said, "Never to underestimate anyone below you, that they have wisdom, life experience, and are introspective." You never know what qualities and experiences your employees can bring to the table.

5. ***Form strong alliances.***

   Just as Dr. King aligned himself with community leaders and national politicians, establishing a network of mutually beneficial relationships is critical to success.

6. ***Learn, then acclimate.***

   Dr. King learned first-hand that no plan survives without making adjustments. Use any obstacles that may arise as opportunities for experimentation and growth.

7. ***Create passionate supporters.***

   Dr. King gained the support of many by sharing his ideas for a brighter future. Painting your vision for others to clearly see and understand helps ensure longevity of the cause.

Patrick Lynch (n.d.) compiled eight leadership lessons from Dr. King's famous "I Have a Dream" 1963 speech:

1. ***Great leaders do not sugar coat reality.***

   Martin Luther King Jr. talked directly about the conflict and brutal reality facing the nation so that he could set the stage for his vision for overcoming these problems together.

2. ***Great leaders engage the heart.***

   While logic may compel the mind, stories and metaphors move the heart. This is the difference between offering information and inspiration. Dr. King chose not to make a fact-based argument and instead decided to make a direct appeal to the hearts of the world. In so doing, he made history.

3. ***Great leaders refuse to accept the status quo.***

   Dr. King refused to accept what was currently acceptable and instead, outlined a bold vision on what needed to be changed, why it needed to be changed, and how it would be changed.

4. ***Great leaders create a sense of urgency.***

   Leaders are impatient—in a good way. They refuse to sit by as change takes its natural course. They have a sense of urgency and communicate it. Dr. King reminded America of the "fierce urgency of now."

5. ***Great leaders call people to act in accordance with their highest values.***

   Dr. King took the higher ground of nonviolent resistance so that his movement would have moral authority in its quest for change.

Like Ghandi and Nelson Mandela, Dr. King believed that his movement could achieve its objectives by taking a higher standard.

6. ***Great leaders refuse to settle.***

   Great leaders know when to be stubborn and when it is better to compromise. Dr. King made a number of compromises on points of lesser impact, but was relentless when it came to achieving his vision.

7. ***Great leaders acknowledge the sacrifice of their followers.***

   Leaders notice the effort their people have expended. Dr. King did not take credit for the accomplishments of his movement. He saw it as a collective effort. From this, he received the loyal engagement of his followers.

8. ***Great leaders paint a vivid picture of a better tomorrow.***

   Leaders can never grow weary of articulating their vision. They must be clear and concrete. They need to help their followers see what they see.

An essay on Bartleby.com (n.d.) captured Dr. King's leadership thusly:

> Dr. Martin Luther King was a great leader, a person with no fear of the outcome. He became an effective leader of the civil rights movement because of his desire and willpower. He instilled trust and confidence in people. He was an effective communicator by helping others understand what he was trying to achieve. He was trustworthy and able to communicate a vision. He sought responsibilities and took responsibilities for his actions. He guided the people who followed him to new heights, and when things went wrong, Dr. King didn't blame others, instead he took the lead.

PeopleTek (2017) noted: "Dr. King influenced so many without being arrogant, without being a bully, without looking down and speaking poorly of others, and without being divisive."

"Our lives begin to end the day we become silent about things that matter."

Key Takeaways

- Leaders need to have courage of conviction and an enduring set of core beliefs and values.
- Leaders must be willing to confront reality and the status quo. They know that complacency is a cancer in an organization. They are willing to be a disruptive force.
- Leaders must be willing to see into the future and the bigger picture. They create a of a better future.
- Leaders must learn and acclimate, adapting as needed.

Jeffrey Preston Bezos

January 12, 1964 –

"I knew that if I failed I wouldn't regret that, but I knew the one thing I might regret is not trying."

Biography

In June of 2018, Amazon CEO Jeff Bezos became the richest man in modern history when his net worth climbed past US$150B. For context, as Bloomberg news service pointed out at the time, that was $55B richer than the famously wealthy Microsoft founder Bill Gates. It's also roughly equivalent to the 2017 GDP of Hungary, greater than the annual tax revenue collected by 44 of the 50 American states, and more than the reported value of Buckingham Palace, the Empire State Building, the Eiffel Tower, the Roman Colosseum, and the Sydney Opera House combined.

As mind-blowing comparisons like those spread across business and mainstream media alike—one website noted Bezos could single-handedly fund NASA for 7.8 years—all eyes were once again on the tech tycoon, as pundits pontificated about what surpassing this milestone meant for one of the world's preeminent business leaders. It was not an unfamiliar place for Bezos, who has long been subject to the type of scrutiny that befalls CEOs of wildly successful, publicly-traded, multinational companies—particularly those executives who share Bezos' flair for innovation and unorthodox decision making.

While some have posited that Bezos' tumultuous childhood birthed in him an unwavering drive to succeed—he was born in Albuquerque in 1964 to a teenage mother who divorced his biological father when Bezos was just over a year old—his early professional development followed a fairly conventional path for burgeoning business talent. After moving to Miami, Bezos graduated as valedictorian of his high school class and made his way to Princeton University, where he earned degrees in computer science and electrical engineering in 1986. His first job was with a telecom startup, but within a few years, he switched course, eventually landing at a New York hedge fund, where he was named senior vice president at just 30 years old.

It was at that time that Bezos first conceived of the idea of launching an online bookstore. As he recounted in a commencement address at Princeton in 2010, "I came across the fact that Web usage was growing at 2,300 percent per year. I'd never seen or heard of anything that grew that fast, and the idea of building an online bookstore with millions of titles—something that simply couldn't exist in the physical world—was very exciting to me."[3]

Despite the inherent risks involved with leaving a successful career for one with unknown rewards (if any), Bezos founded Amazon in 1994. After an expansion of the site's inventory to include music and videos, Bezos harnessed a wave of enthusiasm for online shopping to bring a whole host of products into Amazon's offering. A consumer behemoth was born, and Bezos' place as an industry leader was solidified.

Hand-in-hand with his oft-repeated mantra of leading his business strategy with consideration for consumer needs, Bezos emphasizes a results-driven management style that has come under fire as Amazon continued to grow. After a 2015 *New York Times* article painted Amazon corporate culture as unrelenting in its demands of its employees[4]—a claim backed by other accounts, including a 2013 book by journalist Brad Stone that notoriously received a 922-word negative review on Amazon from Bezos' then-wife, Mackenzie—Bezos sent an internal memo to all Amazon employees. In it, he encouraged any employee who recognized the behavior described in the *Times* piece to email him directly, and noted that the company should have a zero tolerance policy for a lack of empathy for its employees.

Such controversies have not stopped Bezos or Amazon from flourishing. He was named one *Time Magazine*'s Most Influential People in the World in 2018, and his interest in space exploration, primarily through his startup Blue Origin, has garnered him recognition from the Buzz Aldrin Space Exploration Awards and entry into the National Academy of Engineering. Amazon has also expanded into brick and mortar spaces, and Amazon Studios, the entertainment arm of the company, has built a global content development team to create original streaming television series and movies to rival the output of other tech giants like Netflix.

Bezos immense personal fortune remains a subject of both reproach and titillation. After he was named the richest man in modern history, Amazon employees in Europe went on strike to highlight the disparity between Bezos' net worth and their own compensation. Within months, a video game called "You Are Jeff Bezos" debuted online that invited players to spend all $150B of his cash; one critic from the site Motherboard, in writing about the game, described having that much cash as "unfathomable" and "grotesque."

Leadership Insights and Bezos

Bezos is known as a somewhat unconventional leader. IFP (2017) noted: "He is something of an unconventional leader, and has broken away from many of the traditional formats for developing a business." He has long bucked the trend to focus on the short-term and drive quick results to satisfy Wall Street. He, instead, maintained fidelity to his vision and took the long view despite the short-term pressures.

He has shown that he has the willingness and courage to go first and alone. He has a legendary work ethic and drive, using an aversion to complacency—which he described as the "kiss of death" (Umoh, 2018)—as a motivator. He believes the intersection of hard work, innovation, customer focus, and organizational culture is where sustained success lives.

IFP (2017) captured some key lessons from Bezos:

1. ***Ignore the peer pressure.***

   As Bezos once said, "*We are stubborn on vision. We are flexible on details." (Masnick, 2011).* The Amazon boss was confident about his approach to online retail and kept his eye on the prize. He was uncompromising, even though nearly everyone around him doubted his actions.

   In order to succeed, you need to have this same level of confidence in your own business model. Of course, you can change the details of how you're going to reach your overall goal, but it's important that you remain determined about the overall vision for your company.

2. ***Create a "culture of metrics."***

   In a world where defining workplace culture is crucial for many businesses, Bezos bucks the trend. Instead of employee happiness coming first, data does. He has described his company culture as "friendly, but intense" but "if push came to shove, it would be intense."

   What does the data say? This is the key influencer behind all the decisions made at Amazon. Whether it's a new website layout or the launch of a new product, if the data doesn't back it up then it will be swiftly changed.

3. ***Work to charge customers less.***

   "There are two kinds of companies: those that try to charge more and those that work to charge less. We will be the second," Bezos says (Anders, 2012). Most retailers talk about reducing costs so they can charge

customers less, but few do it with the same vigor as Amazon. Frugality is one of the online retailer's official values, meaning they reduce internal expenses as much as possible. This has helped them increase their stock price and reduce the costs for consumers.

John (2013) adds another learning that Bezos champions:

4. ***Hyper-focus on your customers.***

   Very few businesses actually adhere to the adage "the customer is always right." At Amazon, Bezos takes it to heart, believing that the customer is the essential key to growing the business. Amazon puts a lot of stock in its customer feedback, marking the success of website features, products, and even packaging. In fact, Bezos believes that when growing a business, leaders should start with the customer and work their way backward—the customers' needs and concerns should be addressed as a starting point to expand or grow a business. Don't just react to feedback; change to embrace it.

   For example, if customers' feedback indicates that they are using mobile devices to access the website, consider making it mobile-friendly. Or create an app to help customers access the business from their phones and tablets. Customer behavior offers clues to which direction the business should take in order to continue to grow.

Gregersen (2015) highlighted another skill that Bezos displays which has led to many innovations at Amazon—the willingness to experiment.

> In our research interviews for *The Innovator's DNA*, we asked Bezos about the crucial role experimentation plays at Amazon. "Experiments are key to innovation because they rarely turn out as you expect and you learn so much," he told us. "We've tried to reduce the cost of doing experiments so that we can do more of them. If you can increase the number of experiments you try

> from a hundred to a thousand, you dramatically increase the number of innovations you produce."
>
> Innovators like Bezos see the world as a laboratory. They continually seek to answer those "what-if" questions as they search for new solutions. Our research of other high-impact leaders shows that experimentation is the discovery skill that most commonly differentiates innovators from non-innovators. Becoming a master experimenter requires consciously approaching work and life with a hypothesis-testing mind-set.

John (2013) also noted Bezos' focus on the need to "experiment constantly:"

> For any company, experimentation breeds innovation, and it sets a stale business apart from an obvious leader in the industry. Bezos encourages Amazon employees to experiment constantly, and tests promising ideas with the knowledge that they might fail.

Bariso (2017) highlighted another Bezos lesson–the notion of commitment. In his letter to Amazon shareholders, Bezos refers to the company's timeline as Day 1, allowing Amazon to continually move forward. He sees Day 2 as stasis. Followed by irrelevance. Followed by excruciating, painful decline. Followed by death. And *that* is why it is *always* Day 1. Bezos strongly recommends using the following phrase to do good work: Disagree and commit.

Bezos explains that (Barizo, 2017):

> To disagree and commit doesn't mean 'thinking your team is wrong and missing the point,' which will prevent you from offering true support. Rather, Bezos writes, it's a genuine disagreement of opinion, a candid expression of my view, a chance for the team to weigh my view, and a *quick, sincere commitment* to go their way.

> This phrase will save a lot of time. If you have conviction on a particular direction even though there's no consensus, it's helpful to say, *Look, I know we disagree on this but will you gamble with me on it? Disagree and commit?* By the time you're at this point, no one can know the answer for sure, and you'll probably get a quick yes.

John (2013) captured two other lessons that Bezos consistently espouses:

1. ***Be unmovable, but willing to give.***

   This first strategy might seem a bit contradictory. How can you be stubborn and flexible at the same time? The answer is simple—stay focused on your business plans and goals, but be willing to make changes if necessary. A business leader that lacks the ability to be stubborn is likely to abandon plans instead of seeing them through, and a leader lacking flexibility may overlook finding solutions to problems. Amazon became a category leader by paying attention to trends in their industry and adjusting business plans accordingly. An industry inevitably will grow and change in ways that are hard to anticipate. To find success, stay true to the company's goals, but be willing to adapt plans as the industry evolves.

2. ***Follow the "Two Pizza Rule."***

   Bezos believes that if a team can't be fed with two pizzas, the team is too large. Some companies believe that delegating work to larger teams saves time and money, but Bezos found that the opposite is true. Working with large groups of creative individuals can cause more problems than solutions. Bickering between the teams and a lack of communication (caused by size) can cause projects to stall or fail.

   The "Two Pizza Rule," Bezos has found, reduces the risk of stalling projects or repeatedly executing them, which can be costly. A leader needs to identify the key players who can make a project succeed and then offer them the resources to push the project forward. Empowering a small group of talented individuals to work together increases the chances of identifying ideas that help the business innovate.

"What's dangerous is not to evolve."

"Though we are optimistic, we must remain viligent and maintain a sense of urgency."

Key Takeaways

- Leaders must be stubborn and relentless in the pursuit of the organizational vision.
- Leaders must be relentless on improving productivity and efficiency. They measure and monitor constantly.
- Leaders see innovation as a driving energy source.
- Leaders must be willing to experiment and fail, quickly learning and adapting.
- Leaders need to be hyper-focused on the customer.

FEBRUARY LEADERS

For February, we will learn from Abraham Lincoln, Thomas Edison, Sakichi Toyoda and Sara Blakely

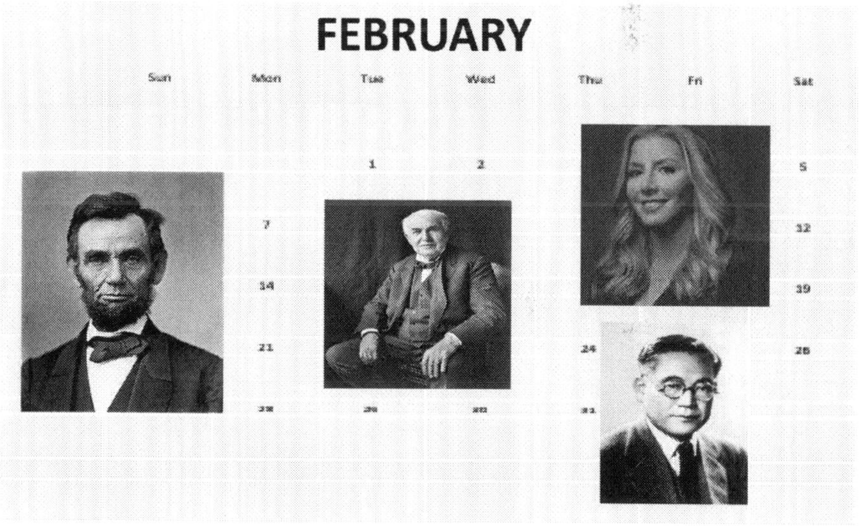

Abraham Lincoln

(February 12, 1809 – April 15, 1865)

"Success is going from failure to failure without losing your enthusiasm."

Biography

The life of Abraham Lincoln is the stuff of American mythology, to the extent that even biographical details of the 16th President of the United States are intrinsically linked to the values that are often touted as central to the country's identity.

Lincoln was famously born in a one-room log cabin in Kentucky in 1809, symbolic of the modest, salt-of-the-earth roots commonly evoked by leaders seeking to emphasize the limitless rewards of hard work. He is said to have earned the nickname "Honest Abe" after walking miles to return the extra change he mistakenly collected from a customer in the store where he worked as a young man—an exemplum of integrity. He was primarily self-educated, demonstrating a strong work ethic, and was known to have wrestled other boys in the frontier settlements where he lived, displaying a brawny competitiveness for when his intellect wasn't enough. He left home in his early twenties to work on a boat transporting goods up and down the country's interior rivers, epitomizing an independent streak and hardy pioneer spirit.

Lincoln's professional and political careers were dotted with both persistent failures and spectacular successes, but his embodiment of these American qualities served him well at critical points throughout his life. After a failed bid at entrepreneurship with a general store left him in debt and a brief stint as a captain in the Illinois militia came to an end, Lincoln campaigned and lost for a seat on the Illinois General Assembly. Despite those setbacks, he slowly built a wave of support that carried him to the Illinois state legislature in 1834. He was praised for both his physical prowess—he stood at 6'4"—and his oratory skills, galvanizing crowds with the type of eloquent storytelling that he would continue to utilize as his political aspirations grew.

In 1836, Lincoln passed the Illinois bar exam and began to practice law, eventually deciding to drum up more business by following the state court as it traveled from county to county. In his time as a prairie lawyer, he tried tax and patent cases, represented manufacturing companies and banks, and worked to have an acquaintance acquitted of murder charges. His reputation was solidified as the state's top lawyer and as a beacon of honesty and fairness in legal matters.

Lincoln was elected to state legislature a total of four times, before setting his sights on the U.S. House of Representatives. He lost a campaign in 1843, but was elected in 1846, serving a single term as a member of the Whig Party. A bill Lincoln proposed to emancipate slaves in the District of Columbia was a non-starter. His most notable achievements during his tenure of the House may have been his opposition to the Mexican War and his full-throated support of Presidential candidate Zachary Taylor.

Neither platform proved fruitful for Lincoln at the time; he failed to secure a position in Taylor's administration after he was elected, and Lincoln's constituents in Illinois did not agree with his position on the war. He largely withdrew from politics for the next five years.

In 1854, a series of political events brought him back into the fold, however. The re-emergence of an old rival—Stephen Douglas—and the passing of the Douglas-led Kansas-Nebraska Act that opened Louisiana Purchase Territory to slavery contributed to the fall of the Whigs in favor of the Republican Party. Lincoln, determined to lead the Illinois Republicans, went head-to-head with Douglas in a Senate campaign that included fierce public debates across the state. Despite his exemplary public speaking skills, Lincoln lost the election; in thanks (at least in part) his performance in those debates, however, he was now a nationally recognized figure. In 1860, he was nominated to the Presidential ballot at the Republican National Convention, carrying the electoral college vote to victory in 1860. By the time Lincoln was sworn in as President the following spring, seven states had already seceded from the Union. Within weeks, the Civil War had broken out.

Lincoln's wartime leadership style has been described as reactive[1], relying on his instincts and common sense to address problems and conflicts as they arose. His oft-cited strategy of building a team of rivals in his Cabinet—to propose and hash out the best course of political action—remained in place throughout the duration of the conflict. One of Lincoln's opponents during the Presidential campaign, for example, the abolitionist Salmon P. Chase, served as his Secretary of the Treasury, and routinely attempted to undermine Lincoln, with the aim of running against him in the 1864 Presidential election. Lincoln's appreciation for Chase's superior war financing ability secured his place in his Cabinet despite the subterfuge; after the war, Lincoln would even appoint him Chief Justice of the Supreme Court.

With the 1862 Emancipation Proclamation declaring slaves free in 10 Confederate states, Lincoln cemented the abolitionist legacy for which he would be remembered and revered. By modern standards, his position would not be considered entirely progressive. Even as the most famous passage from his rousing Gettysburg Address reiterates the Constitutional "proposition that all men are created equal," he had earlier maintained, during the Douglas debates, his belief that white people were superior to black people. Modern day scholars have debated whether or not his intermittent support for the voluntary colonization of territory outside of the United States by freed slaves was rooted in his own racism or in the belief that the others' racism would make true equality impossible to achieve in America.

The black abolitionist leader Frederick Douglass notably addressed this tension in his 1876 Oration in Memory of Abraham Lincoln, during which he acknowledged that from a political perspective, Lincoln's actions regarding ending slavery were "swift, zealous, radical, and determined;" from a strictly abolitionist point of view, however, he deemed them "tardy, cold, dull, and indifferent."

Still, Lincoln's stance—and ultimately, his perceived victory—was decisive enough to make lifetime enemies with Confederate sympathizers. On April 14, 1865, one such person, John Wilkes Booth, shot Lincoln as he attended a play at Ford's Theatre in Washington, D.C. The evening prior, Lincoln had given a speech from the White House during which he voiced support for suffrage for former slaves.

After a brief period in a coma, Lincoln died the morning of April 15. On May 30, 1922, the Lincoln Memorial opened in Washington. At the dedication ceremony, the poet Edwin Markham read his poem *Lincoln, The Man of the People*[2] before a crowd that included then-President Warren Harding, members of Congress, ambassadors, Lincoln's lone-surviving son Robert Todd, and thousands of civilians who had gathered to watch the proceedings.

In it, Markham referred to Lincoln as "a man to match the mountains and the sea," and hearkened back to Lincoln's humble roots. "Up from log cabin to the Capitol, One fire was on his spirit, one resolve," the poem reads, "To send the keen ax to the root of wrong, Clearing a free way for the feet of God."

Leadership Insights and Lincoln

Abraham Lincoln remains America's best President, if the opinion of Presidential historians is anything to go by. In C-SPAN's 2017 survey of

Presidential leadership, which polled 91 Presidential historians, Lincoln retained "top billing" as the country's most esteemed leader. He was also ranked number one in the previous polls in 2009 and 2000. The survey ranked the former leaders on 10 attributes of leadership, ranging from the moral categories of crisis leadership, moral authority, and pursuit of equal justice for all, to the more technical criteria of economic management, administrative skills, performance within context of times, and setting an agenda. The survey also included relations with the public, Congress, and other governments.

In many ways Lincoln was ahead of his time in terms of leadership practices. Tom Peters coined the phrase "management by walking around" in 1980. Lincoln was practicing this as early as 1860. As remarkable as it may seem, in 1861, Lincoln spent more time out of the White House than he did in it. And the chances are good that if a Union soldier had enlisted early in the Civil War, he saw the President in person. Lincoln was probably the most accessible chief executive the United States has ever known. John Nicolay and John Hay, his personal secretaries, reported that Lincoln spent 75 percent of his time meeting with people (Barker, 2014).

Coutu (2009) noted that "Lincoln surrounded himself with people, including his rivals, who had strong egos and high ambitions; who felt free to question his authority; and who were unafraid to argue with him." Lincoln brought Salmon Chase into his cabinet as treasury secretary and kept him there for three years, knowing full well that Chase craved the Presidency and regularly undermined him in communication with other Cabinet members, Congress, and the rest of the country. In Lincoln's view, so long as he was doing a good job at his post, that was more important than personal feelings.

Lincoln came to power when the nation was in peril, and he had the intelligence and the self-confidence to know that he needed the best people by his side—people who were leaders in their own right and who were acutely aware of their own strengths.

Crowly (n.d.) added to this:

> While Lincoln had a fierce personal ambition, he also had "the rare wisdom of temperament that consistently displayed magnanimity toward those that opposed him." He took great pains to re-establish rapport with the men who defeated him in early political races, and famously made a "team of rivals" by appointing to his Cabinet the three men he defeated for the Republican Presidential nomination.

Barker (2014) noted Lincoln's tendency to "persuade" rather than coerce.

> When the conduct of men is designed to be influenced, kind, unassuming persuasion should ever be adopted. It is an old and a true maxim, that a "drop of honey catches more flies than a gallon of gall." So with men, if you would win a man to your cause, first convince him that you are his sincere friend. Therein is a drop of honey that catches his heart, which, say what he will, is the great high road to his reason, and which, when once gained, you will find by little trouble in convincing his judgment of the justice of your cause, if indeed that cause really be a just one.

Coutu (2009) also noted, "What Lincoln had, it seems to me, was an extraordinary amount of emotional intelligence. He was able to acknowledge his errors and learn from his mistakes to a remarkable degree. He was careful to put past hurts behind him and never allowed wounds to fester." He also followed what Barker (2014) called the ability to "lead by being led." Lincoln always gave credit where credit was due and took responsibility when things went wrong.

Barker noted:

> Not only did this satisfy Lincoln's need for honesty, integrity and human dignity; it also gave his subordinates the correct

> perception that they were, in many ways, doing the leading, not Lincoln. If nothing else, it made them feel good about their jobs. It also encouraged innovation and risk taking because they knew that if they failed, Lincoln would not blame them.

Crowly (n.d.) also noted the blend of mind and heart, "the profound lesson to be drawn is that Lincoln led brilliantly, not just from his mind, but also his heart." General William Tecumseh Sherman called it his "greatness and goodness."

Kearns Goodwin (2005) stated, "Life was a school to him and he was always studying and mastering every subject before him." He later told a student seeking advice, "Always bear in mind that your own resolution to succeed is more important than any one thing." Kearns Goodwin also noted his unusual level of empathy: "Lincoln's prodigious influence on friends and foes alike was due to his "extraordinary empathy – the ability to put himself in the place of another, to experience what they were feeling and to understand their motives and desires."

Crowly (n.d.) notes Lincoln's "indomitable sense of purpose." At a very early age, Lincoln reportedly set his sights on "engraving his name in history." "Every man is said to have his peculiar ambition," Lincoln wrote. "I have no other so great as that of being truly esteemed by fellow men, by rendering myself worthy of their esteem."

With the country greatly divided over slavery, and at the height of a Civil War that already had taken the lives of hundreds of thousands of men, Lincoln was certain his purpose was to preserve the greatest democracy the world had ever known, and to ensure its "government of the people, by the people, for the people, shall not perish from the earth."

Tied to the conviction that his work was intrinsically important, it was Lincoln who consistently found the courage to invigorate the spirits of his Cabinet and troops during the country's most dire and desperate hours.

Crowly (n.d.) noted that Lincoln fundamentally cared about people and made every effort to demonstrate that to them. Through kind and encouraging words, and authentic gestures of exceptional thoughtfulness, he assured people of their individual significance. He was most essentially a human being who identified with the challenges people faced and the sacrifices they made.

Lincoln also had a wonderful gift for telling stories and intentionally used his quick and benign wit to soften wounded feelings and dispel anxieties. Barker (2014) noted Lincoln's tendency to influence people through storytelling.

> Lincoln stated, "They say I tell a great many stories. I reckon I do; but I have learned from long experience that plain people, take them as they run, are more easily influenced through the medium of a broad and humorous illustration than in any other way..."

He also was not afraid to display his own humanness. On more than one occasion, he traveled long distances to visit weary troops on the battlefield. Simply by demonstrating to them that their work mattered to him, he earned their unmitigated support. One soldier wrote in a letter home, "Lincoln's warm smile was a reflection of his honest, kindly heart; but deeper, under the surface of that...were the unmistakable signs of care." (Crowly, n.d.).

Schepici (2011) offers five leadership traits **that made Lincoln a successful leader:**

1. ***He built a strong team.***
2. ***He clearly conveyed his message (with stories).***
3. ***He persuaded others rather than coerce them.***
4. ***He was a strong public speaker.***
5. ***He was calm with contradiction and adversity.***

Donald T. Phillips' book *Lincoln on Leadership: Executive Strategies for Tough Times* **(1992) excellently captures much more of Lincoln's transferrable leadership insights.**

"Commitment is what transforms a promise into reality."

"Success is going from failure to failure without losing your enthusiasm."

Key Takeaways

- Leaders must have a sense of purpose and live up to it.
- Leaders should surround themselves with talented people who will tell them what they need to hear versus want to hear.
- Leaders need to get out among their staff and keep a finger on the pulse: they cannot lead from afar.
- Leaders should use storytelling and persuasion to the extent possible to engage hearts and minds.
- Leaders need to acknowledge mistakes and learn from them.
- Leaders need to embrace empathy and show they care.

Thomas Edison

(February 11, 1847 – October 18, 1931)

"Genius is one percent inspiration and ninety-nine percent perspiration."

Biography

When history remembers Thomas Edison, they remember him primarily as an inventor, The Wizard of Menlo Park, NJ, who dreamed up and made reality the motion picture camera, the phonograph, and most famously, the electric light bulb. While those contributions to science and society would have been enough to ensure that his name would live on for generations, at the time of his death in 1931 from diabetes-related causes, he also held a total of 1,093 patents in the United States, either alone or with collaborators.

Yet, for those who have studied his life, Edison can also serve as a case study in how dogged determination can be applied to overcome myriad obstacles. Born in Ohio in 1847, Edison began having difficulties with hearing at a young age, leading to problems in his schooling, which was, commonly for the time, already insufficient and sporadic by today's metrics. On the cusp of his teenage years, Edison left school and began to work on the Michigan railroad system. The American railroad system had begun to rapidly expand during the Civil War era, making use of advances in telegraph technology to coordinate train movements.[1] Edison saw an opportunity for advancement, and within a few years, began to work as an apprentice telegrapher.

However, as telegraph industry trends moved toward the adoption of auditory cues, Edison's partial deafness left him at a severe disadvantage. In response, Edison began to work on creating a system that could send multiple messages along a single wire simultaneously—the duplex telegraph—while also converting telegraph signals into printed messages, rendering his disability moot. Inspired, he left telegraphy behind, and his career as an inventor and innovator took root.

Moving east, Edison initially settled in Newark, New Jersey, where he used his intimate knowledge of telegraphy to secure work with the Western Union Telegraph Company—and its rivals. After selling his quadruplex telegraph innovation to one of Western Union's competitors for $100,000, Edison would have been poised for financial security and prosperity, were it not for a bitter legal battle the deal engendered, and for his own tendency toward poor money management.

Calling upon his father for assistance, Edison established an industrial shop and innovation laboratory in Menlo Park, New Jersey in an attempt to monetize his inventive streak. It was from his Menlo Park lab that Edison and his team developed the phonograph, the carbon button transmitter and the filament bulb, which catapulted him into the sphere of worldwide renown.

In order to attract the attention of business partners and investors (which would include, at various points throughout his career, deep-pocketed financiers like J.P. Morgan and the Vanderbilt family), Edison exploited his Wizard of Menlo Park persona. He cooperated with newspaper editors who could enforce his mythologized image as a scientific genius, generating widespread interest in the man who was dreaming up new ways to improve everyday life in a rapidly changing country.

Edison's flair for public relations was matched by a keen sense of opportunity. While media accounts painted a picture of him as a mad scientist, his Menlo Park lab was often run more like a factory assembly line, with teams of researchers and experimenters testing and tinkering with new ideas until one stuck. His lab's most successful inventions were often developed in conjunction with other systems needed to operate them, grouped for investors and customers as top-to-bottom consumable packages. The light bulb, for example, came alongside concepts for electrical generation and transmission.[2]

Edison's work with electric light formed the basis for establishing the Edison Electric Light Company in 1878, with funding from Morgan and the Vanderbilts, among others. Eventually, Morgan would facilitate the merger of Edison Electric Light and the Thomson-Houston Electric Company, forming General Electric, which then controlled the far majority of the American electrical market at the turn of the century.

In 1886, after marrying the daughter of a wealthy manufacturer—his second wife—Edison built The Edison Laboratory in West Orange, New Jersey. From within this second facility, Edison created the alkaline storage battery—leading to a partnership with Henry Ford—and the phonograph for commercial use. It is also often credited as the birthplace of the motion picture industry, via Edison's work in developing the Kinetograph and Kinetoscope there. Although he tried to coordinate sound to accompany these moving images, existing technology at the time made this a difficult task; thus, Edison pioneered and promoted the genre of silent film.

Around this time, Edison also devoted extensive resources toward creating a process to separate iron from ore and acquired well over 100 ore mines. His attempt to develop efficient means of ore extraction proved fruitless, however, representative of a late in life period of modest success (in comparison to his booming earlier work) that would continue until he retired in his eighties.

After Ford's death, his West Orange estate and lab were eventually transformed into National Historic Sites. The nearby township of Raritan was renamed Edison, New Jersey in his honor in 1954. As had happened throughout his adult life, aspects of Edison's last moments before death have taken on a larger-than-life air. It is said, for example, that, at Ford's beckoning, Edison's son Charles captured Edison's last breath in a test tube.[3] The relic remains sealed and on display at the Henry Ford Museum in Michigan; over the course of the ensuing years, nearly 42 other test tubes allegedly containing Edison's last breaths have been discovered.

Leadership Insights and Edison

Thomas Edison is known as a prolific inventor and this cannot be underestimated, but it could be argued that his greatest contributions were his evangelization of a culture of innovation and his relentless determination to succeed. He saw invention as a means to "do it better." His strong focus on innovation extended beyond just technology or products to include process, as well.

Edison promoted the invention of many technological products, most notably the phonograph and electric light bulb, which contributed to U.S. dominance in industrial production. While Edison was not the first to invent several products closely associated with his name, he improved upon these inventions to make them suitable for practical use.

He was also a skilled and prolific promoter. He married the necessity of attaching a face to his product with a deep commitment to collaboration. Edison inspired a culture of invention where people worked in tandem to develop and improve products. He challenged the notion that inventions result only from of necessity (100 Leaders, 2018).

Caldicott (2013) wrote that the image of a white-coated Edison, alone in his lab, is, thus, a fantasy. Krippendorff (2012) noted:

> From the start, Edison sought collaborators to attain materials to create his prototype and commercialize it. In his lifetime, he founded General Electric and more than 200 domestic and international companies, essentially to bring together investors, engineers, salespeople–collaborators–with a common mission.

Murphy (2018) called Edison a "player-coach," which he defines as "an individual contributor who also manages the work of other employees, you're what is called a Player-Coach."

Henry Ford idolized Thomas Edison, another Player-Coach. Edison reshaped the world with his inventions, but he wasn't a 'mad scientist' working into the wee hours all alone in his lab. Edison also surrounded himself with bright people, creating a collaborative culture that allowed him to innovate at a far faster pace than he ever could have achieved alone.

Murphy wrote:

> Edison's collaborators were craftsmen, and they called each other 'muckers,' reflecting the way they all "mucked in" or pitched in together. They worked long hours, late into the night, punctuated by sessions on the organ at one end of the laboratory and weekend drinking bouts. It was an informal, freethinking atmosphere and Edison was one of the boys.

An astonishing level of collaborative work came out of Edison's Menlo Park lab. This was, in no small part, due to the informal, freethinking atmosphere that Edison created.

Krippendorff (2012) offered a synopsis of Edison's four step approach to collaboration based on Caldicott's review of Edison's process in her book *Midnight Lunch* (2012).

Step 1: Establish Capacity

First, assemble the capacity to innovate. Identify a small group (2 to 8 people) that brings together a diversity of experiences and perspectives. Aim for 5 to 10 collaborators that represent key areas of the company (marketing, operations, HR, etc.).

Step 2: Set Context

This is a two-step approach: First, run what is called a "solo-meld," in which each member individually reads broadly about the collaboration topic, questions assumptions, and conducts initial analyses to create insights, without reaching conclusions. Follow this with a "group-meld," in which members come together to share their insights, experiment with a broad range of potential solutions, and develop prototypes (often today these are narrative prototypes, stories of potential solutions).

Step 3: Maintain Coherence

It's not unusual for any team to get distracted and lose momentum. The key is to inspire the team with the shared purpose, while measuring the progress toward that shared vision. Give the team feedback to keep them engaged.

Step 4: Manage Complexity

Innovative ideas are always inconsistent with prevailing logic and beliefs, so your challenge now is to manage the complexity of converting your idea into reality. This means starting to influence beyond your team so the idea catches on, networking in the broader organization to get people on board, and doing what has been called "footprinting"—building a collection of notebooks, documents, data, videos, pictures, and sound recordings that will serve as a record of your team's work.

Edison was also known for his prodigious work ethic. Throughout his prolific career he was the living embodiment of his own now famous words, that "genius is one percent inspiration, ninety-nine percent perspiration." And, just as much as his legacy is emblazoned by a litany of inventions and technological advances, his tireless work ethic was equally lauded (Brox 2012).

Edison also blended his approach to work ethic with his view on failure. As quoted by Brox (2012), Edison once commented, "I have not failed. I've just found 10,000 ways that won't work." Failure is a state of mind most aptly illustrated by the age old conflict between the glass being half empty or half full. Instead of letting failure define you, it should instead inspire you.

Edison also argued against falling to the trap of complacency, as evidenced by one of his most succinct mantras: "There's a way to do it better—find it." (Brox, 2012).

From this, Edison's successes can be viewed as an argument for the concept of never letting well enough alone. The most innovative companies in the world are driven by leaders who don't settle for passable results. Instead, they are constantly asking "what if?" or "why not?" Your team can't think outside the box if you refuse to open the top. Don't be afraid to take a risk or act on a whim, since, as Edison proved several times over, it could very well lead to something amazing.

"Many of life's failures are people who did not realize how close they were to success when they gave up."

Key Takeaways

- Leaders must be able to create a vision, communicate it to build collaboration, and then turn it into reality.
- Leaders must be consummate collaborators, willing to take input from many sources.
- Leaders need to be willing to fail over and over, seeing the experience as a process and learning opportunity.
- Leaders must be willing to put the work in and be dogged in their determination.
- Leaders should reject the status quo and strive to do it better.

Sakichi Toyoda

(February 14, 1867 – October 30, 1930)

"Workers are treasure of the factory.
They are important to me."

Biography

In effective narrative fiction, it's often said that the more specific a story is, the more universal the lessons derived from it may be. It's why seemingly mundane details of everyday life can often procure profound insights into humanity or relatable dilemmas from which we can all learn something valuable.

The same can be said for business leaders who develop specific methods for their own particular institutional problems that companies in unrelated disciplines can apply to their fields of work. Whether he set out to do so intentionally or not, Sakichi Toyoda, founder of the company that would become the Toyota Industries Corporation, created a new such corporate problem-solving paradigm when he introduced his 5 Whys technique.

In short, Toyoda's 5 Whys uses a cause and effect way of thinking to examine a problem—like, for example, why a car won't start—in an effort to understand its root cause. The answer to each question informs the next question. For example[1]:

> Why won't the car start? The battery is dead.
>
> Why? The alternator is not functioning.
>
> Why? The alternator belt has broken.
>
> Why? The alternator belt was well beyond its useful service life and not replaced.
>
> Why? The vehicle was not maintained according to the recommended service schedule.

When it works successfully, the 5 Whys method points to a human-size problem, providing a path for correction.

Toyoda certainly didn't arrive at this technique through years of corporate training or an Ivy League MBA. Born to a farming family in 1867 in what is known today as Kosai City, Japan, Toyoda began his professional life as an apprentice carpenter, his father's part-time trade. The period in which Toyoda was born is consequential to his eventual career path; Japan in the late 1800's was swiftly changing, with political leaders developing an interest in modernization and moving away from the isolationist policies that had previously kept Western-style industrialization out.[2]

Toyoda's birthplace is also important. Modernization efforts plunged the agricultural community in which he grew up into poverty. Sensing an opportunity for advancement in his late teens and early twenties, Toyoda absorbed information about modern machinery and experimented with ways to update the hand looms used by Japanese farmers for generations. When he was 24 years old, he received his first patent, for a single-hand operated wooden loom. The invention and the patent for it comprised the first step in a series of innovations on the loom.

In 1896, after the development of a winding machine provided him with financial security, Toyoda introduced Japan's first steam-powered loom. The invention would serve as the basis for a thriving textile business.

Toyoda's steady stream of improvements to his looms would occupy his professional life through the 1920s, taking him to England, China and the United States, making a case for Japanese innovation and thoroughly transforming the global textile business along the way.

In 1919, he established a manufacturing facility in Shanghai—an unprecedented move for a Japanese businessman at the time. Once it was running smoothly, he recommitted himself to innovation, building a new Japanese facility for commercial trials. There, he developed his most impactful loom, the Type G. The automatic loom was impressive enough to warrant a patent transfer request from the English textile giant Platt Brothers & Co., Ltd.—yet another as-yet-unheard-of milestone achieved by Toyoda and a significant boost of confidence from Western interests.

In 1926, Toyoda established Toyoda Automatic Loom Works, dedicated to "pursuing related invention and research."[3] Under the leadership of Toyoda's son Kiichiro, the company would establish its first automotive department, setting the stage for its evolution into the Toyota Industries Corporation, a multi-billion dollar auto empire and one of the world's most recognizable consumer brands.

Toyoda died in October 1930 in Nagoya at age 63. In addition to a set of "Toyoda Precepts" based on its founder's principles—including, notably, the directive to always strive to stay ahead of the times—the company maintains Toyoda's 5 Whys method of problem solving. The technique has seen widespread adoption, folded into the leadership philosophies of business leaders as diverse as Henry Ford, General Electric's Jack Welch, and Ricardo Semler of Semco Partners.

Leadership Insights and Toyoda

Throughout his life, Sakichi Toyoda was a great engineer and later was referred to as Japan's "King of Inventors." However, his broader contribution to the development of Toyota was his philosophy and approach to his work, based on a zeal for continuous improvement.

Interestingly, this philosophy, and ultimately the Toyota Way, was significantly influenced by his reading of an article first published in England in 1859 by Samuel Smiles entitled "Self-Help." It preaches the virtues of industry, thrift, and self-improvement.

There are many examples throughout Smiles' article of "management by facts" and the importance of getting people to pay attention actively—a hallmark of Toyoda's approach to problem solving based on *genchi genbutsu* ("go and see to deeply understand"). Toyoda believed the only real way to understand a problem is to go and see it on the ground; when asked to resolve a problem, he expected his managers to do so.

Toyoda's leadership approach was based on these core values:

1. ***Contribute to society***
2. ***Customer first and company second***
3. ***Respect for people***
4. ***Know your business***
5. ***Get your hands dirty***
6. ***Hard work, discipline, teamwork, and constant innovation toward a vision***

He helped craft and embed the "Five Main Principles" into the Toyota culture (Anderson 2015):

1. ***Always be faithful to your duties, thereby contributing to the Company and to the overall good.***
2. ***Always be studious and creative, striving to stay ahead of the times.***
3. ***Always be practical and avoid frivolousness.***
4. ***Always strive to build a homelike atmosphere at work that is warm and friendly.***
5. ***Always have respect for God, and remember to be grateful at all times.***

His values were embodied in what is now one of the pillars of the Toyota Production System: That pillar now called *Jidoka,* sometimes referred to as "smart automation with a human touch" or "autonomation" (Shmula.com, 2010).

Toyoda recognized that although new behaviors always provoke opposition, those who are complacent will be left behind and ultimately defeated. He reminded others often that active engagement with the "new" is the principal business of managers. Toyoda was an innovator who believed that invention only achieved its goal through practical application (Hino, 2006). Everything he invented was the solution to a specific problem, developed through trial and error.

His approach was also influenced by a deep curiosity, strong work ethic, and his belief in the possible. He noted, "I'm not talented more than anybody else. I just put lots of efforts and researches." And has also been quoted as saying, "There is nothing that can't be done. If you can't make something, it's because you haven't tried hard enough." (toolshero, n.d.)

He is also famous for the use of the concept of the 5 Whys: When a problem occurs, ask "why" five times in order to find the source of the problem, then put into place something to prevent the problem from recurring (toolshero, n.d.).

Now famous, the concept of *kaizen* derived from Toyoda's core values and has been a mandate for his successors to constantly improve performance. At the root of *kaizen* is the idea that nothing is perfect and everything can be improved. This is critical to the company, as every leader is taught to remember that the process is never perfect and that the company has never achieved the perfect "lean solution" (Liker & Convis, 2012).

Toyoda's approach is summed up nicely in one of his enduring quotes: "Always stay ahead of the times through research and creativity" (Hino, 2006).

"I'm not talented more than anybody else. I just put lots of efforts and researches."

Key Takeaways

- Leaders must be willing to confront complacency.
- Leaders need to get to root causes and not be distracted by symptoms.
- Leaders need to have a strong work ethic and be willing to invest the needed effort.
- Leaders need to need to understand that nothing is perfect and impossible—hard work and creativity are the engines of progress.
- Leaders need to be respectful and have a ‘human touch.”

Sara Blakley

(February 27, 1971 -)

"Where I get my energy is:
'How can I make it better?'"

Biography

The upward trajectory of Sara Blakely—the founder of the shapewear company Spanx—is the type of business success story that drives ambitious entrepreneurs-to-be to leave their jobs in pursuit of their own million dollar idea. Or, as it turned out to be in the case of Blakely's vast hosiery empire, a billion dollar concept.

Born in Clearwater, Florida in 1971, Blakely's first foray into entrepreneurialism came early, when, as reported in a *Forbes* cover story from 2012, she charged her neighbors admission to enter a haunted house she created. A more formal attempt at building a business when she was still in school—a babysitting service operating out of a nearby hotel—lasted several summers until her lack of appropriate first aid training eventually surfaced and forced her to shut down shop.

By the time she graduated from Florida State University with a degree in communication in 1993, though, Blakely's drive to succeed hadn't yet aligned with a clear purpose or sense of direction. She abandoned plans to attend law school after underperforming on the standardized admission test twice, taking a placeholder job at Walt Disney World, experimenting with stand-up comedy, and eventually selling fax machines door-to-door for the office supply company Danka for seven years.

As she recounted during a summit for *Inc. Magazine* in 2017, a particularly grueling day at Danka led to the realization that she was deeply unsatisfied with her life and career. As a means of taking stock of her life, she listed her skills and her weaknesses; her sales prowess was the lone positive. "I liked providing people with something they didn't know they needed," she said during the forum, before recounting the professional intention she set for herself at the time: "I'm going to invent a product that I can sell to millions of people that will make them feel good."[1]

At 25 years old, Blakely's performance at Danka was strong enough to land her a national sales trainer title. While the job itself didn't engender much passion within her, the wardrobe the role required would prove to be inspirational.

In the intense Florida heat, Blakely thought wearing pantyhose while working was both uncomfortable and unfashionable, although, when layered under her clothes, she found the streamlined effect flattering. Out of frustration, Blakely cut the feet off of one pair she owned so she could wear them to a party with open toed shoes and still keep the hosiery hidden. The result was impractical—she recalls the legs rolling up beneath her pants all night—but the idea for disguised, slimming shapewear that would become her signature Spanx product was born.

After relocating to Atlanta with Danka, Blakely emptied her savings account and spent nights after work researching hosiery and fabric. She relentlessly contacted production mills until finding one who agreed to manufacture her sample prototype. Blakely wrote her own patent and designed the first Spanx logo herself, launching the product officially from her home in 2000.

Calling upon her years of sales experience, she pitched her sole product to the high-end department store Neiman Marcus, which recognized its appeal and immediately placed what became Spanx' first wholesale order; other high-profile retail chains, including Bloomingdales and Saks Fifth Avenue, soon followed.

In another show of dogged persistence, Blakely sent a basket of Spanx to Oprah Winfrey's stylist unsolicited. The gamble paid off in spades when Winfrey selected Spanx as one of her annual "Favorite Things" in November 2000, a consumer goods kingmaking gesture that arrived mere months after the product first hit retail shelves. At the time, Spanx barely had a functioning e-commerce site.

By the end of its first year in business, Spanx made $4M in sales and Blakely resigned from Danka. By 2011, thanks in no small part to a lucrative deal with the home shopping channel QVC, Spanx had become a household name. A year later, as the sole owner of Spanx since its inception—a commitment to autonomy that meant Blakely also never took on outside investors or debt—Blakely became the first female self-made billionaire. Her company had reached nine-digit annual sales numbers without any traditional advertising spend. Spanx has grown to more than $350m in annual sales and has 750 employees.

In the years since its launch, Spanx has expanded its product offering to include an assortment of undergarments for men and women, and Blakely is a U.S. patent holder three times over. In 2015, she and her husband Jesse Itzler purchased a minority ownership stake of the Atlanta Hawks pro basketball team. Blakely—alongside a list of wealthy titans of business that includes fellow billionaires Bill Gates, Michael Bloomberg, and Warren Buffett—has pledged to donate the majority of her net worth to philanthropic causes. In 2013, Blakely became the first female billionaire to join the "Giving Pledge," Bill Gates and Warren Buffett's pledge, where the world's richest people donate at least half of their wealth to charity.

In 2006, Blakely launched the Sara Blakely Foundation to help women through education and entrepreneurial training. Since its launch, The Sara Blakely Foundation has funded scholarships for young women at the Community and Individual Development Association

City Campus in South Africa. More than anything else, Blakely believes in giving back. She created a program called "Leg Up" designed to help other female entrepreneurs grow their business.

Leadership Insights and Blakely

Sara Blakely is an American businesswoman, and founder of Spanx, an American intimate apparel company. In 2012, Blakely was named in *Time* magazine's "Time 100" annual list of the 100 most influential people in the world. As of 2014, she is listed as the 93rd most powerful woman in the world by *Forbes*. She was also inducted into Babson College's Academy of Distinguished Entrepreneurs .

As a self-made billionaire thanks primarily to a solution-led business idea and an underlying trust in her instincts, Blakely is a font of insights and information for aspiring and established entrepreneurs alike. The crowdfunding platform Fundable (n.d.) captured these four quotes from Blakely as points for leaders to consider:

> "Differentiate yourself – why are you different?"
>
> "It's important to be willing to make mistakes. The worst thing that can happen is you become memorable."
>
> "I think failure is nothing more than life's way of nudging you that you are off course."
>
> "Don't be intimidated by what you don't know. That can be your greatest strength and ensure that you do things differently from everyone else."

Schwantes (n.d.) noted that Blakely commented in an interview that she still struggles with doubt and fear. Nevertheless, she pinpointed a single observation that conceivably threatens countless leaders from fully realizing their potential: "Your negative self-talk is the Number 1 barrier to success."

Brody (2018) asked Blakely "You've done this for 18 years. Do you have another venture up your sleeve?" Blakely responded:

> "I'll never say never. I keep an idea book. Right now it's 99 pages, single-spaced, and a lot of the ideas have nothing to do with Spanx.

Blakely also commented:

> "Looking back at the past 10 years, my biggest takeaway is to fire faster. That's a hard thing to do. The other two lessons that just keep getting stronger and louder are: Hire your weaknesses, and stay in your lane. So, I encourage people to delegate and hire where you aren't strong. And realize that the self-awareness of *What are my strengths, and what are my weaknesses?* comes when you are quiet with yourself and you're listening, you're paying attention." (Brody 2018.)

In an interview with Blakely at the Stanford Business School noted these lessons (Briody 2018):

1. ***Start small, think big.***

   "A lot of people want to start big and think big and oftentimes get ahead of themselves," Blakely says. "That can end wildly successful, but it can also cause a lot of problems. You dilute yourself down, and you have people you're answering to."

2. ***Ask questions and be hyper-observant.***

   "I think of a lot of ideas at traffic lights," she says. "I pay attention to things that haven't evolved and why. I ask myself questions all day, every day. I could be looking at a table and be like, 'Why is the table like that? When was the table first created? Is that the actual best design for a table? Or could there be something different?'"

3. ***Share the fails.***

   A key tenet of Blakely's leadership style is admitting to her mistakes and giving her employees room to do the same. She even schedules "oops meetings" at Spanx, during which employees stand up and say how they messed up or describe a mistake they made, usually by turning it into a funny story. "If you can create a culture where [your employees] are not terrified to fail or make a mistake, then they're going to be highly productive and more innovative," she says. "I'm curious about the things that hold power over us. And one is fear of embarrassment. We all have that."

4. ***Be vulnerable.***

   Blakely is no stranger to vulnerability. In addition to admitting to her mistakes, she's open about her process with her customers and shares intimate details about her life as a wife and mother of four on Instagram. "I love the idea of CEOs showing vulnerabilities and the ups and downs," she says. "I don't feel I need to put on a facade to be taken seriously as a leader. When I started Spanx, instead of talking at my customer, I wanted to talk to them. I felt other companies were like, 'We need to be perfect, and you need to see us as the authority. That's how we're going to sell you a product.' They weren't really talking to me, and I didn't necessarily trust them. [Instead], I made myself vulnerable. I was like, 'Hey, I'm one of you. This is why it works.' And I felt like customers became really connected and loyal."

5. ***Use humor.***

   At Spanx, new employees go through a training boot camp, and one of the mandatory activities is doing standup comedy. Blakely does this because it helps employees let go of their fears, loosen up, and use humor when selling Spanx products. "I don't subscribe to the fact that you have to act serious to be taken seriously," she says. "When I started, I wrote, 'Don't worry. We've got your butt covered' right on the package. I named my company Spanx, which made people laugh. All of a sudden you had celebrities like Gwyneth Paltrow and Julia Roberts flashing their Spanx on red carpets and saying, 'I'm wearing Spanx.' I think it's because I chose to do humor, and people wanted to participate in that. When I cold-called to sell fax machines door-to-door, I learned very quickly that if I could make somebody laugh or smile, I'd get another 30 seconds before they'd slam the door in my face."

6. ***Don't underestimate hard work.***

   In the beginning, Spanx was a one-woman operation, and Blakely was in charge of every department at her new company. She was the packer and shipper. She was head of sales. She wrote her own patent to save on legal fees. "I was everything," she says. "I was out in the field talking about the product and sharing the story of why it was better. There's so much about my journey where I was like, 'I am not going to let my success be contingent on other people. As much as I can control it, help it, navigate it, I'm going to.'" That said, she also suggests "hiring your weaknesses" as soon as you can afford to do so. The key is recognizing the difference between both points.

7. ***Break the rules and be relentless.***

   Blakely has never asked permission to do things her own way. She heard "no" for two years from manufacturers before getting her first Spanx product made. She also didn't like how masculine the traditional business environment felt, so she turned tradition on its head. "At a cocktail party after I first started Spanx," she recalls, "one guy came up to me and said, 'Sara, we heard you invented something. I hope you're ready to go to war. Business is war.' I remember looking at him and thinking, 'Why?' I went home that night and sat on the floor of my apartment and thought, 'I don't want to go to war.' Then this voice inside of my head just said, 'Do it differently. Take a different approach."

> Blakely didn't let the being told no deter her from pursuing her vision. She continued to push forward until she heard "yes."
>
> When her product wasn't in a visible space at Neiman Marcus, she took matters into her own hands. "I realized that my product was in the sleepiest part of the department store. It was back in the corner, and nobody was going there. I immediately went and bought envelope dividers, put Spanx in them, and I ran around Neiman Marcus and put them at every register. By the time somebody figured out that nobody else had approved it—because everybody thought somebody else approved it—it was so successful that the head of Neiman's was like, 'Whatever this girl's doing, let her keep doing it.'"

AllBusiness (2018) added this lessons from Blakely:

8. ***Believe in your idea and trust your instincts***

   Blakely has been quoted in Forbes for saying that even if you hear the word "no" a million times, but still believe in your idea 100%, you should not let anyone stop you. In order to develop an entrepreneurial mindset, Blakely visualized her specific goals and developed courage in order to dive deep into the world of business. She knew she was obsessed with her business idea, and that the product was a solution to a problem women everywhere had been dealing with for far too long.

   Blakely was determined to keep going and bring her dream to life; in spite of the initial "no" responses she first heard, she began to hear a chorus of "yeses" from others who believed in her product as much as she did.

9. ***Do your homework.***

   "As a newbie entrepreneur, Blakely didn't have a business degree. She also didn't have any experience in the fashion or merchandising industries. What she did have was the library, books, and her own door-to-door sales experience. The bottom line? You may not know everything about a given industry you want to make your mark in, but that doesn't mean you can't do your due diligence."

"It's important to be wiling to make mistakes. The worst thing that can happen is you become memorable."

"Don't be intimidated by what you don't know. That can be your greatest strength and ensure that you do things differently from everyone else."

Key Takeaways

- Effective leaders are relentless in their focus and hyper-observant.
- Effective leaders must be willing to make mistakes and to share fails.
- Effective leaders hire to their weaknesses.
- Effective leaders are future-facing and are not afraid to break the rules. They fight complacency.
- Effective leaders find ways to differentiate themselves and their organizations.

MARCH LEADERS

For March, we will learn from Albert Einstein, Dr. Seuss, Cesar Chávez and Tammy Duckworth.

Albert Einstein

(March 14, 1879 – April 18, 1955)

"Anyone who has never made a mistake has
never tried anything new."

Biography

Albert Einstein's groundbreaking contributions to modern science have been so celebrated, that even someone who has never set foot inside a physics classroom can likely still tell you that $E=mc^2$ (even if they have no idea what the Special Theory of Relativity actually means). The Nobel Prize-winning theoretical physicist lived in Germany, Switzerland, and Prague before settling in the United States in the 1930's. But, as his news of his discoveries traveled around the world, so did he, bringing his theories and teachings everywhere from Singapore to Palestine, Spain to Japan.

Combined with his outspoken nature, Einstein's travels afforded him the opportunity to acquire the type of mainstream and political clout not typical for academics who toil away in the hard sciences. Pop culture and the casual historian may remember Einstein as a genius professor with a distinctive hairstyle, but during his lifetime, his influence often extended into the realm of politics.

Born in Ulm, Germany in 1879, Einstein and his family moved to Munich when he was just a year old. Einstein would remain there—even after his family relocated to Italy during his teenage years—until just before he reached legal age to serve in the German military service, at which point he fled the country and rejoined his family in Milan. Einstein's academic performance in physics and math was strong enough to gain entrance to the Swiss Federal Polytechnic School in Zurich, affording him the opportunity to complete his secondary education before beginning his university training there (and, in doing so, avoid enlisting in the German military—he would later renounce his German citizenship in favor of a Swiss passport).

Einstein's penchant for disregarding expectations came with him to Switzerland, though. At school, he would often cut class to study physics on his own, which, despite his passing marks, made his professors less than enthused about providing him with the requisite letters of recommendation needed for employment upon his graduation in 1900.

The years following his graduation were difficult for Einstein, as he scrambled to cobble together enough paying work to survive, had a child with Mileva Maric—a fellow physics student whose Eastern Orthodox Christian faith created tension with Einstein's Ashkenazi Jewish family—and saw his father's business sink into bankruptcy. Finally, in 1902, a friend from Zurich helped Einstein secure a job in the Swiss patent office in Bern. The job provided Einstein with the financial stability to marry Maric (although the fate of their first child together remains unknown, with scholars believing the infant either succumbed to scarlet fever or was given up for adoption before the pair wed).

Employment also enabled Einstein the downtime needed to continue his study of physics. Einstein published four papers in 1905, each of which contributed incrementally to his most famous work on the theory of special relativity; the final paper included the equation $E=mc^2$. Far from a bombshell discovery, Einstein's papers largely went unnoticed until Max Planck, the man credited with founding quantum theory, confirmed some of Einstein's work. Suddenly, Einstein was lecturing throughout Europe.

Einstein's ascent in academic circles continued through the outbreak of World War I, which he vehemently and publicly opposed. Around this time, his prominence as a leader began to seep out beyond classroom walls, as well; in 1918, for example, he mediated the release of professors held hostage by a radical student faction at the University of Berlin.[1]

In 1921, while embarking on a world tour, Einstein was awarded the Nobel Prize in Physics. Despite the fact that his marriage crumbled years before and he had already remarried, the money from the prize went to Maric; Einstein was so sure he would win, that he had preemptively signed the Nobel money to Maric as part of their divorce settlement in 1919.

But financial trappings aside, the Prize offered Einstein worldwide fame and access to other leading thinkers of the time; he appeared in public alongside Charlie Chaplin and corresponded with Sigmund Freud. The rise in his profile also made him a target of the Nazi movement that was gaining steam in Germany. Fearing for his life, Einstein sought refuge in New Jersey, where he took up a post teaching at Princeton University.

Despite fleeing personal danger, Einstein could not escape the war. After other scientists proved that his teachings could be used to help develop an atomic bomb, Einstein and the physicist Leo Szilard wrote a letter to then-President Franklin D. Roosevelt encouraging the U.S. to develop their own. Although the country's efforts to build their own atomic weapons—The Manhattan Project—grew from this, Einstein cited his own pacifist beliefs to reprieve himself of participating directly. Regardless, the Emergency Committee of Atomic Scientists, a group Einstein founded with Szilard, was influential in early attempts to navigate peace in a nuclear-enabled world after the bombing of Hiroshima during World War II.

After the war, Einstein's advocacy continued. Now a U.S. citizen (whose socialist leanings had caught the attention of J. Edgar Hoover and the FBI), he joined the NAACP. He was a prominent voice in the American Civil Rights Movement and in the Zionist movement; he helped establish the Hebrew University of Jerusalem and was later offered the Presidency of Israel, which he declined. He also drafted the Russell-Einstein Manifesto with the philosopher Bertrand Russell in 1955, arguing for nuclear disarmament.

Toward the end of his life, Einstein focused on unified field theory—sometimes called the Theory of Everything—that would essentially explain the behavior of all energy and matter. In his later days, he forsook the travels of his earlier career, remaining primarily holed up in Princeton until his death from an aortic aneurysm in 1955.

Leadership Insights and Einstein

Some may wonder why we included Einstein in a compendium of leaders. He was not a leader in the traditional organizational sense. He was a theoretical physicist and mathematician noted for his Theory of Relativity. We included him, however, because many of his core beliefs and practices infuse effective leadership.

Thiran (2018) noted that as a deeply passionate leader in his field, Einstein was obsessed with the work he carried out. This obsession was driven by three main qualities:

1. ***Curiosity***

   "I have no special talent. I am only passionately curious."

   Einstein was constantly asking questions and forever in a state of objective uncertainty. In fact, he once rejected an invitation to become Israel's second President because of his objectiveness, saying that he lacked "the natural aptitude and the experience to deal properly" with people.

2. ***Perseverance***

"It's not that I'm so smart; it's just that I stay with problems longer."

So much of success comes from the ability to keep pushing on in the face of adversity. Often, people fail not because they're not good or smart enough, but because they give up on their goals. Einstein was at the opposite end of the spectrum, tenacious to his last breath.

3. ***Imagination***

"Imagination is more important than knowledge."

While knowledge is useful, it's also limited, and often short-lived when the new replaces the old. On the other hand, imagination can take us anywhere and develop our minds to ask questions that haven't been considered previously. Knowledge can tell us what's impossible—imagination is what helps to transform the impossible into the extraordinary.

Newman (2012) noted that when Albert Einstein said, "The definition of insanity is doing the same thing over and over and expecting a different result," he was merely recognizing the fault in continuing a behavior if your desire is to change course.

Thiran (2018) continued:

> Einstein highlights something you generally hear from great leaders—they know they don't know. And this drives them to keep learning. Einstein's insatiable curiosity and perseverance were driven by his belief that he lacked knowledge. So many times, we read Einstein's journals and letters stating he didn't know the answer, hence he had to keep learning.

He goes further on to say that leaders like Einstein focus on 'simplicity.' Einstein claimed, "Any intelligent fool can make things bigger, more complex. It takes a touch of genius, and a lot of courage, to move in the opposite direction."

In our complex world, a key lesson we can learn from Einstein is to simplify. To him, the best solutions were the simple ones. Great leaders execute seamlessly because they avoid, when possible, complexity in the change they drive and in their communications. This makes it easy for everyone to be aligned (Thiran, 2018).

Einstein was also a proponent of what we now know as servant leadership, once commenting, "The high destiny of the individual is to serve rather than rule."

Despite being a renowned scientist known for his exacting and diligent methodology and experimentation, he also believed in the power of intuition. "The intuitive mind is a sacred gift and the rational mind is a faithful servant," he said. "All great achievements of science must start from intuitive knowledge. At times I feel certain I am right while not knowing the reason." (Umoh, 2017).

He was also a proponent of civil rights and the value of diversity. In the late 1940s, Einstein became a member of the National Association for the Advancement of Colored People (NAACP), seeing the parallels between the treatment of Jews in Germany and African Americans in the United States. He corresponded with scholar and activist W.E.B. Du Bois and the performing artist Paul Robeson and campaigned for Civil Rights, calling racism a "disease" in a 1946 Lincoln University speech.

"Everybody is a genius. But if you judge a fish by its ability to climb a tree, it will live its whole life believing that it is stupid."

Key Takeaways

- Persistence and perseverance are central leadership traits.
- Effective leaders keep it simple and always seek to simplify.
- Leaders need to be curious and imaginative.
- Leaders need to embrace and leverage diversity.
- Effective leaders are constantly learning.

Dr. Seuss

(Theodor Seuss Geisel)

(March 2, 1904 – September 24, 1991)

"Don't give up. I believe in you all. A person's a person no matter how small."

Biography

It's fairly easy to pull relevant leadership lessons from the 60 plus books written and published by Theodor Seuss Geisel—better known by his pen name Dr. Seuss—between 1931 and 1990 (plus two posthumous releases). *How the Grinch Stole Christmas!* praises community over consumption; *The Sneeches and Other Stories* illustrates the value of diversity and compromise. Even the path to getting his first successful children's book published offers inspiration about persistence in the face of adversity, as Geisel's *And to Think That I Saw It on Mulberry Street* was famously rejected by over 20 publishers before making it to print in 1937.

But Geisel's story is also one of innovation and relying on one's natural talents to fulfill personal and professional goals.

Born in Springfield, Massachusetts in 1904, Geisel matriculated at Dartmouth University in 1921. As an undergraduate during Prohibition, he was stripped of his title as editor-in-chief of the school's humor magazine after he was caught drinking on campus. In order to keep writing, he adopted the pen name Dr. Seuss, one of several he would use throughout his career. The pseudonym would eventually take on new meaning as an in-joke after he dropped out of a doctorate program at Oxford University in 1927.

Upon returning to the States from England, Geisel found work as a political cartoonist and an illustrator for other writers' work. He contributed to high-brow publications like *Life, Vanity Fair,* and *The Saturday Evening Post* before securing a staff position at *Judge,* a weekly satirical magazine based in New York. Geisel would also spend 15 years in the advertising department at Standard Oil, even as his career as an author began pick up steam on the side. He gained particular renown for a campaign he illustrated for an insecticide called Flit.

The eventual publication of *And to Think That I Saw It on Mulberry Street* was a turning point for Geisel, after his first foray into children's literature, a short story collection he illustrated called *Boners,* was a flop, as was a book he wrote for adults after *Mulberry* called *The Seven Lady Godivas.* He published one other children's book, *The 500 Hats of Bartholomew Cubbins,* written in non-rhyming prose, before the outbreak of World War II.

Geisel's first genuine success as a children's author and illustrator came with 1940's *Horton Hatches the Egg,* the story of an elephant who steps in for an absentee mother bird on permanent vacation in Palm Beach. The story set the tone for Geisel's whimsical worldview steeped in morality. It was an instant critical and commercial success.

However, with the war raging, Geisel returned to political cartoons, using his platform to criticize Fascism, the United States Congress, the Republican party, famous isolationists of the time like Charles Lindbergh, and the investigation of suspected Communists. It should be noted that while he called out anti-black and anti-Semitic sentiment at home as detrimental to the war effort, not all of Geisel's cartoons demonstrated a belief in racial harmony that would be acceptable today; at least one of his cartoons published in *PM Magazine* also suggested that Japanese-Americans in the Pacific Northwest were traitors "waiting for the signal at home."

Geisel would later address this in 1954, when, after a post-war visit to Japan, he published *Horton Hears a Who!*, an allegorical call for tolerance and equality widely viewed as a reversal of his wartime anti-Japanese feelings.

Geisel also drew propaganda posters for the Treasury Department, illustrated animated wartime films, and served in the U.S. Army's documentary division. He wrote the Frank Capra-directed short *Your Job in Germany*, which was later turned into an Academy Award-winning film called *Hitler Lives*. Geisel traveled to Europe in 1944 as part of Capra's team, and was trapped behind enemy lines in Belgium for three days at the onset of the Battle of the Bulge before being rescued by British troops. He rose to the rank of major, and was awarded the Legion of Merit for his work.

When the war ended, Geisel relocated to La Jolla, California and shifted attention back to his children's stories, entering into a decades-long, highly prolific period that would spawn some of his most beloved and iconic characters, including Yertle the Turtle (1950), the Cat in the Hat (1957), the Grinch (1957), and the Lorax (1971), his stand-in for environmental consciousness in the face of corporate greed.

Geisel died of cancer in 1991. His work would garner him two Emmy Awards, a Peabody, and a 1984 Pulitzer Prize Special Citation. Dartmouth Medical School was named in honor of Geisel and his second wife Audrey due to their continued financial contributions. In 2007, *U.S. News & World Report* wrote that Geisel had "revolutionized the way that children learned to read." By the turn of the century, more than 600 million copies of Dr. Seuss books had been sold worldwide.

Leadership Insights and Dr. Seuss

Dr. Seuss is a renowned American children's author, political cartoonist, and animator, best known for his work writing and illustrating more than 60 books. We included him in this text on leadership because of insights like this:

"It's not about what it is. It's about what it can become."

"Unless someone like you cares a whole awful lot, nothing is going to get better. It's not."

Many of his thoughts are fun, sometimes puzzling, and geared towards children, but his work offers many insightful views on leadership.

As Cocci (n.d.) notes of Geisel's *Yertle the Turtle*:

> **Don't be a Yertle!** Good old King Yertle was an extremely ambitious turtle who had no regard for the people he ruled. He expected his fellow turtles to do exactly what he said, without any disagreements, because he was far superior to them. He didn't listen to or care about the people he ruled, which were the people who created his throne.

Leadership lesson: Don't be King Yertle. Instead, embrace humility as a leader and use your power to serve, rather than exploit, others (Spungin, 2017).

Reilly (2016) added:

> Part of being a great leader is the ability to gain the trust of your team. Leaders who are true to themselves are seen as authentic and inspire loyalty. An authentic leader is genuine and real, as opposed to fake or phony. You can't fake leadership. If you fake leadership, your team will quickly see through it and will be unwilling to follow you and eventually resent you. Engaging

authentically with the members of your team and others around you is the mark of true leadership.

Cocci (n.d.) applied analysis to *Horton Hatches the Egg and I Can Read with My Eyes Shut,* as well:

Be as honest as Horton.

Being honest and straightforward with employees is the quickest way to earn their respect. Even if you're delivering bad news, be honest and upfront about it. Trying to sugarcoat it will only cause decay in your relationships. It's not always easy striking a balance between transparency and honesty, but if you want to earn your employees' respect, it's absolutely necessary.

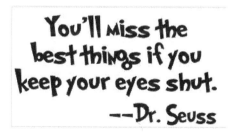

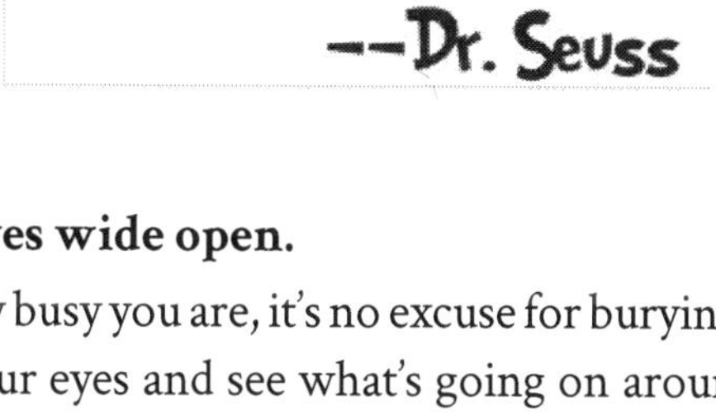
You'll miss the best things if you keep your eyes shut.
--Dr. Seuss

Keep your eyes wide open.

No matter how busy you are, it's no excuse for burying your head in the sand. Open your eyes and see what's going on around you and who's

> doing it, because employees who feel ignored or taken for granted will become more and more unproductive, and eventually quit, leaving even more work to be done. So, open your eyes and pay attention. Are employees doing a good job? If so tell them. Or are there slackers in your midst who are taking advantage of others? If so, take care of them. Encourage your people to think for themselves, grab the bull by the horns, shoot for the moon! People who can think for themselves and don't have to worry about getting hammered for a mistake, stay fresh and excited about work. (Cocci, n.d.).

All team members have unique value. Leaders must be aware of where unhealthy dynamics are festering in their team and learn to unleash the often repressed value that the "out-group" brings through their diversity (Spungin, 2017).

Rielly (2016) added to this:

> Effective leaders don't lock themselves away in their office. If you manage your team all day from your office via emails and instant messages, then it will not be long before you lose touch with your staff and productivity plummets.

On *The Lorax,* Cocci (n.d.) elaborated:

> **When you care, things get better.** You set the tone when it comes to enthusiasm for your work. To a degree, all employees play a role in creating a happy workplace, but you have a special role because as management you have powers (not the abracadabra kind, the motivational kind) and responsibilities.

> Spreading a little cheer is as easy as smiling and saying good morning… and meaning it. So, keep this line from *The Lorax* in mind: "Unless someone like you cares a whole awful lot, nothing is going to get better. It's not." (Cocci, n.d.).

Oh the places you'll go,
Today is your day!
Your mountain is waiting,
So get on your way!
—Dr. Seuss

Also from Cocci (n.d.) on Geisel's seminal book, *Oh, the Places You'll Go!*:

> **Let People Think for Themselves.** To lead and lead well, you have to have confidence. Not just in yourself, but in your team. If your team doesn't believe in themselves, they will be constantly waiting around for you to make decisions. So, don't be afraid to take a back seat and let others shine. You'll be very surprised at what you might find!
>
> If your team doesn't believe in themselves, they will be constantly waiting around for you to make decisions for them, which may make you feel special and important, but it isn't a productive way to operate. Just take it from "Oh, the Places You'll Go!".

Enthusiasm is contagious and effective leader knows how to use that enthusiasm to motivate other members of their team. Enthusiastic leaders are committed to their goals and express this commitment through optimism. Individuals tend to follow people with a "can do" attitude, not those who continually give reasons why something can't be done. Leaders with enthusiasm also demonstrate to the rest of the team that the leader is working toward a common goal alongside their team, and not just "the boss" delegating work (Rielly, 2016).

Reilly (2016) also noted:

Setbacks will happen. Effective leaders nurture the situation to bring out the best in the team. They create a positive environment through praising good work and offering constructive feedback on how to improve when failure or setbacks happen.

All teams need a strong leader to motivate them through a project, regardless of its size. It is your job as a leader to find the best ways to properly motivate your team to reach greatness.

Improvisation. Improvisation is often associated with music or comedy, but it is also important in leadership. Confronted with complex challenges, a good leader uses adaptability skills to surmount obstacles. Effective leaders find opportunity in even the most negative situations and use their improvisational skills to create innovative solutions.

"Don't cry because it's over. Smile because it happened."

Key Takeaways

- Leaders need to have an orientation to serve.
- Leaders should infuse their leadership style with a dose of humility.
- Effective leaders earn respect and trust through consistency, based on a core set of values.
- Effective leaders are genuine, authentic, and real. They are open, transparent, and always honest.
- The best leaders set the direction, expectations, and boundaries and let their teams perform.
- Effective leaders keep a finger on the pulse and establish monitoring mechanisms without getting in the way.
- Leaders must show they care and also lead with optimism and enthusiasm.

Cesar Estrada Chávez

(March 31, 1927 – April 23, 1993)

"Talk is cheap...it is the way we organize and
use our lives every day
that tells what we believe in."

Biography

American agriculture is older than the country itself. Before the arrival of European settlers, native populations dating back centuries cultivated maize, beans, and squash—the so-called "three sisters"—in regions across what would become the United States, working the fertile land that would drive pioneers to venture inward from the coasts to claim it as their own. In the country's early days, the promise of agriculture became a symbol of the promise of America, forming inextricable ties to the nation's moments of great progress and to our most grave sins alike. Farming was at the center of the New Deal; the profits from free farm labor were a motivator for slavery.

And farming—or, more specifically, the plight of migrant farmworkers—provided the context for the emergence of one our nation's most influential Civil Rights and labor leaders, Cesar Estrada Chávez.

Born in Yuma, Arizona in 1927, Chávez, like so many leaders to emerge from Depression-era America, did not complete formal schooling. His family once owned a ranch, a pool hall, and a general store; all were eventually lost to the financial turbulence of the time, forcing Chávez to abandon a conventional education and join his parents and his four siblings in adopting the lifestyle of migrant farmworkers. He and his family frequently lived in temporary camps and harvested in-season crops in California. A physically taxing trade was made more difficult by the era's rampant prejudice against Mexican-Americans.

Chávez had a brief respite from farm work in 1944, but it was far from restful; he enlisted in the U.S. Navy and served for two years during World War II, before returning to migrant farm work in California and Arizona. For the next four years, Chávez toiled in the fields and worked at a lumber yard, until, in 1952, he became an organizer for the Community Services Organization (CSO), an offshoot of activist and organizer Saul Alinsky's Industrial Areas Foundation. The CSO had been founded years before as an advocacy group for Latino Civil Rights in California.

While with the CSO, Chávez set up chapter offices in Oakland and other cities, and drove Mexican-American voter registration throughout the state. In just over half a decade, he progressed from local organizer to national director, delivering speeches in support of labor rights, assembling protests and sit-ins, and exposing corruption. And then, he left the CSO altogether.

Relocating from Los Angeles, Chávez and his colleague, Dolores Huerta, struck out on their own, founding the National Farm Workers Association (NFWA) in Delano, California in 1962. It was alongside Huerta at the NFWA that Chávez' work began its ascent toward maximum critical impact, sparking national interest for the plight of underpaid and mistreated laborers.

Led by Chávez and Heurta, the NFWA worked on behalf of farm workers to establish a minimum wage in California and advocated for the right to collective bargaining, among other initiatives. They also supported a fight spearheaded by Filipino-American grape pickers in Delano in 1965 that led to a strike and a march on Sacramento. As the standoff wore on, the movement won the support of students, truck drivers, longshoremen, and ordinary Americans who refused to buy grapes for their homes.

By 1967, the protestors had reached agreements with several vineyards, after facing countless backdoor deals and strikebreakers. But their struggle was far from over.

As offshoots of the NFWA—which changed its name to United Farm Workers (UFW) after it was incorporated into the American Federation of Labor and Congress of Industrial Organizations (AFL-CIO) in 1972—fanned out across the country, Chávez and his supporters employed many tactics that followed in the tradition of nonviolent protest, most famously that of fasting. Chávez fasted for 25 days in 1968, and 24 days in 1972, during which he was visited by Coretta Scott King in a show of solidarity.

The International Brotherhood of Teamsters, however, didn't always take the same pacifistic stance. In addition to legal tactics and strikebreaking attempts employed by farm owners and legislative bodies, Chávez faced threats from Teamsters seeking to consolidate jurisdictional power over farm laborers in California. As the Delano grape strike was winding down in 1970, Teamsters amped up their efforts to reach an exclusive deal regarding lettuce farmers that locked out UFW members.

In response, Chávez employed a hunger strike; a subsequent deal was reached, but then broken in 1972, causing an estimated 7,000 UFW members to strike, the largest such walk out of farm workers in United States. UFW members were assaulted by Teamsters and a UFW office was bombed in 1970. Chávez himself was jailed for refusing to call off the boycott of iceberg lettuce. Supporters, including Ethel Kennedy, the wife of the late Senator Robert Kennedy, were attacked when they visited Chávez in jail.

Chávez' release was ordered by the state Supreme Court after several weeks, but the Salad Bowl Strike, as it became known, didn't end; a day after he was let out of prison, he called for additional strikes on lettuce growers. The strike formally ceased in 1971, but violence, protests, and marches sprang up for the better part of the decade, during which Chávez continued to practice nonviolent protest tactics. The California Agricultural Labor Relations Act of 1975 was one major milestone, followed, finally, in 1978, with a jurisdictional agreement with the Teamsters the year prior that solely awarded the UFW the jurisdictional right to organize field workers.

Chávez attempted one final hunger strike in 1978—again on behalf of grape workers—this time in response to the harmful use of pesticides. The boycott was deemed unsuccessful, and a weakened body from fasting is believed to have contributed to his death in 1993. Chávez was posthumously awarded the Presidential Medal of Freedom by President Clinton in 1994 for his decades-long commitment to fighting for labor rights through nonviolent protest; his signature black union jacket now sits in the Smithsonian.

Leadership Insights and Chávez

César E. Chávez was a leader and a servant of the people who needed him the most. He triumphed among those who followed him because he knew how to be a servant first. This section highlights the connection between Chávez's life and work, as well as the idea of "servant leadership" (Ortiz, n.d.).

Senator Robert F. Kennedy described Cesar Chávez as "one of the heroic figures of our time." Cesar's motto, "Si se puede!" ("Yes, it can be done!"), coined during his 1972 fast in Arizona, embodies the uncommon legacy he left for people around the world. He was a unique and humble leader, as well as a great humanitarian and communicator who influenced and inspired millions of Americans from all walks of life. Cesar liked to say that his job as an organizer was helping ordinary people do extraordinary things (Cesar Chávez Foundation).

The leadership skills that Chávez acquired were based on the skills approach, a model characterized by effective problem-solving skills, social judgment skills or the ability to work well with people, and knowledge attainment (Northhouse, 2016).

Athie (2001) said of Chávez:

> He never looked for anything for himself. He could see he had been a part of this class of people. He had grown up in the fields; and how many things and how many provisions had been in the life of his parents, his brothers, and family. I think this is what made him see, with compassion, the necessities. He wasn't searching for power, but for solutions; seeking a way of living with people, with the worker, with the owners of the lands.

Ramirez, Diaz, Anderson and Covarrubias (n.d.) identified three leadership qualities that epitomized Chávez' life as a leader: he was caring, he was committed, and he had charisma. They cited his lifelong commitment to workers' rights, his work ethic and perseverance, and his exceptional ability to inspire others.

Ruggiero (n.d.) also noted his ability to connect and inspire, writing, "The standard of excellence that Chávez displayed was his ability to make it possible for members of all races and classes to relate to his cause and his struggle."

The greatest virtue that Cesar Chávez exemplified through his work in adulthood is Justice: "Respecting the human dignity of every individual regardless of their heritage, social class, race or intellectual or physical disability. It involves giving every individual an equal opportunity to flourish, reach potential and achieve success. Chávez worked to allow those around him to thrive and flourish as human beings through the moral ideals of courage and justice" (Ruggiero, n.d.).

"You cannot oppress the people who are not afraid anymore. We have seen the future and it is ours."

Key Takeaways

- Effective leaders are effective communicators who create connections.
- Leaders need to be action oriented and able to get things done.
- Leaders need to have a servant attitude and to consistently demonstrate they care.
- Leaders have to be all-in and committed. They must be willing to persevere and do what it takes.

Bonus Addition – March

Ladda Tammy Duckworth

March 12, 1968 -

Biography

When Tammy Duckworth assumed office as the United States Senator representing Illinois' 8th District in January of 2017, she simultaneously assumed a place at the top of several lists of groundbreaking "firsts." She was the first member of Congress to be born in Thailand, and the first Asian-American woman from Illinois to be elected to Congress. Duckworth, a veteran and double amputee from combat wounds she suffered during the Iraq War, was also the first woman with a known physical disability to be elected to Congress.

But, while the retelling of Duckworth's life may lead with those revolutionary statistics, her inspiring military career and unwavering commitment to public service serves as the foundation of the enduring legacy she is building.

Duckworth was born in Bangkok in 1968, the daughter of a Thai mother with Chinese heritage and a white American father whose family has been in the United States since colonial times. Duckworth's family on her father's side has a history of military service that dates back just as far as their American roots; she has ancestors who fought in the Revolutionary War, and her father is a Marine Corps veteran of World War II and the Vietnam War. When she was young, Duckworth's father worked with the United Nations refugee program, a job that also brought the family to Singapore, Cambodia, and Indonesia. It was a culturally enriching childhood, and occasionally, a tumultuous one. Duckworth has recalled her family—which also includes one younger brother—fleeing Cambodia in the mid-70's, just weeks before the Khmer Rouge took Phnom Penh. Eventually, the family moved Stateside during Duckworth's high school years, settling in Hawaii.

As a gifted student, Duckworth's transition to the U.S. school system was better than seamless—she had previously skipped her freshman year, and graduated from high school in Honolulu with honors, after which she matriculated at the University of Hawaii. After receiving her undergraduate degree in political science, Duckworth pursued a Master's Degree in international affairs from George Washington University. It was during her graduate schooling in Washington, D.C. that Duckworth claimed her place among her family's military heritage, joining the Army Reserve Officers' Training Corps in 1990 and, at least temporarily, curbing her childhood aspiration to become an ambassador.

Two years later, she officially became a commissioned officer in the Army Reserves, where she notably received helicopter pilot training, one of the few combat roles women could hold. Graduating within the top three in her class at flight school qualified her to pilot the Army's Black Hawk helicopters.

After joining the Illinois National Guard, and while pursuing a PhD from Northern Illinois University in 2004, Duckworth was deployed to Iraq within a year of the official start of the United States' war there. In November of 2004, a helicopter Duckworth and a fellow soldier were piloting came under fire from insurgents. A grenade made contact, breaking her right arm and causing irreparable damage to both legs. After undergoing major surgery, Duckworth became a double amputee and received the Purple Heart for her sacrifice.

Duckworth's military career, however, was still a decade removed from its end. Even with her extensive injuries, Duckworth requested a military waiver that would allow her to continue to serve in the Illinois National Guard. Her request was granted, and Duckworth went on to reach the rank of lieutenant colonel before retiring in 2014.

In the period after her recovery, Duckworth became a vocal advocate for veterans affairs, capturing the attention of then-governor of Illinois Rod Blagojevich, who appointed her director of the state's Department of Veteran Affairs in 2006. Three years later, she moved on to the position of Assistant Secretary of Public and Intergovernmental Affairs for the United States Department of Veterans Affairs, a post she held for an additional three years, before she kicked off her campaign for the U.S. House of Representatives in 2011.

Duckworth, who had lost her first Congressional campaign in 2006 by a 2 percent margin, was elected to the House as a Democrat in 2012 after defeating her Republican incumbent rival. In 2014, she was re-elected, defeating fellow veteran Larry Kaifesh. Serving out the remainder of her term, Duckworth then set her sights on the Senate in 2015. In 2016, she was sworn in after defeating former senator Mark Kirk.

Duckworth's tenure in Senate has been marked by her outspokenness about a cadre of issues, including her pro-immigration stance and her support of universal background checks for gun owners. She also serves on the Senate Committees on Small Business and Entrepreneurship; on Energy and National Resources; on Commerce, Science and Transportation; and on Environment and Public Works.

In 2015, Duckworth completed her PhD. Three years later, she and her husband Bryan—a fellow veteran who Duckworth met while at George Washington University—welcomed their second daughter, giving Duckworth the distinction of being the first sitting member of the U.S. Senate to give birth while in office.

Leadership Insights and Duckworth

"I shouldn't even be here, so if I'm here,
I better do something good."

"It's important to have women in leadership positions, because our experiences are different from those of the men we serve with and that helps us identify problems we can fix."

We included Tammy for her unique perspectives as a pilot, wounded combat veteran (and a Purple Heart recipient), and Senator as well as being physically disabled, a mother, an accomplished scholar, and a woman of mixed cultural background. She is still early in her leadership career and much of her perspective has been forged in the military and government positions, but she brings insights worth considering through a larger leadership lens.

In an interview with On Leadership (Washington Post) (n.d.), Duckworth noted:

> Being a leader is identifying who you are, bringing your strengths, but also identifying the strengths of the people that you're working with and really building on that and pulling together a team. And just forgetting about what other people are saying about how you should be and how you're supposed to be, just bring your own strengths to it.

She also noted the importance of understanding and remaining committed to a mission:

> The key part of the soldier's creed is a component called the "warrior ethos." And the warrior ethos is just four lines, it says:
>
> "I will always place the mission first, I will never quit, I will never accept defeat, and I will never leave a fallen comrade behind." Those four things really meant a lot to me.

Khan (2017) also noted this in an interview with Duckworth:

> The two most important lessons the military taught me are to never leave anyone behind—not on the battlefield and not in

> our country—and to never put a service member in harm's way without understanding the costs of war.

In a speech at Georgetown (2018), Duckworth noted some points, which were targeted at the current world events, but offer salient leadership insights that can be applied to organizational leadership:

> While we hope for peace, we must maintain our military readiness and remain prepared for a war.
>
> We need to restore accountability and transparency to how we entangle ourselves in these conflicts, as well as to countless other matters of war and peace.
>
> Our strength doesn't come from the President thumping his chest or flaunting our nuclear weapons... it comes from our people, our values and the global belief that America stands by her word.
>
> It comes from the hard work, the compassion, the courage of Americans serving their country in and out of uniform.
>
> And we cannot afford to take that shared sense of sacrifice for granted.

Duckworth has also spoken about being the first Senator to give birth and to bring her child into the Senate (Jarvie, 2018):

> "It's ridiculous that it's the 21st century and it's such a big deal," Duckworth said. "It should have happened a lot sooner than this. I think it speaks to the fact they we need more women in leadership all across our nation, whether it's in boardrooms or in the Senate chambers and at the very highest ranks of our military."

"That day, I lost both of my legs, but I was a given a second chance at life," she wrote in a 2015 essay for Politico. "It's a feeling that has helped to drive me in my second chance at service — no one should be left behind, and every American deserves another chance."

"I am going to start off assuming that he loves this country as much as I love this country," she told the Axe Files podcast. "If you start off from that point, I think you can learn to work with anyone."

"I shouldn't even be here, so if I'm here, I better do something good."

Key Takeaways

- Effective leaders never lose sight or connection to their stakeholders.
- Effective leaders build on their strengths and the strengths of their team.
- Leaders need to be mission-focused and never quit in seeking its execution.
- Leaders must exemplify accountability and transparency.

APRIL LEADERS

For April, we will learn from Thomas Jefferson, Colin Powell, and Maya Angelou.

Thomas Jefferson

April 13, 1743 — July 4, 1826

"I like the dreams of the future better
than the history of the past."

Biography

Like so many historical figures of his time, the gilded legacy of Thomas Jefferson—the third President of the United States, a Founding Father, and a primary author of the Declaration of Independence—is emblematic of the selective memory of a country built on inequality while touting freedom for all. How can disciples of Jefferson's undeniable and lasting influence on American life reconcile the inclusive nature of his oft-repeated statement that "all men are created equal" with the fact that Jefferson was himself a slave owner and the father of illegitimate children with one slave, Sally Hemmings?

Part of that reconciliation is, of course, to acknowledge the contradiction and to plainly examine the ways in which the actions he took during his lifetime are linked to present day American realities—in ways both positive and negative. A clear-eyed assessment allows for lessons in leadership to be culled from Jefferson's life while still stopping short of endorsing his character and values.

Born in 1743 in Virginia, Jefferson began life on a plantation, one of ten children born to a wealthy family. When he was 17, he left home to attend the College of William and Mary; while there, he took it upon himself to add to his studies by reading law under the tutelage of George Wythe, a prominent local lawyer. From 1767, when he was admitted to the Virginia Bar Association, through 1774, Jefferson enjoyed great success in his legal practice while concurrently pursuing an entree into the political sphere. He was first elected to the Virginia House Burgesses—a colonial legislative body—in 1768.

Jefferson was a proponent of American independence, although his stance wasn't widely known until his essay on the matter, "A Summary View of the Rights of British America," was published in 1774. The popularity of his work led to an invitation to the Second Continental Congress the following year, where Jefferson's role as a leader outside of Virginia took shape.

The Congress, of course, established George Washington as commander in chief of a Continental Army. Jefferson was not considered a gifted public speaker in the vein of his contemporary John Adams, but he was admired for his writing ability. Jefferson, therefore, was asked to take the lead in drafting resolutions, including a first draft of the Declaration of Independence. Reportedly written in the span of roughly two weeks, Jefferson's Declaration was the basis for the final version adopted on July 4, 1776—particularly his preamble outlining the rights of all humans.

Jefferson resigned from the Congress, and opted to turn his focus back to Virginia, where he worked as a member of the Virginia House of Delegates, where he rewrote many state laws to better align with the Declaration of Independence, particularly advocating for religious freedom and the separation of church and state. As the Revolutionary War raged on, Jefferson was elected governor of Virginia for two terms. Rather than pursue a third term, in 1781 Jefferson retreated to

Monticello, the home he built for himself atop a hill near the plantation where he was raised.

While there, Jefferson wrote "Notes on the State of Virginia," outlining his political point of view. Predictably given the time and his previous output, the book included his views on slavery that are contradictory and confusing, if not completely paradoxical. Taken at face value, his stance that slavery contradicts basic human rights can be used as an argument that equality is baked into the premise of America as a country; when combined with the fact that Jefferson is believed to have owned 600 slaves throughout his lifetime and thought black people to be genetically inferior to white people, it is a persuasive piece of evidence of a long history of powerful people speaking out of both sides of their mouth, paying lip service to justice and non-discrimination while actively working to preserve imbalance.

In 1782, Jefferson left Virginia and returned to the Continental Congress—establishing the road to statehood for territories in the West—and then traveled to Paris in 1784 to serve as Minister to France. Historians have characterized Jefferson's time in Paris as decadent and indulgent, and largely inconsequential toward making political headway for relations between the fledgling United States and European nations. Jefferson returned home in 1789, before the French Revolution reached its violent crescendo.

Back in Virginia, Jefferson served as Secretary of State under the first American President, George Washington. Largely absent from Constitutional debates while in France, Jefferson focused on foreign policy, initially favoring an alliance with the French over the British (although later arguing for neutrality). He also held a deep-seated aversion to any form of government that consolidated power in a way that mirrored a monarchy. Through that viewpoint, Jefferson was instrumental in forming the Republican party as an opposition party.

Despite his skepticism toward a powerful national government, Jefferson ran for President and took office in 1801, after serving as Vice President under John Adams. Among Jefferson's most significant achievements as President was the Louisiana Purchase, which doubled the land size of the United States. The deal plunged the country further into debt, but Jefferson argued that the increased land size would help strengthen his long-term vision for a sustainable nation built on agriculture. He retired after two terms of near-constant conflict with opposition at home and fallout from the tense relationship between France and England that resulted in the Embargo Act of 1807, an attempt to force European powers to retool trade deals that backfired, leaving the American economy weakened.

Jefferson lived out his remaining days at Monticello. Before his death in 1826, he established the University of Virginia, one of the United States' most prestigious state universities. Jefferson's visage has been immortalized on Mount Rushmore, and the Jefferson Memorial on the National Mall was dedicated on the 200th anniversary of his birth. In 2012, the Smithsonian National Museum of African American History and Culture would open "Slavery at Jefferson's Monticello: Paradox of Liberty," the first public exhibition on the National Mall to examine the contradictions of Jefferson's stated ideology and his practiced lifestyle.

Leadership Insights and Jefferson

Jefferson is an American leadership icon, in many ways ahead of his in time in terms of leadership practices. He presents a blend of visionary and strategic thinking with pragmatic practices of effective leadership. One example is his understanding of the need to stay grounded and connected, advocating that leaders need to be lifelong learners.

Thiran (2017) noted the ideology outlined Jefferson's *A Decalogue of Canons for Observation in Practical Life.* helped him to navigate various challenges and obstacles throughout his political career.

They are:

1. Never put off till tomorrow what you can do today.
2. Never trouble another for what you can do yourself.

3. Never spend your money before you have it.
4. Never buy what you do not want because it is cheap; it will be dear to you.
5. Pride costs us more than hunger, thirst and cold.
6. We never repent of having eaten too little.
7. Nothing is troublesome that we do willingly.
8. How much pain have cost us the evils which have never happened?
9. Take things always by their smooth handle.
10. When angry, count to 10 before you speak; if very angry, a hundred.

Meacham (2013) noted, "Even the greatest American political leaders—literally the folks on Rushmore, the people we think of as the absolute ideal of political leadership and public service—were, in their time and in their hour, a whole lot more like we are than we might like to think." He added, that they often demonstrate a willingness to sacrifice ideology for a commitment to an overarching principle. In the case of Jefferson and the other Founding Fathers, that overarching principle was survival of the country that they had created—a nation they believed was the world's best hope for human liberty. "They were devoted to the principal vision of the country, but never let the qualms about the means of accomplishing their ends get in the way," he said. "These were constantly practical people. If they hadn't been, we'd be living in a very different world."

Leaders must be in-tune with their culture. Meacham offered Thomas Jefferson as a prime example of someone who had a deep understanding of his times and culture. Great presidents and leaders make time to have conversations that have nothing to do with the day's immediate agenda.

Yaeger (2015) notes:

> In short, Jefferson exhibited leadership over decades, even if he was not the person ultimately in charge. He voiced his concerns and his ideas; he argued and advocated for what he believed was the best policy; he researched, sought out advice, and prepared for the day when he would be in a place to make the call. And, when that day finally came, he was ready to act judiciously.

Jefferson offers an important lesson in long-term leadership for all of us. Even though the process was a frustrating one—and would continue to be so for several years, even after he sent the first fleet of American ships to the Mediterranean in a show of force—Jefferson did not give up when his suggestions were rejected the first, second, or tenth time. Instead, he strengthened his position through personal investment in learning. But what was more, by implementing his plan in stages and allowing Congress and the American people to come alongside him and see the reasoning behind the action, he ultimately won more sympathy and support than if he had simply ram-rodded his agenda through.

Like many historic leaders, Thomas Jefferson was a man who didn't fit into a specific mold, sometimes favoring ideas that were unpopular at the time. Jefferson was considered to be a visionary, often going against the grain in order to achieve the greater good for the country. Jefferson forged ahead, despite personal tragedy and despair (n.d.).

Wikihow (n.d.) captured some leadership lessons from Jefferson:

1. **Broaden your knowledge**. A polymath by nature and experience, Jefferson spoke five languages, and was passionately interested in philosophy, science, religion, architecture, and invention. He was well read and always had a thirst for knowledge. Never assume that you are "above" digesting popular information sources as well. A leader should know the pulse of what the majority of the public is thinking and following by

way of trends, fads and curiosities. Knowing what matters to the people you lead (whether it's a team or a company) will always help you to tailor your ideas and visions to make them resonate with those you're guiding. Be curious and genuine in your desire to understand what moves people.

2. **Speak your mind, even if your opinion isn't popular.** Looking beyond the status quo for a better way of doing things and for ways to improve society as a whole may not be popular initially-- resistance to change, however beneficial, is a human certainty. During Jefferson's times, free America was not fully realized and many Americans did not fully grasp the concept of a completely free society. However, Jefferson turned his frustration into determined persistence and talked to anyone who would listen about his vision of a free U.S. He pushed and persuaded until his dream came to fruition. Stick to your principles. Don't allow others to influence or sway you from your original intent.

> "On matters of style, swim with the current; on matters of principle, stand like a rock." –Thomas Jefferson

3. **Focus on your strengths.** There is much said and written about overcoming your weaknesses. While there is always room for tightening up aspects of yourself that aren't working the way you want them to, it is a fool's life to pursue anything that relies principally on your weaknesses. Realize that focusing all the time on weaknesses leaves less time to focus on strengths and in many cases, can cause you to feel "less than" rather than to celebrate what you're brilliant at. If you believe you're in a position that isn't a good fit or you aren't qualified enough, don't bluff or "wing it."

4. **Acknowledge your imperfections without fostering them.** Even the greatest leader understands that he or she is not perfect. Although Jefferson is considered to be one of the

country's greatest leaders, his character is riddled with imperfection and inconsistency. A good leader will continue to learn and grow, will seek to be less defensive of his or her own ideas and be more open to the perspectives of others.

Use your mistakes as a learning experience. If you don't learn from your mistakes, you cannot build and further your leadership. By acknowledging your errors and studying them, you can fortify your ability and credibility as a leader and avoid the same pitfalls and shortcomings in the future. Although it is widely known that Jefferson made many mistakes, future Presidents turned to him for advice and lessons, well beyond his actual life.

5. **Learn from others, even if it means you must follow for a while.** Great leaders learn skills by not just forging ahead without knowledge but by identifying mentors or guides, studying their strategies and molding their techniques to their advantage.

   Stay aware throughout your life that you don't always know everything, not even in your own field of expertise. Even seasoned leaders understand that always improving your knowledge is the real source of power––and that it is impossible to know everything.

   Gain motivation and insight from your mentors. Although Jefferson asked Adams to create the draft, it was Adams who provided Jefferson with the necessary motivation and encouragement, which led him to pen his draft. Adams pointed out Jefferson's strengths, one being that he was a better writer. Sometimes it takes other people's observations of you to point out your strengths.

"In matter of style, swim with the current; in matters of principle, stand like a rock."

"I am a great believer in luck and I find the harder I work the more I have of it."

Key Takeaways

- Effective leaders are visionaries, informed by doses of pragmatism and practicality.
- Effective leaders build on their strengths. They acknowledge their weaknesses, but invest more in what they do well for leverage.
- Effective leaders stay grounded and connected, willing to listen and learn from a wide variety of sources.
- Effective leaders do not 'wing it,' they prepare.
- Effective leaders practice determined persistence.
- They are willing to go first, even with unpopular positions, for the greater good.

Colin Powell

April 5, 1937 –

"Trust is the glue that holds an organization together and the lubricant that keeps it moving forward."

Biography

Colin Powell's professional accomplishments—which include holding the titles of the 65th United States Secretary of State, National Security Advisor, Chairman of the Joint Chiefs of Staff, and four-star general in the United States Army—have become known across the country, if not the world, as a particularly aspirational example of a devotion to service. But, his childhood may be most relatable to a smaller set of people: namely, those who grew up in and around New York City.

Born in Harlem in 1937 to Jamaican immigrants of mixed ancestry, Powell lived in the South Bronx throughout his youth, where he attended the city's public schools. His parents both worked in Manhattan's garment district, while Powell found employment in local shops in his neighborhood. Thanks to the oft-cited "melting pot" nature of 20th century New York, he also served as a Shabbos goy for his Jewish neighbors.

In 1958, he graduated from the City College of New York. His bachelor's degree was in geology, but, while at CCNY, he enrolled in the school's Reserve Officers' Training Corps (ROTC), setting the stage for his military career. Upon graduation, he left New York for Fort Benning on the Alabama-Georgia border to complete his basic training as a second lieutenant in the Army. Soon after, he was sent to West Germany and then to Fort Devens in Massachusetts. In 1962, the same year he married his wife Alma, Powell was deployed to Vietnam, the first of two tours he would complete there.

Neither of Powell's tours in Vietnam were without incident. In his first, he was injured by a booby trap, for which he was awarded a Purple Heart. In his second, he survived a helicopter crash; his efforts to rescue three fellow soldiers from the wreckage garnered him a Soldier's Medal. Even after his subsequent accomplishments continued to build after the war, Powell's time in Vietnam has been revisited often, particularly surrounding the veracity of his findings from an investigation he led into a whistleblowing letter sent by a soldier regarding the My Lai Massacre, in which a reported 300 Vietnamese civilians were killed by U.S. forces. Powell found the letter to be without merit, a claim that others have consistently refuted then and since.

Upon returning from Vietnam, Powell completed his MBA at George Washington University in 1971. He continued to rise in rank in the Army for the next two decades. He had served a tour of duty in Korea and worked at the Pentagon, when, in 1989, President Ronald Reagan appointed him National Security Advisor. Reagan's successor, George H.W. Bush, also found a place for Powell in his administration. After receiving the title of four-star general and serving as Commander in Chief, Forces Command, Powell was appointed Chairman of the Joint Chiefs of Staff. He was the first black person to hold this title.

Powell received more national attention than ever before for his role as military strategist in the Bush administration, due in large part to the United States' war in Iraq known as Desert Storm. The so-called Powell Doctrine was implemented there, advocating for a swift and powerful exertion of force to minimize casualties during war, only after exhausting all other diplomatic means of conflict resolution.

After serving for a brief time in the Clinton administration, Powell retired from the military in 1993 and shifted his attention toward philanthropy through the youth-focused nonprofit organization America's Promise. In 1996, he officially joined the Republican party, and, five years later, he re-entered politics when President George W. Bush appointed him Secretary of State. He was confirmed unanimously by the Senate and, once again, made history as the first black person in that position.

Powell's tenure as Secretary of State was defined by controversy surrounding the invasion of Iraq in 2003, for which he attempted to leverage his reputation and largely positive public perception to rally support. He would later admit that much of the evidence he presented in his advocacy for military action and the overthrowing of Iraqi leader Saddam Hussein was based on faulty intelligence. That ultimately became the impetus for his subsequent resignation and retirement.

Since then, however, Powell hasn't shied away from speaking out on political issues, lending his considerable clout toward lobbying for causes he supports. He famously broke with his Republican peers when he endorsed Barack Obama for President in 2008. He has also pursued inroads into the business world, serving on the board of multinational corporations while remaining active in charitable causes. Despite steady rumors throughout the 2000's that he would run for President or serve as a Cabinet member, he has yet to formally enter politics again.

Leadership Insights and Powell

Powell brings a wide perspective to our leadership discussion. He had a very successful military career, reaching the pinnacle of military leadership as Chairman of the Joint Chiefs of Staff, before pivoting into a global role as U.S. Secretary of State. He was the 65th United States Secretary of State, serving under President George W. Bush from 2001 to 2005, the first black person to serve in that position. He also led a non-profit, became a partner in a venture capital firm, and serves on several Boards of

Directors. As Chairman of the Joint Chiefs, he oversaw 28 crises, including Operation Desert Storm during the 1991 Persian Gulf War.

Powell is the recipient of numerous U.S. and foreign military awards and decorations. Powell's civilian awards include two Presidential Medal of Freedom, the President's Citizens Medal, and the Congressional Gold Medal.

Lynch (2016) noted that just before assuming his role as Chairman of the Joint Chiefs of Staff, Powell published a list of 13 principles of leadership, which are as follows:

Rule 1: It Ain't As Bad as You Think. It Will Look Better in The Morning.

Time provides perspective. Many terrible events that we have had as professionals do not seem as devastating when we revisit them the next day. This is a valuable reminder not to over react to adverse circumstances.

Rule 2: Get Mad Then Get Over It.

Anger can derail judgment and cloud objective thinking. We are humans and will get mad. The key is to control the anger by letting it happen and then pass. Holding grudges and vendettas will prevent you from rebuilding alliances and moving forward.

Rule 3: Avoid Having Your Ego So Close To Your Position That When Your Position Falls, Your Ego Falls With It.

It is vital that we do not define who we are by what we do. It is important to recognize that our roles are means for us to accomplish many things and are not ends in and of themselves.

Rule 4: It Can Be Done.

Leadership is about making things happen. Leaders challenge the status quo, ask the deeper questions, provide inspiration to succeed, and build confidence among others that they can do great things. This can also be said for any individual contributor in an organization. The power to influence by believing it can be done is powerful.

Rule 5: Be Careful Who You Chose.

The people you hire and advisors you chose are vital to your success. None of us can succeed on our own.

Rule 6: Do Not Let Adverse Facts Stand In The Way Of A Good Decision.

Leadership is challenging because in the end you will have people that can strongly agree and vehemently disagree with your decision. This can be lonely and challenging. Leaders have to do their best to seek the best sets of data, arrive at the truth and accept that their decisions, while necessary, will have detractors.

Rule 7: You Can Not Make Someone Else's Decisions. You Should Not Let Someone Else Make Yours.

In the end leaders have the ultimate responsibility to make the final decision. They can secure great input and advice but cannot defer the decision to those who report to them. They need to accept accountability.

Rule 8: Check the Small Things.

Having a big picture perspective is great, but leaders cannot ignore the importance of the details. This balancing act is one of the biggest challenges professionals face as they advance in their careers. In the end, strategy is vital but worthless without execution.

Rule 9: Share Credit.

Let's hope that the age of the rock star hire is over and we are now more focused on the servant leader.

> **Rule 10: Remain Calm and Be Kind.**
>
> Leaders need to inspire and build confidence in others. Running down the hall with your hair on fire will not help. Leaders also have to be respectful and kind to everyone. Those around them take their cues from those in leadership roles.
>
> **Rule 11: Have A Vision and Be Demanding.**
>
> While leaders can be empowering and humbly serve those around them they also need to have a vision and be demanding on fulfilling it. This means holding people accountable, not accepting mediocrity, and expecting more out of everyone.
>
> **Rule 12: Do Not Take Counsel of Your Fears or Naysayers.**
>
> Paralysis by analysis can inhibit us from decisively acting. Leaders have to recognize that counter/negative inputs can often come with agendas.
>
> **Rule 13: Perpetual Optimism Is A Force Multiplier.**
>
> Leaders who are positive, who believe that great things can be done, are the ones we are all attracted to and are the most successful. An analysis of past presidential campaigns (let us exclude the 2016 race) has shown that the more positive message almost always prevails. Perpetual optimism will generate exponential results because everyone will have the shared belief that it can be done.

Murphy (2016) also commented:

> Powell's emphasis on humility and appreciation of the value of teamwork still stands as a model for public service, and indeed for all leaders. Powell understood that just as no man is an island, so too is no leader. Leaders serve as the heads of organizations,

> but are also still simply a part of the whole. Appreciating the contributions of all the parts to the whole makes the organization run better, which is the overarching goal. Powell understood this, and even when no one was watching, went above and beyond to ensure organizational success.

Powell himself commented (n.d. Military Transition):

> No matter what your job, you are there to serve. It makes no difference if it is government, military, business, or any other endeavor. Go in with a commitment to selfless service, never selfish service...get off the train before somebody throws you off, go sit in the shade with a drink, and take a look at the other tracks and trains out there. Spend a moment watching the old train disappear, then start a new journey on a new train.

Stanford GSB (2005) hosted Powell at a "View from the Top" Lecture Series and noted on Powell's leadership insights:

> Successful leaders know how to define their mission, convey it to their subordinates, and ensure they have the right tools and training needed to get the job done.
>
> Powell said: "Leadership is all about people...and getting the most out of people." It is about conveying a sense of purpose in a selfless manner and creating conditions of trust while displaying moral and physical courage. "Never show fear or anger," he added. "You have to have a sense of optimism."
>
> Effective leaders are made, not born, Powell said. They learn from trial and error and from experience. When something fails, a true leader learns from the experience and puts it behind him. "You don't get reruns in life," he said. "Don't worry about what happened in the past."

A false leader is someone who fails to get the necessary resources for his or her staff to do their jobs, Powell said. The first way you take care of the troops is to train them, he said. Then you have to trust them and let them get on with their work. The best leaders are those who can communicate upward the fears and desires of their subordinates, and are willing to fight for what is needed. If not, the organization will weaken and crumble.

"Leadership is solving problems. The day soldiers stop bringing you their problems is the day you stopped leading them. They have either lost confidence that you can help or concluded you do not care. Either case is a failure of leadership."

"If you are going to achieve excellence in big things, you develop the habit in little matters."

Key Takeaways

- Effective leaders are bold, decisive, and action oriented, but still display humility.
- Effective leaders know they are only as good as their team.
- Leaders need to embrace selfless service, putting their people first.
- Effective leaders are mission-focused and bring a sense of optimism to execution.
- Effective leaders balance mission and execution, paying attention to the small things without micro-managing.
- Effective leaders are obstacle removers and problem solvers.
- Effective leaders earn trust by doing what they say what they will do.

Maya Angelou

(Marguerite Annie Johnson)

April 4, 1928 – May 28, 2014

"A leader sees greatness in other people.
He nor she can be much of a leader if all she sees is herself."

Biography

Politicians and CEOs are often studied and analyzed in MBA programs for their strategic thinking and business acumen. But stopping there omits some of our most impactful leaders who exert their influence through less structured means, using the arts to shift culture. There may be no better example of this in contemporary history than the life and work of writer, poet, and activist Maya Angelou.

Angelou's birth coincided with the start of the Great Depression in 1928, one of many factors working against her from the beginning of her life. Her parents' tumultuous marriage ended when she was a toddler, and she and her older brother were sent from their home in St. Louis to live in rural Alabama with their grandmother. While the conditions of Angelou's life in Alabama were in stark relief to the harsh financial constraints others faced at the time—thanks to her grandmother's successful general store—she was an African American in the segregated South; racism was rampant.

Angelou's time in Alabama was short lived. Four years after her arrival, she was unceremoniously collected by her father and returned to St. Louis to live with her mother. At only eight years old, Angelou was raped by her mother's boyfriend. After she told her brother about the assault, her assailant was convicted, but released from prison shortly thereafter; once he was freed, he murdered days later in what is believed to have been retaliation by Angelou's family members. The course of events were so traumatic for Angelou, that she didn't speak for five years.

Angelou returned to live with her grandmother again for a time, before moving in her teenage years to be with her mother—this time in Oakland, California. Throughout the 1940's in San Francisco, Angelou worked various jobs while she studied dance and acting at the California Labor School. These included gigs as a waitress, a prostitute, a stripper, and the city's first black female cable car conductor. It was while working at a strip club that Angelou was discovered by a theater group, landing her a role in an international touring production of *Porgy & Bess.*

Angelou visited Europe and Africa with the production, and continued to act and sing for a living, moving to New York in the late 1950's. There, she joined the Harlem Writers Guild, providing her with access to other prominent black artists and activists of the time. She utilized her platform and prominence to organize the Cabaret for Freedom, a benefit for the Southern Christian Leadership Conference—which would go on to name her Northern Coordinator, solidifying her role as a leader of the Civil Rights Movement. After brief stints writing for publications in Cairo and Ghana—where she met Malcolm X, with whom she worked to facilitate the Organization of Afro-American Unity—Angelou returned to California, where she wrote and performed in a series of works for television, film, and theatre that explored the African American experience.

In 1968 she agreed to help Martin Luther King, Jr organize a march that would never come to fruition; he was assassinated on her birthday that year. Channeling her grief and reflecting upon her childhood trauma, Angelou published her seminal work, *I Know Why the Caged Bird Sings*, the following year. The memoir catapulted her into a rare echelon of international renown and admiration, setting the stage for a decades-long career as a lecturer, a professor at Wake Forest University, and one of the country's most prominent literary voices. The work was viewed as a paradigm shift in autobiographical writing, for its mastery of the form and boundary pushing stylistic flourishes, but also for its role in giving black women writers the space to interrogate their lives and share their experiences with unapologetic candor.

In the coming years, Angelou would publish seven autobiographical works, and gain much recognition for her poetry. She would also continue to actively engage in American politics. She recited a poem at President Bill Clinton's inauguration in 1993 (a recording of which later earned her a Grammy Award), and campaigned for Hillary Clinton in 2008 before shifting her support to President Barack Obama's campaign after he won the Democratic primary during that election cycle. In 2011, she was awarded the Presidential Medal of Freedom; in 2013, she was commissioned by the U.S. State Department to write a poem eulogizing Nelson Mandela.

Before her death in 2014, Angelou had received over 50 honorary degrees from colleges and universities recognizing the influence she had on the arts and Civil Rights activism. She was nominated for a Tony Award and a Pulitzer Prize, won two NAACP Image Awards, and, in 2000, was given the National Medal of Arts.

Leadership Insights and Angelou

Maya Angelou is one of the most revered poets in American history. But, given her prolific output and ability to articulate many facets of the American experience, her voice reverberates well beyond the sphere of the arts. She published seven autobiographies, three books of essays, several books of poetry, and is credited with a list of plays, movies, and television shows that span over 50 years. We included her in this text because much of her work contains keen leadership insights worthy of adoption.

Slaughter (2014) noted:

> What was so moving to me about Maya Angelou, and I believe to most people, was her authenticity. And it was her authenticity, along with the wisdom she shared, that made her such an endearing leader. She was often the voice of reason in a world that's sometimes full of unreasonableness. As leaders, we can all learn from someone who stood up for what she believed in with grace, dignity, and courage.

"I've learned that people will forget what you said, people will forget what you did, but people will never forget how you made them feel."

"Nothing can dim the light that shines from within."

Schnall, M. (2018) interviewed Angelou and offered these leadership lessons from her time with her:

> **1. Speak with confidence and power.**
>
> First off, there was her voice. Slow, thoughtful, deliberate, commanding, and so eloquent. She delivered each word thoughtfully, as though it was a gift—and it was. My default nature is to speak quickly and reactively, so I learned from Maya the importance of slowing down to carefully consider each word and speak with confidence and power. She did not speak off the top of her head, but from the depths of her soul. She knew who she was and stood firmly within her truth.
>
> Maya also taught me the importance of taking pride in who you are and talking with authority as an expert. This skill comes

from within, not from someone else granting us this ability. She used her powerful voice (as we all can) to share her stories, to advocate for tolerance, justice and equality, and to move people to feel more beauty, peace and love.

2. Don't be afraid to be vulnerable and share your story.

Maya's lessons and leadership feel particularly timely considering the #MeToo moment we are in, which signifies a new era of women speaking their truth, baring their souls, and telling their stories. That is another thing I learned from Maya and her writing: the importance of sharing our stories, struggles, and vulnerabilities rather than hiding them away. She told me, "We need to not be in denial about what we've done, what we've come through. It will help us if we all do that. Have a sense to look at yourself and say, 'Well, wait a minute. I'm stronger than I thought I was.'"

3. See hard times as opportunities for growth.

Another lesson I learned from Maya is that the most powerful leaders are often those who have overcome incredible obstacles. It is often within the darkest moments and pain of life that we learn and grow. As she told me, "We may encounter many defeats, but we must not be defeated. It may even be necessary to encounter the defeat, so that we can know who we are. So that we can say, 'Oh, that happened, and I rose. I did get knocked down flat in front of the whole world, and I rose. I didn't run away; I rose right where I'd been knocked down.' That's how you get to know who you are." I think that is so helpful for us to remember as we ride life's unavoidable waves, knowing we will get knocked down—this is a necessary part of our evolution and how we develop valuable reserves of wisdom and strength that serve us as individuals and as leaders.

Schnall, M. (2014) in an earlier interview also noted the importance of courage:

> One of the most inspiring virtues Maya often spoke of was the importance of courage, which she bravely displayed in her own tumultuous life, and to see our setbacks and challenges we encounter as an opportunity for growth. She told me,
>
> "We may encounter many defeats, but we must not be defeated. It may even be necessary to encounter the defeat, so that we can know who we are."
>
> Eikenberry, K. (2014) noted this of Angelou's passing: "It is three simple lines and the words I most connect to Maya Angelou. After I heard of her passing, they are the words I thought of . . ."
>
> "If you don't like something, change it. If you can't change it, change your attitude. Don't complain."
>
> He then went on to note: "In your workplace, in your organization, there are things that are broken or things that are good but could be better. Changing them is the work of leadership."

Marcus, L. (2014) also shared some leadership insights from Angelou:

> All of us knows not what is expedient, not what is going to make us popular, not what the policy is, or the company policy—but in truth, each of us knows what is the right thing to do. And that's how I am guided.
>
> Whatever you want to do, if you want to be great at it, you have to love it and be able to make sacrifices for it.
>
> Words mean more than what is set down on paper. It takes the human voice to infuse them with deeper meaning.

"If you are always trying to be normal,
you will never know how amazing you can be."

"Each of us has a power and responsibility to become
a rainbow in the clouds."

Key Takeaways

- Effective leaders do the right things for the right reasons.
- Leaders must be authentic and consistently true to themselves.
- Leaders must have courage of conviction.
- Leaders can and should learn from defeats, but not be defeated.
- Words matter; leaders need to use their voice powerfully, but appropriately, with dignity and grace.
- Leaders should not be afraid to show vulnerability.

MAY LEADERS

For May, we will learn from Golda Meir, Florence Nightingale, and James Dyson.

Golda Meir

(Golda Mabovitch)

May 3, 1898 – December 8, 1978

"I never did anything alone. Whatever was accomplished in this country was accomplished collectively."

Biography

In pop culture, the nickname "Iron Lady" may be most closely associated with former British Prime Minister Margaret Thatcher, who led the United Kingdom throughout the '80s with an uncompromising will and singular point of view. But, the moniker has been applied—fairly or not, and with varying degrees of both derision and admiration—to any number of female political leaders who assert the power they've earned. One such recipient of the title was Golda Meir, Israel's first female prime minister—the nation's fourth PM overall—who served in the role from 1969 to 1974.

Meir was born in 1898 in Kiev, in what was then a part of the Russian Empire. Her father, a carpenter, emigrated to the United States to look for work in 1903, calling for his family to join him three years later in Milwaukee when he had saved enough money to fund their travel. The timing was pivotal, as anti-Jewish sentiment was reaching a fever pitch at home and violent pogroms were becoming increasingly commonplace.

As a child in the Midwest, Meir displayed an early interest in activism and politics. When she was in elementary school, she is said to have organized a fundraiser for classmates who couldn't afford textbooks. In high school, a rebellious visit to her sister in Denver—who frequently hosted a circle of local intellectuals discussing politics—engrained in her a deep connection to the Zionist movement advocating for a Jewish state in Palestine. Her conservative parents wanted her to lead a traditional life as a wife and mother; while Meir did receive her teaching credentials from what is now the University of Wisconsin-Milwaukee and went on to marry a man she had met in Denver, her parents' hopes for a conventional life for their daughter would go unfulfilled.

In 1924, Meir and her husband left the United States for a kibbutz in Palestine, where her commitment to Zionism grew. She became head of the political department of Histadrut, an organization representing trade unions, and was a delegate to the World Zionist Organization. She frequently spoke publicly on behalf of Zionist causes throughout World War II, eventually becoming acting head of the Jewish Agency—the most prominent Jewish authority in Palestine at the time—after the arrest of its leader at the hands of the British attempting to enforce the White Paper policy that limited Jewish immigration. She would also test her diplomatic mettle during a covert trip to Amman to convince the Jordanian king not to attack the Jewish community in Palestine.

Finally, in the aftermath of the war, Meir was on hand for the declaration of Israeli independence in 1948, becoming one of just two women to sign the declaration and the first to receive a makeshift passport from the fledgling state. She first served Israel as the foreign minister in Moscow, but returned in less than a year. She was elected to Israeli parliament as the country's Minister of Labour, and, in 1956, after a failed run at becoming Mayor of Tel Aviv, became Foreign Minister.

After a tumultuous tenure that included Israeli military action in Egypt to regain Western control of the Suez Canal and surviving a bomb attack in Jerusalem—and a brief retreat from politics after being diagnosed with lymphoma—Meir was elected Prime Minister upon the unexpected death of previous leader Levi Eshkol. She assumed office in March of 1969.

Meir's Premiership was, unsurprisingly, far from peaceful, although she traveled far and wide meeting with world leaders across the globe on the platform of promoting peace in the Middle East. In keeping with her history of Zionism, most of her support at home came from radicals who shared her belief that land seized and occupied by Israel in the Six Day War in 1967—including the still-contested Gaza Strip and West Bank—should be preserved for Israeli settlement. Moderates willing to compromise with neighboring countries for the sake of peace offered her little resistance, however.

Meir was in power during the massacre of Israeli athletes at the 1972 Olympics in Munich and a hostage crisis involving Jewish emigrants at the Austrian-Czech border. She decided against a preemptive strike on mobilizing Syrian forces in 1973, fearing it would alienate Israel from foreign allies. In turn, Israel was attacked by Syria and Egypt, in what has become known as the Yom Kippur War. The conflict lasted three weeks, but criticism over her decision to remain on the defensive rather than launch an attack before Israel was invaded was instrumental in her resignation in 1974.

Meir died of lymphoma four years later in Jerusalem. She published an autobiography before her death, entitled *My Life,* which became a *New York Times* bestseller. A library was named in her honor at the University of Wisconsin-Milwaukee, as was a nearby public school and a performing arts center in Tel Aviv.

Leadership Insights and Meir

Meir was elected prime minister of Israel on March 17, 1969, after serving as Minister of Labor and Foreign Minister. She was, at the time, the world's fourth and Israel's first and only woman to hold such an office. She led Israel through a succession of trying times, including the Munich 1972 Olympics massacre and the Yom Kippur War.

McKinney (2008), noted:

> Meir had that rare quality of seeing things precisely as they are. Her vision was in sharp focus. Her mind was capable of piercing through the extraneous and confusing details to the central important point. She remained unconfused by the labyrinth of branches and twigs, and had the trunk of the tree in clear view.
>
> She worked tirelessly and used her gifts of charm and oratory to promote her causes. Some of her personal characteristics—self-confidence, intransigence, myopic vision, doggedness—brought her much criticism later in life, but they were exactly what was called for at that time and place in the formation of a country.

Klagsbrun (2017), noted four attributes leaders can learn from Meir:

1. **Hard Work:** From her earliest involvement in political life, Golda undertook the most difficult tasks.
2. **An Ability to Listen.** Even at the height of power, Golda Meir would sit through hours of meetings hardly saying a word, but listening to every side of every argument before reaching a decision about what needed to be done. "Instead of throwing an idea at us," recalled a former staff member, "she would say, 'You tell me what to do,' allowing people to feel they had been heard and their views considered."
3. **Confidence in Herself**. Once she made up her mind, after listening to all viewpoints, almost no one could change it. That trait gave her great credibility, said Amos Manor, former head of the Shin Bet, Israel's internal secret service. "People felt that she believed in what she said and that she spoke with the authority

of that belief, even if she turned out to be mistaken. That was her strength."

4. **Integrity.** Of the many leadership traits Golda Meir embodied, her integrity stands above everything. She devoted herself tirelessly to building a homeland for the Jewish people, never once seeking personal gain for herself or her family. And when out of office, she declined any perks, riding buses and shopping in the supermarket like anyone else. Her integrity gained her the respect of even her severest critics.

Hard work, a willingness to listen to others, confidence in her decisions, and utmost integrity are traits of Golda Meir that any leader would do well to emulate.

Provizer (n.d.) noted:

> Many leaders, in the words of Richard Nixon, whose time in the White House corresponded with Meir's tenure as prime minister, drive to the top by the force of personal ambition. They seek power because they want power. Not Golda Meir. All her life she simply set out to do a job, whatever that might be, and poured into it every ounce of energy and dedication she could summon.
>
> Meir never seemed to seek power. Instead, it appeared she only responded to the call to take it and, by so doing, became a political symbol of special importance.
>
> Beyond optimism and grimness, Meir also displayed other dualities. She was a person who could both laugh and cry, be both hard and sentimental, as well as both wise and simplistic.
>
> She was blunt yet prudent, firm yet careful and intransigent (she would say that was her middle name) yet compromising.

In Syrkin's (1969) words, "Her peculiar virtue lies in a fierce moral assurance always translated into action to which her whole life testifies." And, importantly, that virtue never erased Meir's problem-solving orientation toward leadership—an orientation that was not without its adaptive dimension, though of the incremental kind.

"Trust yourself. Create the kind of self that you will be happy to live with all your life. Make the most of yourself by fanning the tiny, inner sparks of possibility into flames of achievement."

"It isn't enough to believe in something; you have to have the stamina to meet obstacles and overcome them, to struggle."

Key Takeaways

- Effective leaders get right to the heart of matters; they are not distracted by noise. They can connect the right dots.
- Leaders must be authentic and consistent. They earn credibility by being true to their values.
- Effective leaders are dogged and do what it takes to get the job done with laser focus.
- Effective leaders listen to a wide variety of sources, trying to understand all points of view.
- Leaders never lose sight of the higher purpose.

Florence Nightingale

May 12, 1820 – August 13, 1910

"So never lose an opportunity of urging a practical beginning, however small, for it is wonderful how often in such matters the mustard-seed germinates and roots itself."

"I think one's feelings waste themselves in words; they ought all to be distilled into actions and into actions which bring results."

Biography

In 1820 Victorian English society, when trailblazing nurse and medical reformer Florence Nightingale was born, maintaining one's social standing was of the utmost importance (if you were fortunate enough to have it). Nightingale was one of the lucky ones in that sense, born in Florence, Italy to a wealthy landowner father and a mother who came from a family of successful merchants.

The Nightingales relocated back to England the year after Florence's birth, living between two inherited estates. Nightingale enjoyed the trappings of wealth—in addition to comfortable homes, she received a proper education and the opportunity to practice philanthropy, often caring for local villagers who had fallen ill. Ironically, the access afforded to her by her standing would prove to be the reason she rejected much of what her privileged position would have otherwise required of her, a sentiment that reflects her lifelong drive for change.

When Nightingale reached her mid-teens, she was certain that God had called her to pursue nursing as her life's purpose. Pointedly, this meant working toward a goal other than marrying into another wealthy family and keeping her bloodline alive, as was expected of aristocratic women at the time. Nightingale's family was unsupportive of this decision, and Nightingale respected their wishes for some time, until 1844, when she enrolled in a nursing school in Germany. (Nightingale had conveniently been taught German, French, and Italian in school.)

Nightingale's commitment to nursing was put to a test arguably tougher than familial pressure when she returned to England upon completion of her training. After a swift promotion to superintendent at the hospital where she worked in London, Nightingale was faced with an outbreak of cholera that unsanitary conditions made difficult to contain. Rather than stand down to an early obstacle, Nightingale doggedly worked to improve the health and safety practices at her hospital. In doing so, mortality rates there improved markedly.

Still, early success under her belt didn't allow time to rest on her laurels; England was part of an alliance of nations that had become entangled in the Crimean War against the Russian Empire, and a group of nurses Nightingale had trained (along with a handful of Catholic nuns) were deployed to Crimea in 1854 to treat the wounded and aid in the war effort on the ground.

The British army hospital near Constantinople was—quite literally—a cesspool, overrun with rodents, understaffed, understocked, and full of hurt and sick soldiers who were only getting sicker. Using her experience improving the state of her London clinic, Nightingale worked day and night to get the facilities in working order. Her tireless after-dark rounds earned her the nickname "The Lady with the Lamp." The death rate dropped, and Nightingale became an instant hero among wartime soldiers. Before she had even left Crimea, The Nightingale Fund had been established at home to fund nurses' training.

When Nightingale returned to England in 1856, she discovered she had become a hugely popular figure there and that the fund established in her name had been flooded with donations as news of her work in Crimea spread throughout Britain. Queen Victoria had already awarded her a sizable cash prize for her efforts, which she used in part to fund a new hospital—St. Thomas'—and a nurses training school. She also seized upon the onslaught of attention as a way to forever change nursing and hospital standards. In 1858, she published a massive report entitled *Notes on Matters Affecting the Health, Efficiency and Hospital Administration of the British Army*, in which she detailed statistically that the types of hygienic practices she implemented in Crimea were necessary to avoid losing more soldiers to wartime illness spread through poor conditions than to even battle injuries.

The report sparked massive reform. England established the Royal Commission for the Health of the Army, and underwent intensive internal restructuring regarding military administration. Nightingale also influenced the social stigma of upper class women entering the nursing field, pushing public perception toward nursing as a desirable and honorable trade for women across social strata.

By the time Nightingale had reached her late 30's, she was largely bedridden due to what is believed to have been a bacterial infection she contracted in Crimea. That hardly slowed down her will to initiate change, however. She turned her attention to civilian hospital reform, publishing *Notes on Hospitals* in 1859. She maintained a correspondence with Queen Victoria, consulted on sewage systems in India, and provided guidance on field hospitals during the United States' Civil War. In 1907, King George conferred upon her the Order of Merit, making her the first woman to receive the country's highest civilian honor.

Nightingale succumbed to illness in 1910. Nurses trained at The Nightingale School went on to establish new training schools in North

America, Africa, and Australia. Today, it is part of King's College, and a museum housing artifacts from her life sits across the Thames River from Big Ben and the Houses of Parliament, on the site of the original hospital and school she founded.

Leadership Insights and Nightingale

Florence Nightingale was a pioneer and considered the founder of modern nursing. In 1860, Nightingale laid the foundation for professional nursing with the establishment of her nursing school at St Thomas' Hospital in London. She also was a prodigious and versatile writer. In her lifetime, much of her published work was concerned with spreading medical knowledge. She was a pioneer of the use of infographics, effectively using graphical presentations of statistical data to articulate her point of view.

Tye (2015) outlines 10 lessons from the work of Florence Nightingale—lessons that she herself would more likely have described as calls to action.

> **Lesson 1 - Attitude:** Nightingale would have agreed with the statement that attitude is everything. She had an intuitive understanding that emotions are contagious, and would never have tolerated the gossip, complaining, and other forms of toxic emotional negativity that are prevalent in many hospital break rooms (and too often in public places). Even in the horrendous circumstances that prevailed at Scutari (British Army Hospital in Turkey in the Crimean War), Nightingale insisted that people be treated with dignity.
>
> **Lesson 2 - Commitment:** Nightingale had a mission, not a job. She did not inquire about pay and benefits before leading her team of young nurses off to the Crimea, and she endured working conditions that would be considered intolerable in today's world. Yet she never experienced "burnout," and through

devotion to her calling she changed the world of healthcare forever. Her legacy reminds us that caring for the sick is more than just a business—it's a mission, and that being a caregiver is more than just a job—it should be a calling.

Lesson 3 – Courage: Florence was courageous, and she was unstoppable. She did not allow opposition from the British aristocracy or the antiquated views of imperious physicians and military leaders to prevent her from doing her work. When she ran into a brick wall, she found a way around or over.

Lesson 4 – Discipline: Nightingale was a disciplined pioneer of evidence-based practice. Less well-known than her contributions to hospital and nursing practice was her pioneering work in medical statistics; her painstaking efforts to chart infection and death rates among soldiers at Scutari gave weight to her demands for improved sanitary conditions, first at military hospitals, and later in civilian institutions. She demonstrated that if you want to be effective, it's not enough to know that you're right—you must be able to demonstrate that you're right with the facts.

Lesson 5 – Empathy: Long before Daniel Goleman coined the phrase "social radar" in his book *Emotional Intelligence,* Nightingale appreciated that awareness and empathy are central to quality patient care, and effective leadership. At the Scutari Barrack Hospital, Nightingale established the first patient library in hopes of giving the soldiers under her care something to do other than drink. While she was at first ridiculed by the military brass, they were astonished when in fact this act of empathy in action achieved the desired result.

Lesson 6 – Loyalty: Nightingale was a team-builder who cared passionately about the nurses under her wing and the soldiers under her care. She was a demanding leader, but also showed uncompromising commitment to the people she led. Upon her return to England from Scutari, she personally endeavored to

> make sure that every nurse who had served with her there would find employment upon their return home. Her legendary loyalty to the soldiers she served was reflected in the fact that when she was buried, her coffin was escorted by octogenarian veterans of the Crimean War.

Tye (2018) added:

> But one of the most remarkable—and most often overlooked—attributes of Nightingale's leadership was her intense and enduring loyalty to those she served and led. One of the greatest qualities of the greatest leaders is the way they earn the loyalty of those that they presume to lead. And as Nightingale's example shows, the best way to earn such loyalty is to give it. As was the case with Nightingale, a leader's loyalty is not just a mushy emotional attachment—it requires hard work and sacrifice on behalf of those one presumes to lead.

Tye (2015) continued:

> **Lesson 7 – Humor:** Nightingale's contemporaries reported that she had a wonderful sense of humor and was often able to defuse tense situations with the light touch of laughter. I think she'd say that if she could laugh in the hell-on-earth environment of the Scutari Barrack Hospital, then no matter what the world throws at us, we can't forget the restorative and healing power of laughter.
>
> **Lesson 8 – Contrarian Toughness:** We need to see opportunities where others see barriers. We need to be cheerleaders when others are moaning doom-and-gloom. We need to face problems with contrarian toughness, because it's in how we solve those problems that we differentiate ourselves from everyone else.
>
> **Lesson 9 – Initiative:** Nightingale attributed her success to the fact that she "never gave or took any excuse." When told there

was no money to repair a burned-out wing of the Scutari Barrack Hospital that was scheduled to receive hundreds of new casualties, she hired a Turkish work crew, and before anyone could stop her, had the wing refurbished. The acid test of an "empowering" workplace is whether people—regardless of job title—can take the initiative to do the right thing for patients and coworkers without seeking permission or worrying about recrimination.

Lesson 10 – Aspiration: Nightingale never rested on her laurels, but rather continuously raised the bar. After proving that a more professional approach to nursing care would improve clinical outcomes, she helped found the first visiting nurses association, chartered the first modern school of professional nursing, and through her writing, helped establish professional standards for hospital management. She remained active virtually until the end of her life at the age of 90.

"I attribute my success to this: I never gave or took any excuse."

"Let whoever is in charge keep this simple question in her head (not, how can I always do this right thing myself, but) how can I provide for this right thing to be always done?"

Key Takeaways

- Effective leaders have a positive outlook and infectious attitudes.
- Leaders must demonstrate and inspire commitment to the mission.
- Effective leaders have courage of conviction and persevere through challenging times.
- Leaders are loyal and care deeply for their teams.
- Leaders show initiative and do not make excuses.
- Effective leaders are relentless in the pursuit of their aspirations for the organization.

James Dyson

May 2, 1947 -

"If you want to do something different, you're going to come up against a lot of naysayers."

Biography

When paired with conviction and curiosity, even the simplest idea can have far-reaching, transformative effects. For British engineer and inventor Sir James Dyson, his life-changing proposition was borne from frustration around one of life's most mundane tasks: tidying up. In 1978, Dyson's irritation with the poor performance of his household vacuum cleaner set him on a path to rework the design of the appliance from the inside out, laying down the foundation for a multi-billion pound empire rooted in innovation of everyday tools.

It helped, of course, that Dyson had an education in design by the time he set out to revolutionize housework. Born in coastal Norfolk, England in 1947, he attended the Byam Shaw School of Art for a year before studying furniture design at the Royal College of Art in London. Prior to even graduating in 1970, he had already worked on the design of the Sea Truck—a boat capable of supporting three tons of weight at relatively high speeds. The concept was initially created by engineer Jeremy Fry, who took Dyson under his wing, showing him how to take an invention from a plan to a consumer-friendly product.

Dyson's fateful vacuum cleaner design was based on technology he had put into place in the factory where he produced the first marketable invention he created on his own. In 1974, he introduced a wheelbarrow with a pneumatic ball for extra stability in front, rather than the traditional wheel. Air filters in the factory that produced the Ballbarrow (as it was called) were routinely clogged; inspired by a cyclone system that had previously been implemented in larger production facilities, Dyson adapted a mechanism that used centrifugal force to separate dust particles from the air. Dyson realized that the bags in the vacuum cleaner he used at home would clog in similar ways, so he co-opted the cyclonic design in his vacuum prototype, eliminating the need for disposable bags to collect dirt and dust and allowing suction to remain consistently strong after use.

It took him five years and over 5,000 prototypes before he landed on his final model, supported during this time by his wife Deirdre's earnings as an art teacher. Despite the perfection he strove for, Dyson's G-Force vacuum cleaner was hardly an instant hit with appliance companies in the UK, who uniformly expressed no interest. After a failed licensing agreement with Amway in the United States, Dyson borrowed nearly $1,000,000 and manufactured the G-Force vacuums himself.

In 1991, his product made its way to consumers' homes for the first time through a partnership with a Japanese mail-order catalogue, and Dyson was awarded the top prize at the country's International Design Fair that same year. Several additional catalogue clients improved his cash flow, and Dyson was able to open his own factory and research center in England in 1993. A serendipitous visit from a former British foreign secretary would help his business change course. The politician's wife sat on the board of Comet—England's leading electronic retail chain—and helped get him in the store in 1995. Comet carried the

Dual Cyclone model, and it became the best-selling vacuum cleaner in the UK within a year.

In the next decade, Dyson's retail exposure expanded globally; today Dyson product is currently sold in over 65 countries worldwide. Dyson engineers in the UK, the US, Singapore, and elsewhere expanded their efforts into other products, as well, designing bladeless fans first sold in 2009, and introducing energy efficient hand dryers in 2006 for use in public restrooms.

Dyson has remained committed to fostering advances in technology and design. His company dedicated a reported £7,000,000 a week in 2017 to research and development[1], including studies into artificial intelligence. Dyson opened The Dyson Institute of Engineering and Technology in 2017 to foster the next generation of design talent, and in 2019 became Britain's wealthiest person with an estimated net worth of nearly $14 billion.

Leadership Insights and Dyson

Dyson is a British entrepreneur known for disruptive innovation. He has brought his creativity into the consumer markets in vacuum cleaners, air purifiers, and hair dryers, among other household appliances. He has used design and an unrelenting focus on creativity to build his businesses, always opting to take the long view.

Gottlieb (2004) noted Dyson's continued eye for innovation and creativity.

> The key to the company's success to date is its culture of creativity, an appreciation of sheer novelty that springs from Dyson himself and extends through every level of the organization. Nothing is prized more highly within the firm than the willingness and ability to generate and develop new ideas, to take chances, even to fail miserably, if that failure comes in the pursuit of an exciting potential innovation.
>
> "Everyone is empowered to be creative," says Dyson, who points out that the idea of putting the company's customer-assistance

> phone number on a label on the handle of each vacuum came not from a manager, but from an employee on the service desk. "You are just as likely to solve a problem by being unconventional and determined as by being brilliant," he once wrote. "Be a bit whacko, and you shake people up...And we all need shaking up."

AIB (2015) noted the associated element of risk taking. Although Dyson has formally stepped down as Chairperson of the organization, risk taking remains a priority within the management and engineering departments of the company. Dyson believes that "risk taking is an essential building block for innovation and invention. To compete, companies must take risks. Without taking risks, you don't generate long-term wealth."

The main point to take away from Dyson's risk taking is how it is a holistic stance: It encourages innovation in employees and is also reflected in the leadership style built by Dyson. In his current role as Chief Engineer, he is known to offer praise, encourage workers to take the difficult route rather than the obvious one, and ensures he takes an active role in the innovation process. This attitude is quite the contrary to other business leaders who remain in their office; however, it demonstrates why risk-embracing entrepreneurs often run the most innovative organizations.

"Everyone gets knocked back, no one rises smoothly to the top without hindrance. The ones who succeed are those who say, right, let's give it another go."

Dyson spoke of the need to "foster an environment where failure is embraced. As a small business owner, it isn't failure itself that should be feared, but the day failure stops inspiring the recovery."

Dyson himself wrote in 2018 about the importance of taking a long-term view:

> Dyson is a family business. We haven't cashed in our chips as many have. That allows us to take a long-term view. We take

risks every day. By extending your timescales, the problems of today fade in significance; you can get through them by seeing the (far greater) opportunity of the future.

"Enjoy failure and learn from it. You never learn from success. Successes teach you nothing. Failures teach you everything. Making mistakes is the most important thing you can do."

"There is no such thing as a quantum leap. There is only dogged persistence - and in the end you make it look like a quantum leap."

Key Takeaways

- Leaders must be forward-facing, fighting complacency every day.
- Leaders must be agents of change, willing to shake things up.
- Leaders must embrace risk and be willing to fail. Fail miserably to fuel recovery.
- Leaders learn from failures and move forward; without failure there is no growth.
- Leaders must be willing to learn from others.

JUNE LEADERS

For June, we will learn from Vince Lombardi, Katharine Graham, and Lewis B. Puller.

Vince Lombardi

June 11, 1913 — September 3, 1970

"The achievements of an organization are the results of the combined effort of each individual."

"It's not whether you get knocked down, it's whether you get up."

Biography

"Winning," famed American football player and coach Vince Lombardi once said, "is a habit." Lombardi, it seems, would know. Over the course of his seven years as head coach of the Green Bay Packers, the Brooklyn native led the team to two Super Bowl wins and five NFL Championship titles in all. He was named NFL Coach of the Year twice and maintained a pro sports coaching career streak of never ending a season with a losing record. He is so closely associated with victory in the game that the trophy awarded to the Super Bowl champions each season is named in his honor.

Lombardi's football career has much less illustrious roots, however. One of five children born on the cusp of the Great Depression to first-generation Italian-American parents in Sheepshead Bay, New York, he got his first introduction to the game through a local recreational league. He continued to play football—and dabbled in baseball and basketball—while studying to become a priest, an aspiration he eventually abandoned when he left seminary school and enrolled in a nearby Catholic high school in 1932. He joined the football team there as a fullback and performed well enough to garner an athletic scholarship to Fordham University the following year.

Winning, however, wasn't yet a habit for Lombardi exactly. Upon graduating in 1937, economic circumstances made well-paying jobs hard to come by; Lombardi didn't find much stability in failed bid as a debt collector or a semi-pro football player, and a stint in law school at Fordham was similarly short-lived. Motivated to land a steady job so he could marry his then-girlfriend Marie, Lombardi accepted a position in 1939 as assistant football coach at St. Cecilia High School in Englewood, New Jersey, where he also taught science and Latin. In 1942, he took over head coaching duties, leading the school to six championships.

His success at St. Cecilia caught the attention of his alma mater, and Lombardi made the leap to collegiate sports first as coach of the Fordham freshman team in 1947, and, the following year, of the varsity squad. His tenure at Fordham, in turn, gave Lombardi the opportunity to serve as offensive line coach at West Point, beginning in 1949.

West Point, a military academy and football powerhouse, provided Lombardi with experience and exposure at a higher level of athletic coaching, serving under future College Hall of Fame coach Earl "Colonel Red" Blaik. It also put Lombardi in the crosshairs of controversy in 1951, when the majority of the team was discharged from the academy after they were caught cheating on schoolwork, a violation of the institution's Honor Code. The scandal—complicated by the fact that America was embroiled in the Korean War at the time and that Army football was considered the height of the game—received national attention. Still, neither Blaik nor Lombardi resigned, and by 1953, after weathering two seasons of weakened rosters, West Point once again ended with a winning season as Lombardi's role as coach grew in prominence.

Lombardi's persistence paid off in 1954, when he accepted his first position in the NFL, as offensive coordinator for the New York Giants.

Despite winning a national title with the Giants in 1956, the title of head coach eluded him. He was unable to secure a post at the top from the Giants or at the collegiate level, despite attempts to move up in rank, until, in 1959, the Green Bay Packers offered him a general manager and head coach role.

The Packers were weak, both on and off the field, with a losing record and diminishing fanbase. Lombardi angled for a five year contract, then buckled down, making sweeping and demanding changes to the team's training program. His efforts led them to a winning record by the end of his first season at the helm, and he was named NFL Coach of the Year. In 1960, the Packers won the NFL Western Conference divisional title. Under his stewardship, the Packers won the first two Super Bowls ever played, in 1966 and 1967, five of the championships the team would claim in the seven years Lombardi served as head coach.

After stepping down from the lead role (but remaining general manager) in 1968, Lombardi took his talent to the Washington Redskins in 1969. As was now truly habitual, the Redskins had their first winning season in over a decade that year. In September of 1970, just months after a cancer diagnosis, Lombardi passed away at age 57.

In the time since his passing, Lombardi's name has become synonymous with both gridiron success and compassionate leadership; biographers and colleagues have noted on the record Lombardi's support of Civil Rights and his vocal intolerance for discrimination based on race and sexual orientation. In addition to induction into the NFL Pro Football Hall of Fame, Lombardi received equivalent honors from the Washington Redskins, the Green Bay Packers, Fordham University, the American Semi-Pro Football Association, and the states of New Jersey and Wisconsin.

Leadership Insights and Lombardi

Vince Lombardi was a straightforward choice to add to this compendium on leadership insights. Lombardi is considered by many to be one of the greatest coaches in football history, and he is more significantly recognized as one of the greatest coaches and leaders in the history of any American sport (ESPN Poll 2017). In his 15 seasons as an NFL assistant and head coach, his teams never had a losing season. He was also prolific in his principles of leadership, including the "Lombardi Rules," a set of guidelines for individuals and leaders alike.

Michael of Leadership Geeks (2016) offered these Lombardi leadership lessons:

1. Winning is a habit.

Lombardi saw winning as a mindset and habit that had to be cultivated. He famously said, "Winning is a habit. Watch your thoughts, they become your beliefs. Watch your beliefs, they become your words. Watch your words, they become your actions. Watch your actions, they become your habits. Watch your habits, they become your character." As a leader, you should have the desire to win and not fall into the trap of mediocrity. Start thinking of winning as a habit, and notice if the sum of your words and actions are leading you toward success or away from it. Make small changes in your words, actions and habits so that they take you closer to your goals. If you don't believe you will succeed, you are sabotaging your own growth as a leader.

2. Pay the price it takes.

Lombardi was known for telling his team to "run it again." He knew that the discipline of hard work and doing more than what others are doing would give his team a competitive advantage. Lombardi meticulously planned every training session and put his team through an extremely tough training regimen. Professional athletes make their job look easy, but the truth is that 99% of the work that goes into winning a championship takes place before the game.

You cannot bypass hard work on the way to success. Remember that the bigger the success you desire, the harder and smarter you'll need to work. Are you willing to pay the price for your success?

3. Take responsibility for your role as a leader.

When Lombardi first became head coach for the Green Bay Packers, he set out to define the role of his players and his own role as coach. Instead of putting the responsibility of winning on the players, he assumed that duty himself. He communicated to his team his expectations on their commitment and hard work during training, but also outlined what he would be responsible for—teaching them and pushing them to maximize their potential.

By taking on the burden of winning, Lombardi removed pressure from the players and allowed them to focus on being their best on the field. This also built trust between him and his team—trust that if both sides focused on their roles, they could achieve success.

Ambrose (2015) noted that Lombardi led from the front:

> What made Vince Lombardi among the most successful and trusted leaders? He led his team from the front. He was an active participant who led by motivating, developing and persevering alongside his teams, rather than by pushing them from behind. Trustworthy leaders do not ask or expect employees to assume risk or perform tasks they would not also assume or perform.

Kelly (2014) added:

> Despite being linked to the "winning is everything" stigma, he actually favored preparation and instilling the will to win among his team. The greatness of Lombardi is that he realized football

players faced plenty of obstacles in order to achieve success. He understood that his leadership directly impacted their motivation, and in essence, the success of everyone. Eventually, the men that followed him found satisfaction, value in their work, and the rewards associated with a winning team.

Lombardi, Jr. (2001), offered this "Lombardi Model of Leadership."

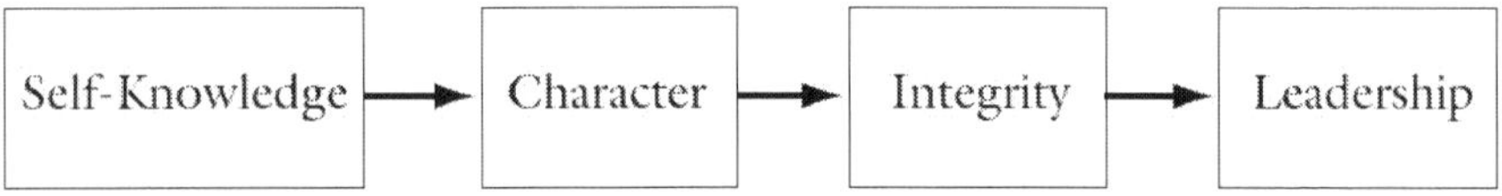

Leadership starts with self-knowledge: Self-discovery leads to self-knowledge. Only by knowing yourself—your principles and values—can you hope to become an effective leader.

Self-knowledge is the basis for character: Once you understand yourself, you can start to grow and write your character.

Along with good habits and competence, this creates the skills required for effective leadership.

Character is the root of integrity: Without character, asserts Vince Lombardi, there can be no integrity.

Integrity provides the foundation of leadership: Character and integrity are the two pillars of effective leadership.

Lombardi (2001) also offered a series of *"Lombardi Rules"*.....on how to build a system of success based on his Father's leadership practices.

Lombardi Rules		
1	**Own Your Habits**	Search out and identify your beliefs and the habits that grow out of them
2	**Use your courage**	When necessary, pick flight – but otherwise, be brave. Fight!

3	**Embrace your passion**	Jump into your passion with both feet – and bring others along with you
4	**Be prepared to sacrifice**	Sacrifice and self-denial lie behind every success
5	**Demand total commitment**	Demand it first from yourself and then from others around you
6	**Weed out the uncommitted**	The organization that wins is populated by winners
7	**Work at it**	Don't buy the myth of the overnight success. Invest in your talent
8	**Be disciplined on and off the field**	Discipline takes different forms – but it always pertains
9	**Be mentally tough**	Use your toughness to beat setbacks. Use your toughness to seek out new challenges

Lombardi (2001) also offered a set of related rules for Leaders…

Lombardi's Rules for Leaders		
1	**Be authentic**	Act your integrity. Be predictable. Make amends when you foul up
2	**Earn trust through investment**	Use your authority to build the organization's trust in you
3	**Use your mission**	Define the goal. Pursue the goal
4	**Create a shared vision**	"We can do better" is a good place to start

5	**Align your values**	Bring espoused values into congruence with practices - or else!
6	**Know your stuff**	When the time comes, show that you know it
7	**Generate confidence**	Set the stage psychologically, and give people the tools they need
8	**Chase perfection**	Settle for excellence along the way
9	**Live what you teach**	And live what you coach. And sell what you teach and coach
10	**Strike the balance**	Be as close as you can- and as far away as you have to be

"The only place success comes before work is in the dictionary."

"The difference between a successful person and others is not a lack of strength, not a lack of knowledge, but rather a lack of will."

Key Takeaways

- Leaders take responsibility, lead from the front, and are consistent exemplars.
- Effective leaders share their vision and are mission-focused.
- Leaders prepare and chase perfection; they get things done.
- Leaders know themselves and their values. They earn trust through consistent displays of character and integrity. They are authentic.

Katharine Graham

June 16, 1917 – July 17, 2001

"A mistake is simply another way of doing things."

Biography

By nearly any metric, Katharine Graham was born into incredibly lucky circumstances. Her father was a wealthy investment banker, and his father was, too. Her mother rubbed shoulders with artists and intellectuals like Gertrude Stein, Georgia O'Keeffe, and Auguste Rodin. By the time Graham—known as Kay—was born in New York in 1917, it was something of a foregone conclusion that her childhood of nannies and multiple homes would lead to an expensive education, a family of her own, more nannies, and more homes.

Graham did, indeed, attend a prep school in suburban Virginia, then Vassar and the University of Chicago, graduating in 1938. She briefly moved to San Francisco, where she worked as a reporter for the *San Francisco News*. Even that wasn't entirely unexpected; her mother had previously worked as a journalist, and while she was still in school, Graham's father had purchased the *Washington Post* during a bankruptcy auction. Within a year of graduating from college, Graham returned East, working at her father's paper in both the editorial and circulation departments.

In 1940, she married a Supreme Court clerk, Philip Graham, and within the decade shifted her focus from professional aspirations to raising the couple's children, a family that would eventually include a daughter and three sons. In 1946, Graham's husband took over from her father as publisher of the *Post*, the first step in building a media empire that included the eventual acquisition of television and radio stations and *Newsweek* magazine. Graham and her husband enjoyed life as Washington society figures and political insiders. The couple socialized with the Kennedys and became adept at political maneuvering in the nation's capital.

Then, in late 1962, the Grahams' marriage unraveled when Graham discovered Philip's extramarital affair with a *Newsweek* employee. The following year, battling mental illness and alcohol abuse, Philip suffered a public meltdown during a press conference, was subsequently hospitalized, and took his own life at the couple's home that August.

Facing public embarrassment and pressure to sell the *Post*, Graham, instead, opted to step into the role of president in September, the first in a series of gutsy decision making that would alter the course of American publishing and American politics.

An early pivotal move Graham made as the hiring of reporter Ben Bradlee as managing editor of the paper in 1965, giving him room to pursue investigative reporting that routinely challenged the federal government at the highest levels. In 1971, two years after Graham had formally become the paper's publisher, Bradlee received excerpts from the Pentagon Papers, leaked classified reports exposing the depth of the U.S. government's involvement in Vietnam—including aiding in the assassination of Vietnamese President Ngo Dinh Diem—and previously undisclosed motivations for engaging in war there that contradicted public talking points. *The New York Times* had already published excerpts from the papers and was in the midst of a costly legal battle with the U.S. Department of Justice to suppress further reporting on the documents.

Facing the threat of lawsuits that could bankrupt her company and potential jail time for what the Nixon administration argued constituted a violation of the Espionage Act, Graham approved publishing Bradlee's reports, justified by the First Amendment and the responsibility of a free press. Her decision was eventually upheld by the Supreme Court.

Graham's mettle was tested again shortly thereafter, when the *Post* published reporting by Bradlee and other staffers on the Watergate scandal, involving a string of illegal activities undertaken by the Nixon administration against political opponents. Graham herself received (and the paper published) an obscene, sexist threat from Nixon's attorney general. The *Post*'s reporting incited a national uproar and was instrumental in the initiation of the impeachment process that led to Nixon's resignation in 1974.

Over the course of her tenure, Graham grew the *Post* into one of the country's most trusted and widely-read news sources, cementing its reputation for dogged journalism in defense of the truth. Upon becoming CEO of the Washington Post Company in 1972, Graham also held the distinction of being the first female CEO of a Fortune 500 Company.

Graham retired from the position in 1991—ceding the role to her son, Don—but continued reporting on world affairs. Her biography, *Personal History*, garnered her a Pulitzer Prize in 1998. Graham died in 2001 after sustaining injuries from a fall and was posthumously awarded the Presidential Medal of Freedom the following year.

Leadership Insights and Graham

Katherine Graham was an American publisher and the second female publisher of a major American newspaper, following Eliza Jane Nicholson's ownership of the *New Orleans Daily Picayune* (1876-1896). We have included her in this compendium based on her groundbreaking role as a woman leader.

When Graham became the first female Fortune 500 CEO in 1972, she had no female role models and faced difficulty being taken seriously by many of her male colleagues and employees. Graham outlined in her memoir her lack of confidence and distrust in her own knowledge.

The convergence of the women's movement with Graham's control of the *Post* bolstered Graham's resolve and also led her to promote gender equality within her company. This also infused her insights on leadership in general.

In a speech at Harvard (HBS, 1998), Graham dismissed the idea that she is a role model, explaining to the HBS audience:

> "Your generation of women has to meet much higher expectations than I did." But based on her own career, Graham did offer five personal qualities that are essential for enduring leadership: strong personal values; self-confidence; courage and tolerance in the face of failures; the ability to delegate to the right people; and the willingness to make changes when changes are necessary. Finally, she added, "Caring about and loving what you do for a living will make you feel like the luckiest person in the world.

Moore (2018) captured these points from Graham:

> The best leaders know that you cannot just talk about priorities; you have to exhibit what you care about by taking action. You can show your priorities in five ways:
>
> **Get out of the office and into your employees' ecosystem.**
>
> Graham spent time in the newsroom each day. Ben Bradlee, the editor Graham hired who directed the paper through the Pentagon Papers and Watergate dramas, said that Graham had "round heels for reporters." For her, "writing the first draft of history" (journalism) was at the center of her company. Employees felt she recognized their work because she observed it as it happened. In addition, Graham intensified her understanding of jobs in the newsroom by her direct observation, by listening, and by asking questions.

Be proactive in building competence and knowledge.

Graham held lunches for reporters in her private dining room, and welcomed experts for briefings. Journalists coveted being invited to these luncheons, which permitted them to deepen their knowledge of both their subject area and their publisher's mentality.

Show that you are willing to jump in when needed.

Graham built her resources by adding news bureaus worldwide, and boosted editorial budgets and staff, but she always saw herself as an operational part of the team. She would eagerly call in tips she picked up at social occasions and take excellent and extensive notes of speeches. During a violent press operator's strike, which nearly shut down the paper, Graham lived inside the *Post* building. She did everything from taking classified ads to stuffing newspapers in bags, getting ink on her designer dresses. She was undeterred, and after the strike, directed the paper to its greatest financial success.

Stand up for your employees.

One Sunday afternoon Graham heard that the Chinese government ransacked the room of one of her foreign correspondents and held the woman for questioning. Graham did not pick up the telephone or ask for a letter of protest to be written. She put on her heels and single strand of pearls and drove to the Chinese embassy, marching up to the door and insisting on a justification. Her actions were not lost on her reporters.

Follow your core convictions—even in small matters.

In writing about Katharine Graham, Robin Gerber tried to get an interview with Warren Buffett, who had been Graham's friend and mentor. In a final attempt, she sent Buffett the draft manuscript with a note saying that she hoped he enjoyed it. Two weeks later, he called her and talked about Graham, her leadership, and his relationship with her. He told Gerber about an occurrence he felt she had gotten wrong and gave her a quote for the book cover. Why did the CEO of Berkshire Hathaway take time to talk to Gerber? He could have dictated a note about the error, or asked his assistant to call. It is because the legacy of his friend is important to him.

There were some related notes from Family Business Magazine (2018) that added to the five priorities above:

She was "the ideal boss," wrote *Post* staff writer Robert G. Kaiser in a tribute to Graham. She wasn't perfect, he wrote — her insecurities could be troublesome, and he thought she was "too easily impressed by people with big titles." Nevertheless, she was interested and engaged in what her staff members were doing, and she backed them up. Sometimes family business owners manage employees too tightly and don't give them room enough to do their jobs. But, noted Kaiser, "Katharine Graham gave her employees at the *Washington Post* the ultimate journalistic gift: absolute independence."

Most successors have an opportunity to learn their family's business over a long period, working in it and being brought along by members of the older generation. Graham, who had worked at the *Post* only sporadically as reporter, had to learn quickly — and in a corporate environment where women were neither expected nor welcomed.

She set about educating herself in every way she could, seeking advice and knowledge from the circle of company executives as well as from others prominent in the news industry.

"A mistake is simply another way of doing things."

"Whatever power I exert is collegial."

Key Takeaways

- Enduring leadership demands: strong personal values; self-confidence; courage and tolerance in the face of failures; the ability to delegate to the right people; and the willingness to make changes when changes are necessary.
- Leaders keep a finger on the pulse and get out amongst staff, customers, and other stakeholders consistently. They are visible and approachable.
- Leaders are lifelong learners and open to learning from a variety of sources.
- Leaders have the backs of their staff.

Lewis B. "Chesty" Puller

June 26, 1898 - October 11, 1971

"Hit hard, hit fast, hit often."

"If you want to get the most out of your men, give them a break! Don't make them work completely in the dark. If you do, they won't do a bit more than they have to. But if they comprehend, they'll work like mad."

Biography

Over the course of almost four decades of service in the United States Marine Corps, Lewis Burwell "Chesty" Puller developed a reputation for bravery and heroism in the face of adversity, ultimately becoming the most decorated American Marine in history.

Puller was born June 26, 1898 in West Point, Virginia. From a young age, he was determined to serve in the Armed Forces. He joined the Marines in August 1918, having spent the previous year enrolled in the Virginia Military Institute, and completed boot camp at the Marine Corps Recruit Depot in Parris Island, South Carolina; though Puller hoped to be able to see combat during World War I, he was ultimately never involved in any fighting for this cause.

After the end of the war, Puller graduated from Officer Candidate School on June 16, 1919, and was placed in the reserves as a corporal.

Puller's first experience with active duty happened during the Banana Wars, a period of American engagement in Central America and the Caribbean that was most heavily supported by the United States Marine Corps. He served in the Haitian Gendarmerie to start, spending five years there before returning to the United States in March 1924 and receiving his commission as a second lieutenant; subsequent years saw him traveling around the United States for various postings in Virginia, Hawaii, and California.

He returned to international service in November 1928, when he was sent to Nicaragua to fight against rebel forces. It was here that he received his first Navy Cross. After going back to America in July 1931 to complete a 12-month Company Officers Course, Puller resumed his duties in Nicaragua in September 1932 and was awarded another Navy Cross for his actions.

Following his time in Central America, subsequent years saw a combination of domestic and international engagements, with Puller going first to China, and then returning to the United States in 1936 to act as an instructor at The Basic School for new United States Marine Corps Officers in Philadelphia. After serving as an instructor for several years, he went back to China in 1940 and would remain abroad until the end of August 1941, when he assumed command of a battalion in North Carolina.

Puller was drawn into the Pacific Theater of World War II and was involved in engagements across the Solomon Islands, New Britain (now part of Papua New Guinea), and Palau, including the Battle for Henderson Field, the Battle of Cape Gloucester, and the Battle of Peleliu, recognized as one of the most devastating battles for the Marines. During the action in the Pacific, Puller received his third and fourth Navy Crosses, the Bronze Star Medal, his first Legion of Merit, and was also promoted to Colonel.

During his service in the Pacific, Puller sadly suffered a personal loss: His younger brother Lieutenant Colonel Samuel Duncan Puller of the United States Marine Corps was killed by a sniper in Guam on July 27, 1944.

Puller returned to the United States to train more recruits in November 1944 and would continue to serve domestically until the onset of the Korean War in June 1950, when he was drawn into the Battle of Inchon in September of that year. During his tour in Korea, Puller continued to demonstrate exemplary leadership and valor; for his efforts he received the Silver Star Medal, his second Legion of Merit, the Distinguished Service Cross (awarded to him by the United States Army), his fifth Navy Cross, and was also promoted to brigadier general.

His time in Korea marked the end of Puller's international service, and he returned to the United States in May of 1951. During the final years of his military career, he was promoted to major general in September 1953 and took command of the 2nd Marine Division at Camp Lejeune in Jacksonville, North Carolina in July 1954.

Puller suffered a stroke in 1955, which led to his retirement from the United States Marine Corps on November 1 of that year, after having devoted nearly four decades of his life to the Armed Forces; he retired as a lieutenant general. Ever the patriot, he requested that he be returned to duty in 1966 so he could fight in Vietnam. However, this request was denied because he was in his late sixties at the time.

Puller lived out the rest of his retirement in Saluda, Virginia with his wife, Virginia Montague Evans. He passed away on October 11, 1971 and is buried in the cemetery of Christ Church Parish nearby.

To this day, Puller holds the distinguished honor of being only one of two servicemen to have received five Navy Crosses. His story has become embedded within the culture of the United States Marine Corps, taking on the tenor of near folklore. Marine tradition includes repeating, "Good night, Chesty, wherever you are!" at the end of each day during boot camp. Although even Puller himself was never sure of the exact origins of the nickname Chesty, that, too, lives on as the name of the English bulldog that serves as Marine Corps mascot.

Leadership Insights and Puller

Lewis Burwell "Chesty" Puller is the most decorated United States Marine in American history. He had a legendary 37 year career in the Marines with combat duty in Haiti, Nicaragua, China, the Pacific, and Korea.

Puller never shied away from a fight, and his quotes are just as gutsy as the legend himself. Puller's legendary tactics earned him the respect of Marines everywhere. His most famous quote embodies his philosophy on the battlefield: "Hit hard, hit fast, hit often."

Marines try to live up to Chesty Puller's reputation as a Marine's Marine. Puller made sure every member of his unit was taken care of, no matter what. He talked the talk, but he also walked the walk when it came to the best chances of survival for men under his command. This formed the foundation of his insights on leadership.

Landking (2010) noted that elements of Puller's leadership style can apply to management.

1. **Be visible.**

   Get out from behind the desk and make sure your people see you. The less you're hidden away in meetings, or at your computer, and the more you are engaging and encouraging your people, the better off you'll be.

   Schick (2015) noted: Chesty instinctively knew what his Marines wanted to hear—a confident commander who would stop at nothing to get the mission accomplished. That is why when his unit found itself surrounded by an enemy division in Korea, Chesty was able to reassure his Marines by explaining to them how this was, in fact, a blessing in disguise. As Chesty pointed out, "We've been looking for the enemy for several days now. [And] We've finally found them. We're surrounded. That simplifies our problem ..." As one battalion commander later recalled "[Chesty] kept building up our morale higher and higher, just by being there."

2. **Make your team's welfare a priority** — Its possible to demand results while looking after the best interests of individuals.

   Schick (2015) noted Chesty lived with his men. There were no officers' messes in Puller's outfit and he fell in line with the privates, carrying his own mess gear. In combat, he rigidly refused comforts unattainable for his men, and in training, he carried his own pack and bedding roll while marching at the head of his battalion.

3. **Share the tough times** — Whether its working nights and weekends to make a deadline, or doing grunt work to set up an event, your people will go the extra mile if you do.

   Schick (2015) pointed out Chesty spent most of his time fighting alongside his Marines at the front, and this earned him their respect. Leading from such close quarters enabled Chesty to gain critical insight into what motivated his Marines.

Schogol (2017) offered some insights into Puller's leadership:

> In Nicaragua in particular, he led the charges against the enemy himself rather than telling his men to charge while he held back. It is a style of leadership common across the history of warfare, but one which he continued up through a relatively high level of command.
>
> His forceful leadership and gallant fighting spirit under the most hazardous conditions were contributing factors in the defeat of the enemy during this campaign and in keeping with the highest traditions of the United States Naval Service.

As a battlefield commander, Puller did not wait for orders when things went wrong. He took initiative and responded aggressively and quickly. He used his initiative to figure out what to do and then make it happen, while others were preoccupied with other issues or simply unable to come up with a solution to this difficult problem of a battalion surrounded behind enemy lines."

What would Chesty Puller think? (NEA, n.d.)

Every Marine learns the USMC history and traditions. This rhetorical question is about making sure the current Marine Corps lives up to his standard.

"If there is a single trait which could make you a true leader...I would have to call it *'Stick-to-it-ive-ness'—the ability to finish each job begun."*

"If you want to get the most out of your men, give them a break! Don't make them work completely in the dark. If you do, they won't do a bit more than they have to. But if they comprehend, they'll work like mad."

Key Takeaways

- Leaders must be visible, engaged, and in among the staff.
- Leaders should not ask the team to do things they are unwilling to do.
- Leaders show initiative and tackle challenges head on. They persist.
- Leaders share the glory and the tough times.
- Leaders must be exemplars of what is expected.

JULY LEADERS

For July, we will learn from Nelson Mandela, John Glenn, Richard Branson and Ginny Rometty.

Nelson Mandela

July 18, 1918 – December 5, 2013

"I learned that courage was not the absence of fear, but the triumph over it. The brave man is not he who does not feel afraid, but he who conquers that fear."

Biography

As the most famous figure associated with the decades-long fight against South Africa's racist apartheid policies, Nelson Mandela is remembered not only for his leadership in times of struggle, but also for his subsequent work to reunify and heal a fractured nation.

On July 18, 1918, Rolihlahla Mandela was born in Mvezo, a village in what was then known as British South Africa. A member of the Madiba clan, he was given the name Nelson years later by a teacher. After his father passed away when he was a child, King Jongintaba Dalindyebo of the Thembu people became Mandela's guardian.

After finishing his secondary education, Mandela went first to study at the University College of Fort Hare, before ultimately completing his degree at the University of South Africa in 1943; initial study for a law degree at the University of the Witwatersrand was left unfinished in 1952.

Mandela's political activism began in earnest when, in 1944, he joined the African National Congress (ANC), and was involved in forming their Youth League. As a result of the 1948 South African general election—which saw the National Party rise to power and the beginning of their implementation of apartheid—the ANC adopted their Programme of Action in 1949, calling for public acts of defiance and disobedience in support of the struggle for black rights in South Africa.

In 1952, Mandela and Oliver Tambo opened the first black law firm in South Africa, aiding black clients who were otherwise poorly represented. It was during this year that Mandela received his first legal charge as a result of his political activity, ending up with a sentence for nine months of labor that was ultimately suspended for two years; he also received his first legal ban, which restricted his abilities to travel and socialize with others.

His legal struggles continued throughout the late 1950s and early 1960s. In 1956, Mandela was arrested with 155 others and charged with treason in what would come to be known as the Treason Trial; he was ultimately acquitted in 1961. During the state of emergency that was declared following the Sharpeville Massacre on March 21, 1961, Mandela was detained, and the ANC was banned, alongside the Pan Africanist Congress.

Mandela's experiences during these years caused him to abandon his initial belief in non-violent resistance, and in 1961, he co-founded Umkhonto weSizwe ("Spear of the Nation"), which would provide the ANC with an armed branch that could be used in their continued fight for freedom and justice. Mandela left South Africa under an assumed name in January 1962 to drum up support for the cause; shortly after his return in July of the same year, he was arrested and sentenced to five years in prison.

In October 1963, Mandela was brought to court again as part the of the Rivonia Trial, during which defendants were accused of sabotage and plotting for a violent overthrow of the government. Facing the death penalty, on June 11, 1964 he was sentenced and convicted instead to life in prison, alongside seven other defendants. He was sent to Robben Island, off the coast of Cape Town, which had been used for as a prison for centuries.

He would spend 18 years on Robben Island, during which time both his mother and his eldest son would pass away. Initially allowed to write only two letters per year, over time his rights as a prisoner improved in that regard, and he was able to correspond with the outside world more frequently. This allowed him work on a law degree correspondence course, and he dedicated his nights to the program after days spent performing mandatory manual labor. In March 1982, he was moved to Pollsmoor Prison, where he remained until a diagnosis of tuberculosis sent him to the hospital. After receiving treatment, he went to Victor Verster Prison in December 1988, where he stayed for the rest of his imprisonment.

While incarcerated, Mandela remained a prominent figure in the struggle for black rights in South Africa, and over the years there was an increasingly loud call from the international community for him to be freed, alongside global pressure put on the South African government to end their apartheid policies. On February 11, 1990, Mandela was released, having spent a total of 27 years imprisoned. During his captivity, the government had made several conditional offers of freedom, all of which Mandela had rejected.

Following his release, he travelled internationally to speak against apartheid with various world leaders, and in 1991, he was elected President of the African National Congress, which had been reinstated prior to Mandela's discharge from prison. His work with the South African President F.W. de Klerk to bring an end to apartheid garnered them both the Nobel Peace Prize in 1993, and ultimately led to the democratic elections of April 27, 1994, during which Nelson Mandela was elected as the first black President of South Africa.

His time in power was heavily focused on reconciliation and forging a new sense of unity amongst the citizens of South Africa, who had been scarred by decades of separation, segregation, and violence; it was important to Mandela that everyone, including the white population, feel invested in the future of their country. Improving the living conditions of black and other non-white South Africans was a key goal, as they had suffered disproportionately under apartheid.

Mandela resigned from his ANC position in 1997, and at the end of his Presidential term in 1999, he did not seek re-election, choosing instead to establish the Nelson Mandela Foundation to devote his time to different humanitarian causes.

Much of his work post-presidency was spent supporting the fight against HIV/AIDS, a cause that he had previously been criticized for not doing enough to support while serving as President. In 2003, he also oversaw the establishment of the Mandela Rhodes Foundation at the University of Oxford. He largely retired from the public eye in 2004, although he still made occasional public appearances.

Mandela passed away in Johannesburg on December 5, 2013, at the age of 95, having lived his life in pursuit and service of equality for all, regardless of a person's ethnicity. As he noted in his 1994 autobiography, *Long Walk to Freedom,* "No one is born hating another person because of the color of his skin, or his background, or his religion. People must learn to hate, and if they can learn to hate, they can be taught to love, for love comes more naturally to the human heart than its opposite.

Leadership Insights and Mandela

2018 was the Year of Mandela—the year the independence leader would have turned 100 years old. Although he died in 2013, at the age of 95, his entire life still stands as a testament to the power of the human spirit. Confronted by the challenges of apartheid, physical imprisonment, and doubt, Mandela nonetheless wielded his inimitable spirit to improve the lives of millions of his fellow countrymen and women, as an activist, scholar, leader, and, ultimately, one of the world's most celebrated humanitarians. It would be hard to take a leadership insight compendium seriously if Mandela was omitted; his legacy is so impactful and his presence rarely matched.

The big truth is that Mandela, like Lincoln, achieved the historically rare feat of uniting a fiercely divided country. The feat is rare largely because of the abundance of ordinary politicians who seek power by highlighting differences between the people they govern and fueling antagonism. Mandela sought it by appealing to people's common and shared humanity.

Schoemaker (n.d.). noted:

> Mandela's extraordinary achievement was to encourage racial harmony, forgiveness without forgetting, power sharing, and a strong focus on the future, not the past. As a master of symbolism, Mandela supported his strategy by being magnanimous towards his former enemies.

Dhliwayo (2018) compiled seven reasons why Mandela was a great leader:

1. **Self-sacrifice**

   A Messiah-like figure to his people, Nelson Mandela spent 27 years of his precious life in prison on Robben Island, hammering on rocks in the scorching heat during the day, only to retire to a tiny eight-by-seven-foot concrete cell with only a straw mat to sleep on. When he was offered freedom in 1985, he refused, saying: "I cannot and will not give any undertaking, at a time when I and you, the people, are not free. Your freedom and mine cannot be separated!"

2. **Compassion**

   It is easy to forgive a stranger, and easier to forgive a friend, but how difficult it is to forgive an enemy. Nelson Mandela forgave his greatest adversary, the apartheid government, which not only caused tremendous suffering to himself and his family but also to his countrymen. He could have demanded the heads of those who murdered thousands of innocent indigenous South Africans, but he chose the higher route instead. Setting up the Truth and Reconciliation Commission, he left a legacy of forgiveness and reconciliation, not only for his people but also for the world.

3. **Learner.**

   While in prison, he not only threw himself into the routine of daily exercise, but he also read smuggled books as much as he could. A lover of learning, although he was restricted from access to political books he liked, he ordered books on gardening and horticulture, eventually cultivating food that fed not only his fellow prisoners but also prison officials. He also continued his legal education while in prison, often giving legal advice to both prisoners and prison staff. His zest for learning and teaching was so great that Robben Island became known as "Nelson Mandela University."

4. **Ethical.**

   In today's increasingly competitive world, people care less about how you acquire money, power, and wealth, just as long as you amass them. Mandela, on the other hand, put people and honor before worldly gain. At a time when most African presidents were corruptly amassing fortunes during their tenures, Mandela's estate was roughly just US $2.9 million. And, he not only left money for his family, but for his staff as well.

5. **Unifier.**

As the old adage goes, "United we stand, divided we fall." When Mandela took power, he sought to bring whites, blacks, and other minorities together. Some expected him to favor blacks, particularly those from his Xhosa tribe, but because of his vision for a rainbow nation, South Africa is currently benefiting from its rich diversity economically, intellectually, and culturally. The last president of apartheid-era South Africa, F.W. Deklerk, hailed Nelson Mandela as a "great unifier" who displayed a "remarkable lack of bitterness."

6. **Servant.**

He focused on the needs of others, not his own, listening to those who society had ignored and sought out those who society had cast away. He served the poor and the rich; he served the educated and the illiterate. There is no one Mandela did not care for. He saw everyone as his brother and sister—even his enemies. While rulers all over the world were busy empowering themselves and their friends, he was busy empowering his people.

7. **Human.**

The media put him on a pedestal, classifying him as an infallible saint—an incorrigible angel who could do no wrong. He became a man of mythical proportions to many in Africa and all over the world. The reality, however, was far from it; Mandela himself never denied his humanity, given to the same weaknesses as everyone else. His first marriage broke down, and so did his second; he was unable to balance being a leader in the home and in the nation. He also failed to raise the kind of children befitting a man of his nobility. He said in an interview, "My first task when I came out was to destroy that myth that I was something other than an ordinary human being." In the end, although disappointing, people were still drawn to him. In fact, his humanity made him even more appealing.

Freiberg (2018) offered some more insight on Mandela as a leader:

1. **Passion produces perseverance**

   When you find a cause worth fighting for you become passionate and passion fuels the fires of perseverance. Opposed to the policies of his country's white minority government, Mandela led a non-violent action against apartheid in South Africa. It was a choice that landed him in prison for 27 years.

   As with most innovators, Mandela's road to change was paved with enormous challenges, but he never gave up the fight. His passion for the cause was bigger than the bitterness and shame of his failures. He said, "The struggle is my life. I will continue fighting for freedom until the end of my days."

2. **Expect change to be messy.**

   Business is wrought with obstacles. Innovation and change rarely follow a nice, neat linear path. Driving change often causes sacrifice, misfortune and pain. If it were easy and didn't require tremendous backbone, everyone would be doing it, right?

   Solving a problem that really matters, change that is truly worthwhile is hard to come by. It requires nerve to push through the trials and ultimately make your vision a reality. This is why many change efforts that fail can be traced back to a "failure of nerve."

3. **Forgiveness is key to focusing forward.**

   When he was President of the United States, Bill Clinton had a conversation with Mandela when he was President of South Africa. Years earlier, Clinton woke his family up at three o'clock in the morning to watch the press coverage of the historic day Mandela was released from prison. As the television cameras pressed in, Clinton observed the sheer anger and hatred on

Mandela's face as he walked from his cellblock to the front of the prison. Then in a heartbeat, Mandela's rage seemed to vanish.

Nelson Mandela's emotions naturally gravitated toward anger and resentment. Whose wouldn't? Until he recognized what was happening. Then, he made a different choice. Mandela didn't "choose" to live in a world full of racism, but he was able to choose how he would respond to that world. He said, "We don't have to be victims of our past, that we can let go of our bitterness, and that all of us can achieve greatness."

4. **End Right vs. Being Right**

   In marriage, in social justice and certainly in business, you can focus your energy on being right or ending right. The former is often about ego and focuses on the past. The latter is future-oriented and focuses on what you are ultimately trying to achieve.

   Strong-willed and determined, Mandela never cowered. He vehemently fought for what he believed in, but he was also humble and kind. "You mustn't compromise your principles, but you mustn't humiliate the opposition," he said. "No one is more dangerous than one who is humiliated." Mandela understood that you can't make peace with your enemy if you aren't willing to work with them and treat them with dignity. Here, he taught us about the power of collaboration and compromise.

   A good leader can engage in a debate frankly and thoroughly, knowing that at the end he and the other side must be closer, and thus emerge stronger. You don't have that idea when you are arrogant, superficial and uninformed.

5. **Change begins from the inside-out.**

   If there was a silver lining to his years of imprisonment, Mandela said it was to look in the mirror and create within himself that which he most wanted for South Africa: peace, reconciliation, equality, harmony and freedom. Perhaps his most profound impact and greatest legacy was to teach us, through vivid, living, personal example, to be human before anything else.

Self-awareness is a sign of great leadership. Mandela understood that if he was going to lead his nation out of racial discrimination and into a peaceful democracy he would have to "be the change."

Mandela understood that this difference starts with who we are and how we land on others as leaders. His joyful and infectious character sparked hope for millions of people who want to dream big and pursue their dreams without oppressive limitations, who want to live in a world of tolerance, inclusion and hope.

Great leadership is generative. That is, it is concerned about the care and growth of future generations, helping them live with dignity and raising them to new levels of morality and motivation.

"It always seems impossible until it's done."

"A good leader can engage in a debate frankly and thoroughly, knowing that at the end he and the other side must be closer, and thus emerge stronger. You don't have that idea when you are arrogant, superficial, and uninformed."

Key Takeaways

- Effective leaders learn from the past, but are forward-facing.
- Effectives leaders are masters of symbolism and storytellers creating vivid imagery.
- Leaders have to be willing to sacrifice for the greater good.
- Effective leaders are unifiers, not dividers.
- Leaders have to be lifelong learners.
- Effective leaders are compassionate, empathetic, service oriented, and values-driven.

John Glenn

July 18, 1921 – December 8, 2016

"To sit back and let fate play its hand out and never influence it is not the way man was meant to operate."

Biography

John Herschel Glenn Jr.'s professional life was marked by success and achievement at nearly every stage. Starting as a noted military pilot, he would go on to become one of NASA's original seven astronauts and the first American to orbit the Earth, before dedicating more than twenty years to his career as a United States Senator.

Glenn was born on July 18, 1921 in Cambridge, Ohio, and spent time at Muskingum College before leaving school to enlist in the Armed Forces during World War II. After joining the Naval Aviation Cadet program in March 1942, he transferred to the United States Marine Corps and was commissioned as a second lieutenant in March of the following year.

In 1944, Glenn was sent to the South Pacific, ultimately flying 59 combat missions in the Marshall Islands and receiving two Distinguished Flying Crosses. Following the end of his tour in 1945, he returned to the

United States, where he remained until 1946. After that, Glenn's missions took him to China and Guam. He would finally go back to America in 1948, spending the next few years honing his skills as a pilot through advanced flight training and working as a flight instructor.

Glenn was promoted to the rank of major in 1952, and by early 1953, he was back in combat during the Korean War. Over the course of the year, he flew a total of 63 combat missions as a part of the Marine Corps and 27 missions as an exchange pilot with the United States Air Force, earning another two Distinguished Flying Crosses for his bravery.

After finishing in South Korea, Glenn headed to the United States Navel Test Pilot School in Patuxent River, Maryland in January 1954, undergoing a six-month training course before graduating in July of the same year. Working as a test pilot throughout the mid- to late-1950s, Glenn achieved particular acclaim on July 16, 1957 with Project Bullet, his successful effort to fly from the West Coast of the United States to the East Coast in just three hours and 23 minutes, averaging supersonic speed across the journey.

Glenn earned his fifth Distinguished Flying Cross as a result of Project Bullet, and the success of the mission helped to raise his profile as a potential candidate for joining Project Mercury, the NASA program that aimed to successfully orbit a man around the Earth. At the time of Project Mercury's announcement at the end of December 1958, the Space Race against the Soviet Union was accelerating, and NASA was looking to assemble a team of men to take part in missions for the program.

In April 1959, Glenn was promoted to lieutenant colonel and selected as one of the Mercury Seven, thus becoming part of the first class of American astronauts. After the group underwent extensive training, plans were finalized for the first two Project Mercury flights. Glenn was chosen as the backup pilot for both missions, taking place in 1961; it wouldn't be until the following year, however, that Glenn would actually get the opportunity to go into space.

By the end of 1961, the Soviet Union had already sent two men into orbital flight, and there was mounting pressure on the United States to prove it could match the Soviets' capabilities and technology. Glenn was selected for Project Mercury's first orbital flight mission, and on February 20, 1962, was launched into space on the *Friendship 7*, taking off from Cape Canaveral, Florida. Though he encountered unexpected problems with the spacecraft's internal control system and an error with a sensor for the heat shield, Glenn successfully managed the situation, and the *Friendship 7* ultimately completed three orbits of the Earth, spending nearly five hours in space before landing in the Atlantic Ocean.

Glenn's spaceflight was a historic moment for the United States during the Space Race. As the first American to perform an orbital flight, he was feted as a national hero and earned a sixth Distinguished Flying Cross for his efforts. He also received the NASA Distinguished Service Medal from President John F. Kennedy.

Though Glenn continued to work on Project Mercury, there were no more space missions planned for him, and he resigned from NASA in 1964 to pursue a career in politics at the suggestion of Robert F. Kennedy. He also resigned from the Marine Corps, ending his military career in January 1965 at the rank of colonel. He intended to run for a seat in the 1964 Senate elections, seeking to represent Ohio as a Democratic candidate. However, an injury he sustained that year brought an early end to his first campaign, and he was unable to proceed.

Glenn instead pursued a career in business, working first as vice president and then president for Royal Crown Cola. He didn't give up on his dreams of becoming a U.S. Senator, running unsuccessfully in 1970. However, in 1974, he won his campaign and embarked on a political career that he would continue for more than two decades.

During his time in office, Glenn would sit on the Special Committee for Aging, and serve as the chairman of the Senate Government Affairs Committee, re-elected to his position as senator three times. He would also seek nomination as the Vice-Presidential candidate in 1976 and as the Democratic Presidential candidate in 1984; neither of these attempts were successful, however.

Generally regarded as being of strong moral character, his reputation suffered in the late 1980's and early 1990's when he was involved in the Keating Five corruption scandal alongside four other United States Senators; the charges against Glenn were dropped, but he was criticized for exercising poor judgment. He retired from the Senate in 1999, having devoted 25 years of service to politics.

In 1998, Glenn became the oldest person to fly in space after he completed a nine-day mission aboard the Space Shuttle *Discovery* at age 77, undergoing various tests to compare the effects of spaceflight on the aging process.

After his retirement, Glenn became involved in the foundation of what is now known as the John Glenn College of Public Affairs at The Ohio State University. He received the Presidential Medal of Freedom from President Barack Obama in 2012.

Glenn died in Columbus, Ohio at the age of 95 on December 8, 2016 and was interred in Arlington National Cemetery on 6 April 2017, having outlived the other Mercury Seven astronauts. He is remembered for his dedication to serving the United States, both through the military and through politics, and for his bravery in the face of the unknown during his time at NASA.

Leadership Insights and Glenn

John Glenn demonstrated through several career transitions and roles in his life that he was a leader in the deepest sense. He was a United States Marine Corps aviator, engineer, astronaut, businessman, and politician. He was acclaimed widely in these roles for both his accomplishments and for his character. By way of example, he received Congressional Gold Medal, National Aviation Hall of Fame, National Geographic Society's Hubbard Medal, Presidential Medal of Freedom, and the International Air & Space Hall of Fame. He also helped found the John Glenn College of Public Affairs.

Courage weaves itself through Glenn's life—as a combat pilot, test pilot, astronaut, and Presidential candidate. His character was framed by his courage of conviction, consistent values, and the balance of humility with extraordinary accomplishment.

Baldoni (2016) noted about Glenn:

> Service was paramount to men like Glenn. And from his example, we can learn what it takes to put yourself at risk for a cause. First in combat. Later in space. He also took that sense of service to the U.S. Senate. There he applied himself to mastering the issues of the day and later championing the rights of the elderly. To prove that final point, he went into space aboard the Space Shuttle, becoming, at age 77, the oldest person ever to do so.
>
> There was something old fashioned about Glenn, rooted, no doubt, in his rural Ohio upbringing. While he cut a bold figure, he was a down-to-earth man. People recall his common touch. His basic human decency. He spoke well of others ignoring his own accomplishments. He was a patriot not because of his feats in space, but his example of national service.

Lalonde (2016) offered some leadership lessons from the life of Glenn:

1. **Leaders quit.**

   When the Japanese attacked Pearl Harbor in 1942, John Glenn dropped out of college and enlisted in the U.S. Army Air Corps. He quit something important to join an organization he believed in.

   People will often think leaders never quit. That's far from the truth. Like Glenn, leaders quit. And they can quit often if the course of action isn't working.

2. **Leaders transition.**

   Glenn transferred from the U.S. Army Air Corps to the U.S. Marine Corps. From there, he transitioned to NASA (though he remained an officer in the Marine Corps). Finally, he transferred careers once again to become a politician. Watching Glenn's life, you can see multiple transitions. The U.S. Army, the Marine Corps, and politics. He kept moving. Leaders don't stay in one position forever. They transition roles and move on. Whether that's upwards in the organization or sideways to another organization, leaders transition.

3. **Leaders do good.**

   Yes, John Glenn served in the military. He fought for the country. He served the country in politics.

   Yet his contributions went beyond serving. He also helped found John Glenn Institute for Public Service and Public Policy at The Ohio State University, which later became the John Glenn College of Public Affairs in 2015.

   John knew he wanted to leave a lasting impact on the world. And he did that by creating an organization that outlived his life.

   Leaders look to do good and contribute to the community around them. They give to wonderful organizations, they volunteer for causes they believe in, and they care for those they serve.

Clark (2016) noted after spending time with Glenn:

> During our discussions, he told me something that changed my life, and might change yours. He told me that whenever he arrived at a crossroads in his life—when it was time to decide whether to, say, return to NASA or run for public office—he would sit down with his wife and discuss: "What is the best use of me?"

> That approach to his role in life—always looking for the best use of his particular abilities and talents—was a revelation to me. I've tried to keep that, and his example of courage, humility and decency, foremost in my mind as I proceed through the years.

Goforth (2016) commented: "With his intellect, his physical and mental courage, his work ethic, his dedication to his country, and with his humility, Glenn set an example."

Braden (2016) offered these leadership values of Glenn:

> **The foundational value of John Glenn was serving others.** He placed a high value on serving others with his life, as an astronaut, a senator, and as a loving husband and father.
>
> **John Glenn was a practical optimist.** He knew what he wanted to achieve and was open to different ways of getting there. Many people don't realize he learned to fly as a Marine pilot. He, like many men of his time, chose the military to pursue their dreams of flight. The military provided him and many men of his generation the opportunity to pursue their passion of flight.
>
> The third value John Glenn shared was fighting for the underdogs in our society. He did this throughout his political career. He understood firsthand the distance between farm and fame. His votes in the Senate focused more on supporting others and helping give others an equal choice in life. John Glenn believed in empowering others through example and deeds.
>
> John Glenn was a man of quiet courage. He went from being a national hero for his trip to outer space to a man who could no longer fly because of a slip and fall in his bathroom. He knew there was something out there for him outside of space travel. He and Annie raised their children here in the Midwest, with Midwest values. It was his children who chose the name

Friendship 7 for his Mercury space capsule. It reminded all of the importance of friendship in a life well lived.

If this is all John Glenn accomplished, it would be enough. But he chose to return to space in his 70s to provide us all incredible inspiration for the second half of life.. He broke through the gray glass ceiling of living a life of passion.

The most powerful lesson I learned from John Glenn: he always was striving and never completely arriving. He continued to grow, but along the way tripped over questionable circumstances in trying to find a better life. He didn't know at the time how a single act could severely damage a lifetime of good and achievement. Serving leaders must always be aware of who they invest their time in.

John Glenn taught us you can reach and touch the stars while remaining connected to the people and values that keep you on the ground.

"If a man faces up to the [unknown] and takes the dare of the future, he can have some control over his destiny."

"Don't give in to complacency and cynicism. Don't ignore what is bad, but concentrate on building what is good.

Key Takeaways

- Effective leaders are always striving and moving forward.
- Effective leaders have a deep sense of duty and service.
- Leaders need to maintain a "common touch" and create connections across and down the organization.
- Leaders need to be practical optimists and need to have "quiet courage."
- Leaders need to create a lasting impact, leaving things better than they found them.

Sir Richard Branson

July 18,1950 -

"Complexity is your enemy. Any fool can make something complicated. It is hard to keep things simple."

Biography

As the story goes, when British entrepreneur Sir Richard Branson was a student at the prestigious English boarding school Stowe, his headmaster told him he would either go on to be a prisoner or a millionaire. While the educator was half right—Branson would briefly serve jail time for tax evasion in the early '70s—his prediction about Branson's wealth missed the mark. By 2018, Branson would be worth an estimated $5.1 billion. His fortune was largely thanks to the empire of 400 companies he formed under the Virgin Group umbrella.

Born in London in 1950, Branson was hampered by dyslexia during his school days, failing out of Scaitcliffe School before eventually dropping out of Stowe at age 16. His entrepreneurial tendencies were evident early on, however, as an early venture founding a magazine called *Student* proved financially viable in 1966 thanks to advertising revenue. *Student* was a useful entree into London's music scene, and from that beginning, he launched a mail order record catalogue, which he in turn flipped into a record store on London's bustling Oxford Street.

Branson used funds from his retail venture to open his own recording studio and record label, named Virgin Records as a nod to the lack of music industry experience Branson and his business partner Nik Powell had amassed before launching the company. Despite having no familiarity with the finer points of running a label, success came quickly. An early Virgin signee, Mike Oldfield, released the single "Tubular Bells" in 1973, and it was a near-instant smash. Soon, Branson signed deals with era-defining artists including The Rolling Stones and the Sex Pistols, and grew the business into a formidable independent label with enough cache to take on established major labels on an international scale. By the late 1970s, Branson was a millionaire.

Emboldened, Branson diversified the Virgin portfolio. He expanded into London nightlife when he purchased the gay nightclub Heaven in 1982. After he chartered a plane to cart fellow passengers to Puerto Rico when a commercial airline canceled their flight, Branson formed Virgin Atlantic Airways in 1984.

By the dawn of the '90s, however, Branson ran into a major setback when he was forced to sell Virgin Records to EMI to help stem the company's financial losses. The deal reportedly left him in tears.

But the Virgin empire rolled on, this time quite literally, with an expansion into UK rail services under the Virgin Trains banner. He made a return to the recording industry with a new record label in 1996—aptly named V2—and broadened his airline offering with a short haul European carrier called Virgin Express.

Air travel would prove to be a major battleground when Branson accused British Airways, the reigning stalwart of UK aviation, of engaging in what came to be known as a series of "dirty tricks," including hacking Virgin computers and planting negative stories in the press. British Airways eventually agreed to a multimillion dollar settlement, Branson's portion of which was distributed as a bonus payment to his staff. The two companies would grapple once more, this time when

Virgin reported a joint price-fixing scam to government authorities on both sides of the Atlantic. Virgin walked away unscathed; BA was fined over £270 million.

Never one to settle down, Branson forged ahead with a telecom division, Virgin Mobile, and, in 2004, launched a space tourism company called Virgin Galactic. He also engaged in high-profile missteps, including an ill-fated soft drink brand called Virgin Cola and even an attempt to enter the wedding industry with Virgin Brides. Virgin Voyages (a cruise line), Virgin Media, Virgin Comics, Virgin Healthcare, and Virgin Hotels have been introduced or announced, as well, and Branson has invested avidly in robotics and clean energy.

He has also embraced his position in the public eye to advocate for young entrepreneurs in South Africa and the UK, nuclear disarmament, carbon emissions regulation, universal access to broadband internet, wildlife preservation, and an end to both capital punishment in the United States and anti-LGBT legislation in Uganda. He also served as "litter czar" under UK Prime Minister Margaret Thatcher to encourage proper waste disposal. He has crossed the Atlantic and the Pacific by hot air balloon, and broke the world record for fastest crossing of the English Channel in an amphibious vehicle in 2004.

Branson was knighted in 2000 and has published eight books that detail, among other things, his life, work, and leadership philosophy.

Leadership Insights and Branson

Branson is an English business magnate, investor, author, and philanthropist. He is an extraordinary entrepreneur, having founded the Virgin Group in 1972, which today contains over 400 companies. For his many accomplishments, he was Knighted for "services to entrepreneurship" and also named to *Time magazine*'s list of the 100 Most Influential People in The World.

He has a flamboyant style and has become somewhat of a "celebrity" CEO, leveraging social media quite effectively. He is also an active and engaged humanitarian, supporting a wide range of causes including global warming, sustainable energy, exploited children, hunger and digital development. He also promotes entrepreneurship through programs such as Virgin Startup, an official delivery partner for the UK's Start Up Loans program and the Branson School of Entrepreneurship in South Africa.

What makes Richard Branson a successful leader is captured in how he is often ascribed with these attributes: fun, anti-establishment, warm, friendly, a risk taker, adventurer, opportunist, fast, competitive, hard negotiator, and workaholic. The eclectic entrepreneur also believes that a great leader is someone who is genuinely interested in people and who strives to bring out the best in them.

Branson is a transformational leader. He has experienced failures and learned from them. What makes Branson a transformational leader is that he is able to rise and adapt in times of distress and major changes.

Bradt (2014) noted several aspects of Branson's leadership philosophy:

Environment/where to play: Listen out there

Listen, take lots of notes and keep setting new challenges.

"One of the keys to 'the way' we do things is nothing more complex than listening – listening intently to everyone. Ask why with a wide-angled lens."

Turn off that laptop and iPhone and get your derrière out there.

Branson has never had an office in the office. He never summons people to *"come unto me"*. Instead he stops people where they work and asks them questions about the good things they are doing to learn and encourage.

Values/what matters and why: Do good

Make a positive difference and do some good.

Branson founded Virgin *"to make people's lives better."* Businesses have the opportunity and the responsibility to do good things in their communities. They have to create and *"creators are never satisfied: they believe they can always do better."*

Attitude/how to win: Turn dreams to actions grounded in beliefs

Follow your dreams and just do it.

Branson told PrimeGenesis partner Roger Neill that *"The difference between me and many others is that I write down all my ideas – and then make them happen."* He's convinced that *"everything that's really worthwhile in life involves some degree of risk."* So, he loves being the underdog, finding holes in the way the *"big dogs"* do things and then beating them by changing the game.

Believe in your ideas and be the best.

This passion for being the best is why Virgin Air traded its "typical" earphones for high-quality digital earphones that each passenger could keep, why Branson values capability over expertise and why culture is so important to Virgin. You can't be the best as an individual. You have to be the best as a team.

Relationships/how to connect: Communicate to build your team

Communicate, collaborate and communicate some more.

Relationships are about personal connections fueled by communication. As Branson puts it, *"great leaders are...simplifiers...that can communicate...in terms that are universally understood."* This is why Steve Jobs focused Apple's new headquarters on a central piazza – to enable random interactions, collaboration and communication.

Have fun and look after your team.

The core of Virgin's magic is *"a youthful joie de vivre and great people skills, combined with a relentless focus on great service and succeeding,* (and a) *never-failing sense of humor."* This creates a culture in which employees feel *"valued, empowered and trusted"* so they can *"go out and make amazing things happen."*

Behaviors/what impact: Delegate and follow through

Turn off that laptop and iPhone and get your derrière out there again

When a Virgin train had an accident, Branson dropped everything to be in the hospital with those injured. He didn't wait until the dust had settled, the analyses were done and he could answer questions. It's not about answering questions. It's about showing up.

Don't give up.

Roman philosopher Seneca said *"Luck is what happens when preparation meets opportunity."* Branson has adds a dose of persistence to that. Not surprisingly, Branson has a history of what Jim Collins describes as "return on luck."

Delegate and spend more time with your family.

Leadership is not about you. It's about inspiring and enabling others to do their absolute best together to realize a meaningful and rewarding shared purpose. Be BRAVE. Delegate. And spend more time with your family.

Branson offered a few insights on leadership in a Virgin blog (n.d.):

The difference between leadership and management:

While a good manager will have the ability to supervise others, keep them within company guidelines, play by the rules and read the maps they're handed, all this tells you nothing about how comfortable they will be going off-road and breaking new ground.

Striking out in new unexplored directions takes a whole different mindset and one that often means breaking, or at least massaging, a few of the old rules. Management is much more about maintaining processes, disciplines and systems than about changing them.

Strong leaders, on the other hand, while maintaining stability, must have vision, creativity and perhaps most importantly, the ability to influence others to follow and support them in the challenges of moving an organization into unchartered and often highly risky territory.

Good leaders vs. bad leaders:

Good leadership is by definition all about taking the venture forward and finding viable new avenues where the business can evolve and prosper. Poor leadership, on the other hands, typically tends to be static, much more about protecting the status quo and, if there are any around, resting on laurels.

This 'don't rock the boat' approach may have been a viable business model twenty years ago, but at the frenetic pace of business today it is no longer an option. To stand still today is to go backwards—and quickly.

While I have found that outstanding leadership tend to come in a huge range of very different and often quite quirky and eccentric packages, poor leadership usually displays a lot of common denominators.

The art of delegation

There seems to be a lot of confusion around the subtle but critical difference between 'delegation' and its first cousin 'relegation.' Simple stated, 'delegation' is handing on the responsibility for a situation together with the authority to resolve it. Relegation on the other hand is simple pushing a problem away

> but without including the power to really do anything much about it —except perhaps to shoulder the blame. In short, one of the most common mistakes to be found in poor leaders is an inability to understand the difference between these two ways of working. In the same way that this kind of leader is skilled at relegating blame, they are usually very good at holding their people accountable - everyone, that is, except for themselves.

In 2015, Warrell spent a week with Branson and came away with these five lessons all under the frame of how to lead purposefully:

> **Be Approachable:** *Be someone others find it easy to be around.*
>
> **Be Real***: Give up pretense and ditch the ego.*
>
> **Be Playful***: Laugh more, stress less, and stop taking everything so seriously (yourself included).*
>
> **Be Curious***: Be open to unlearning what you think you know so you can re-learn what you need to know.*
>
> **Be Passionate***: Find what you're passionate about and then find a way to do more of it.*

Thompson (n.d.) added more on the insights of Branson after Branson's home island was badly damaged by a hurricane:

> **Burn the house down.**
>
> If you lost everything tomorrow, would you rebuild your home exactly the same way? Would you fill it with all the same stuff? If your business were incinerated and you were given the opportunity to start over, would you go about it the exact same way? Would you create all the same products and services? Would you hire all the same people back? Probably not. "I'd not wish it on anyone," Branson told me, "but sometimes the best way to get clear about what matters is to imagine starting over from scratch!"

Track your insights.

The biggest heartbreak about the blaze for Branson was losing his prize notebooks. He's scribbled ideas, insights, and to-do's in a set of bound blank books in almost every meeting I've ever attended with him. He's been doing that for decades. "You need to have some way to capture what matters, what you're learning, and what you might find important later."

1. **Don't take the bait.**

   Our primal brains are hard-wired by fight-or-flight urges, which means that we're easily seduced by anything that feels remotely like a crisis rather those less exciting things that have longer-term strategic impact. "We're too easily driven by instant gratification," Branson told me, "in good things and bad." It's too easy for those of us who are busy to respond like Pavlov's dog, leaping at anything that shows immediate threats or rewards. Be wary of urgent things that trump long-term commitments.

2. **Pick who, not just what.**

   No one builds a great house or business alone. Success depends on the people you recruit to share your vision. Branson was once recognized as one of the world's most remarkable thought leaders by Thinkers50 founders Des Dearlove and Stuart Crainer. When I asked him about honors like that, he's always given credit to others "who make each dream possible." He feels "grateful and lucky" to have attracted hundreds of leaders "whose passion is equal" to his own in every single organization that lives under the Virgin brand.

   "You have to think about who you will spend your time with based on what you care most about," Richard once said as he stirred the open fire and we sat barefoot on the sandy beach near his home on Necker in the British Virgin Islands. Dark clouds suddenly extinguished the brief Caribbean sunset we had been enjoying, as if to signal another storm on its way. "Life is short. Embrace the people who make you a better person," he mentored. Consider someone a friend when he or she helps you become who you aspire to be, and help them do the same. "You need fewer of those people who zap energy and you need more of the kind who help you stay on track--true friends who help you find joy and meaning."

"A company is people ... employees want to know... am I being listened to or am I a cog in the wheel? People really need to feel wanted."

"Engage your emotions at work. Your instincts and emotions are there to help you. "

Key Takeaways

- Leaders need to be approachable, genuine, real, and authentic .
- Leaders need to be always listening, engaged, and asking questions.
- Leaders need to make a positive difference and make things happen.
- Leaders need a prudent mix of passion and perseverance.
- Leaders need to be thoughtful risk takers.
- Effective leaders create connections and build relationships.
- The best leaders attract talent, set the parameters, and get out of the way.
- The best leaders are not afraid to fail.

Bonus Addition – July

Virginia M. (Ginni) Rometty

July 29, 1957 –

"You make the right decision for the long run. You manage for the long run, and you continue to move to higher value. That's what I think my job is."

"Never protect your past, never define yourself by a single product, and always continue to steward for the long-term. Keep moving towards the future."

Biography

Virginia Rometty—or, as she is more commonly known, Ginni—is a rarity in business as one of the few female American tech CEOs. But, having initially joined IBM in 1981 as a systems engineer before rising through the company ranks to the top position in 2012, she also boasts a decades-long career at a single company, an increasingly unusual feat at a time when the ever-evolving tech ecosystem draws top talent from one business to another or to younger, disruptive startups. Rometty's tenure at IBM has been marked by transforming the company toward a data and software focus, and in the process, keeping it competitive against fellow tech giants like Apple and Microsoft.

Rometty's work ethic was formed at a young age. One of four children born into an Italian-American family in Chicago, Rometty was left to fend for herself and her siblings while her mother worked multiple jobs after her father left the family in the early 1970s. Despite the hardship, Rometty secured a scholarship from General Motors that enabled her to attend the prestigious Northwestern University, graduating with high honors in 1979 with degrees in electrical engineering and computer science.

The scholarship led to internships with GM during her undergrad days, and, upon completing her degree, full-time employment with the company in their systems development division in Detroit. In two years, however, she would make her fateful move to IBM, as an analyst and engineer. For the duration of the '80s and '90s, Rometty's trajectory at the company continued upward as it expanded to include sales experience with clients across industries, from telecom to healthcare.

By the time Rometty reached the rank of general manager, she was ready to play a pivotal role in one of IBM's most high profile business moves, the acquisition of PricewaterhouseCooper in 2002. The sale marked a shift in direction for the company, positioning it as a service provider and software company, rather than a hardware business. Rometty was credited with executing some of the finer points of the deal, particularly with orchestrating the smooth transition of PwC consultants into the IBM fold despite significant cultural differences between the two companies. For her efforts, Rometty was recognized by *Time* as an influential global business leader.

With the PricewaterhouseCooper deal under her belt, Rometty was named Senior Vice President of Global Business Services before becoming Group Executive of Sales, Marketing and Strategy. Her accomplishments included expanding the IBM business globally, with a particular focus on growth markets, forging into cloud computing, and overseeing the commercial roll out of Watson, IBM's natural language-compatible computer system.

When, in 2011, it was announced that Rometty would succeed Sam Palmisano to become IBM's first female CEO, Rometty had already logged 30 years at the company and played a vital role in the company's future planning and strategy, the oversight of which she would now command. In her first years as CEO—she would also become president and chairman—Rometty led deals with companies like Twitter and Apple and pushed ahead with IBM's research and development into forward-looking, emerging areas of the tech industry like cybersecurity, artificial intelligence, and blockchain.

She also pushed to create a more progressive work environment at IBM, with employee benefits that include breastmilk delivery and longer paternity leave. The company's community outreach programs have expanded under Rometty's watch, as well; there are now more "new collar" jobs at IBM—those that make room for employees without college degrees—as well as integrated mentorship opportunities and pipelines for tech training and employment.

Her reign as CEO has not been without negative press and ample criticism, however, primarily around a stretch of financial loss for IBM over a staggering 22 quarters. She eventually turned the slump around to post sales growth of 1% in the last quarter of 2017, primarily driven by cloud computing success.

Still, Rometty's leadership has just as frequently been praised, with repeat honors as a top tech executive from a range of business publications, including *Bloomberg*, *Fortune*, and *Forbes*. She serves on the Council of Foreign Relations, is on the Northwestern University board of trustees and the board of Memorial Sloan-Kettering Cancer Center, and has been a co-chair at the World Economic Forum. She holds honorary degrees from Rensselaer Polytechnic Institute and Northwestern, and her commitment to diversity was also honored with a Catalyst Award in 2018.

Leadership Insights and Rometty

Virginia (Ginni) Rometty became the first women to head IBM in 2012. She has been with IBM since 1981. She has faced several challenges including criticism of financial results (22 quarters of revenue decline), executive compensation, and outsourcing. While managing these challenges, she also has been leading a transformation of IBM to focus more on analytics, cloud computing, and artificial intelligence. She has led the acquisition of more than 30 companies and the divestiture of some of IBM's more commoditized assets. She led IBM back to financial growth in 2018.

She has been awarded the KPMG Inspire Greatness Award and been listed in the Bloomberg 50 Most Influential People in the World, *Fortune*'s 50 Most Powerful Women in Business, and *Time*'s 20 Most Important People in Tech, as well as *Forbes*' America's Top 50 Women in Tech for her leadership.

Husain (2018) noted several leadership qualities of Rometty that have infused her initial time as IBM CEO:

> **Taking Risks**
>
> Heading a leading conglomerate like IBM in different managerial and executive positions during volatile times, such as the Dot Com Bubble burst in 2001 and the worldwide market turmoil in 2007-8, can be a tough nut to crack. And taking risks by applying sweeping changes/strategies to beat your rivals is Ginni Rometty's forte. She has always been aware that growth and comfort don't usually coexist. She knows that the best way to grow is to try new things and break the glass ceiling.
>
> Dealing with artificial intelligence and cloud computing is one way how IBM successfully maintained its supremacy over its competitors in a fierce market. Nicknamed Big Blue, IBM continues to grow under Rometty's charismatic leadership. Even though she has been facing the wrath of the critics for being too blunt and bold in her decisions the acquisition of PricewaterhouseCoopers by IBM, when Rometty was leading IBM's

consulting group in 2002, was a testament to the fact that she knows how to take calculated risks that pay off well in the future.

In an interview at Stanford Business School (2018), she noted: "Don't protect your past; don't define yourself as a product."

Action Speaks Louder than Words

Ginni's humble beginnings and a simple but hard-fought childhood was one of the many reasons she molded into a tougher version of herself. She knew right from the day when she joined IBM that her job won't be a bed of roses, and the hard work and diligence she put into her work speak volumes about her industriousness. Over the last 5 years under her leadership, IBM witnessed continuous change and evolved with the times. IBM used to spend billions of dollars on research and development each year. In the year that Rometty was named the CEO of IBM, that amount escalated to 6.9 billion dollars.

In 2014, Rometty allocated $1 billion dollars to create a business unit for Watson and $3 billion dollars to fashion a next-generation semiconductor. She doesn't lust after fame by regularly corresponding with media or tweeting to solicit cheap attention from the media. Her actions embody her desire to make IBM the best IT and technology company in the world through a focus on innovation.

In an interview at Stanford Business School (2018), Rometty commented: "Our license to operate is based on trust," Rometty said. "Society and business will decide if they want to trust you." She expressed her belief that companies should adhere to three values constituting what she called "principled stewardship": purpose, transparency and explainability.

"In addition to being passionate, I feel really strongly, whatever you go do, do something with purpose," she says.

Aligning the Workforce

Right after taking charge of IBM in 2012, she made sure to align the workforce and motivate employees to the fullest.

Rometty explained in an interview how she successfully aligned the huge workforce at IBM worldwide (380,000 as of 2016). She achieved this by following long-term strategic beliefs around which employees can jointly focus. She made sure her employees come to work each day brimming with confidence and self-belief to achieve a common goal and purpose.

Reinventing the Company

Constantly reinventing themselves is the mantra for all of the employees at IBM. And Rometty is the person behind this idea. She thinks that Data is what the world will be looking for in the future as without correct and precise data, nothing can be done. According to her, "20% of the world's data is searchable. Anybody can get to that 20%. But 80% of the world's data is where I think the real gold is, whether its decades of underwriting, pricing, customer experience, risk in loans – that is all with our clients. You don't want to share it. That is gold."

IBM has recently acquired the Weather Company and has collaborated with Salesforce.com to refine IBM's AI program, Watson. These are just two of the examples that prove how IBM is taking huge strides to keep pace with its competitors.

In an interview with Fortune (2014), Rometty noted:

Look, all of these changes are rooted in this belief that you've got to constantly reinvent yourself, and all the big changes have been around the major points of our strategy: around reinventing industries and professions for data, around remaking the enterprise era for cloud, and all around this theory of engagement.

What makes this time different is that the three of those things are happening at one time, at a speed we haven't seen before. So, you're going to get a shift that's faster and more profound. And it impacts every industry. You've got to keep reinventing. You'll have new competitors. You'll have new customers all around you. To me, those three together is what's driving all of the change in the industry.

This change is happening faster than it has ever happened before, and so it does put a premium on speed, and speed of change, and being bold. And a bit of experimentation. To try things and then course-correct along the way.

Jacksonville University (n.d.), in a profile of Rometty, noted:

Rometty is a charismatic speaker. Her open, frank communication style invites an audience to share her vision, which she articulates succinctly and well. While being an accomplished public speaker does not necessarily translate to becoming a successful leader, it is clear that Rometty combines both of these qualities to great effect.

Yet, what truly sets her apart is the substance of her message. "You have to get comfortable being uncomfortable," Rometty told Benioff and their audience. "Ask yourself: When did you grow the most, and did you feel at risk? Almost 100 percent of people will say yes. It's true for people, it's true for companies and it's true for countries.

"Be first and be lonely."

"I learned to always take on things I'd never done before. Growth and comfort do not coexist."

Key Takeaways

- Leaders must lead with purpose.
- Leaders need to be highly communicative —open, frank, and transparent
- Leaders need to take the long view and be willing to make calculated risks.
- Leaders need to be consistent in words and actions, but actions and results best define leaders.
- Leaders need to be comfortable being uncomfortable.

AUGUST LEADERS

For August, we will learn from, Mother Teresa, Warren Buffett, and Fred Smith.

Mother Teresa

(Anjeze Gonxhe Bojaxhiu)

August 26, 1910 - September 5, 1997

"Not all of us can do great things. But we can do small things with great love."

"We ourselves feel that what we are doing is just a drop in the ocean. But if the drop was not in the ocean, I think the ocean would be less because of the missing drop."

Biography

Motivated by her faith and her belief in acts of service and charity, Mother Teresa spent almost fifty years caring for the poorest and most ostracized members of society, in the process creating a global network of centers and hospices that continue to provide care to this day.

Born to an Albanian family on August 26, 1910 in Skopje, now the capital of Macedonia, Teresa was originally known as Agnes Gonxha Bojaxhiu. Religion was a central part of her life even as a child, and following a pilgrimage to a shrine in modern day Kosovo at the age of 12, she resolved to devote her life to Christianity.

At the age of 18 in 1928, she moved to Ireland to join the Institute of the Blessed Virgin Mary, also known as the Sisters of Loretto; it was here that she received the name Sister Mary Theresa, in honor of the French Saint Thérèse of Lisieux. She remained in Ireland until the end of the year, before travelling on to India to begin her career of service in earnest, arriving in Kolkata on January 6, 1929.

Initially, her primary focus was education, and she taught at a girls' school called St. Mary's for years, becoming the school's principal in 1944. During this time, she also began the process of becoming a nun, starting with her First Profession of Vows in May 1931. This culminated with her Final Profession of Vows on May 24, 1937, after which point she took on the name that would later become famous—Mother Teresa.

She experienced a transformative moment on September 10, 1946 while travelling between Kolkata and Darjeeling, when she felt an undeniable calling to go beyond the work of her convent and dedicate her life to seeking out and aiding the indigents of society. In 1948, she began wearing the white and blue sari that would come to be synonymous with her public image, and left the convent to work with the poor of Kolkata. The first center that she opened as part of her outreach was a school for the children of the slums.

With the permission of Pope Pius XII, Mother Teresa established the Missionaries of Charity on October 7, 1950, a religious order specifically focused on aiding and assisting society's outcasts and rejects. Over time, additional branches would be opened to include other members of the clergy, such as priests. A group called the Co-Workers of Mother Teresa became officially connected to the Missionaries of Charity in 1969, allowing laypeople to join in the charitable work of the association and help expand its reach.

The organization worked to open centers that would provide comfort and care to those in need, including hospices for the terminally ill, orphanages for abandoned children, and places for the homeless to receive food and shelter. Originally providing support to the people of

Kolkata, by the early 1960s, Mother Teresa began sending religious sisters to other parts of India. In the following years, the Missionaries of Charity expanded its global presence, opening centers across the world, including one in New York in 1971. By the late 1990s, they were serving people in more than 100 countries, and nearly 4,000 sisters were involved in the work.

A pillar of Mother Teresa's mission was a belief in, and emphasis on, the dignity and humanity of everyone, even the poorest of the poor. By showing compassion to those who society had chosen to ignore, she believed she was truly fulfilling her mission from God to spread love and shine light on people who were otherwise forgotten.

Though she received much international acclaim for her work, Mother Teresa always maintained she was not worthy of such praise and emphasized that she was being recognized on behalf of the people that she served. Among other honors bestowed upon her, Mother Teresa received the Pope John XXII Peace Prize in 1971, the Nobel Peace Prize in 1979, the Bharat Ratna in 1980 (India's highest civilian award), and the honorary Order of Merit in 1983.

It is important to note that while many have come to view her as the ultimate symbol of peace and charity, Mother Teresa's work was not without criticism during her own lifetime. Her organization's hospices were noted as being lacking in adequate medical care and medical professionals, as well as appropriate pain medication for patients with terminal conditions. She was also criticized for her outspoken opposition to abortion and contraception; many saw the latter as a tool that, alongside proper education, could have helped to alleviate some of the issues that stemmed from overpopulation in the places she served, in addition to the spread of sexually transmitted diseases like HIV. (HIV patients are among those, however, who receive shelter at facilities founded by Mother Theresa's order.)

Suffering from health problems later in life, in particular issues with her heart, she spoke with Pope John Paul II in 1990 before announcing her intention to step down from leading the Missionaries of Charity.

However, no successor was appointed, and she would remain in the role until March 13, 1997.

Mother Teresa died on September 5, 1997 in Kolkata, at the age of 87. Since her death, she has become a saint, beatified by Pope John Paull II on October 19, 2003 and canonized by Pope Francis on September 4, 2016.

Leadership Insights and Mother Teresa

Including a proclaimed saint in this text on leadership was an easy decision, especially given that many of us were able to see, hear or read about Mother Teresa in our lifetimes.

From a leadership perspective, aside from her compelling personal example, she was also the Founder of the Missionaries of Charity (1950), a Roman Catholic religious congregation which has over 5,000 nuns, 400 Brothers, 750 Missions and is active in 139 countries. There is much to learn from Mother Teresa from her spiritual life as well as her exemplary record of building and leading a global organization.

Thiran (2017) noted about Mother Teresa:

> What has always struck me about Mother Teresa is how this diminutive lady with a big heart and powerful spirit was able to effect so much positive change around the world.
>
> She truly epitomized the saying that "you're never too small to think big," and it was through her example that I realized there is nothing that can't be achieved if you have the right focus, passion, and determination to make it happen.
>
> One of the other striking qualities about Mother Teresa was that she never talked much about what she was going to do—she simply went ahead and carried out what she felt was necessary.

> One key insight that from Mother Teresa is that we all have our critics—it's an inescapable part of life. There is a choice: We can either yield under the pressure of criticism, or we can rise above it and succeed in spite of it. Mother Teresa chose the latter.
>
> Thanks to her choice, she ensured a powerful and positive legacy that is sure to live on for generations and inspire many people to push towards their unique greatness, and to share their gifts with the world.

Jacobson (n.d.) noted:

> One of Mother Teresa's great strengths was her relentless focus on the core mission of her organization: helping the poorest of the poor. She spent much of her own time helping individuals in extreme need. Her personal example still serves as the model for the Missionaries of Charity. Mother Teresa was completely focused on helping one person at a time.

Russell (2018) added to this:

> Mother Teresa's leadership role was a complex one. On the one hand she understood the benefits of high profile leadership and became a prominent leadership figure driving change on a national and international level, yet believed that the true route to change was achieved on a local level, helping one person at a time.
>
> The Saint experienced a time of darkness whilst carrying out her work, yet retained the veneer expected of her. Mother Teresa said: "Do not wait for leaders; do it alone, person to person," and from this quote we can perhaps get to the crux of her thoughts about leadership: be a good leader, but first be a good person.

Bose & Faust (2011) captured eight leadership principles of Mother Theresa:

> PRINCIPLE 1: Dream it simple, say it strong. Create a vision that is simple. Say it strongly with words and actions at every possible moment.
>
> PRINCIPLE 2: To get to the angels, deal with the devil. Develop a framework to make decisions on ethical issues.
>
> PRINCIPLE 3: Wait! Then pick your moment. Before beginning, be prepared emotionally, financially, and operationally.
>
> PRINCIPLE 4: Embrace the power of doubt. Relentlessly question your business.
>
> PRINCIPLE 5: Discover the joy of discipline. Discipline can bring you joy.
>
> PRINCIPLE 6: Communicate in a language people understand.
>
> PRINCIPLE 7: Pay attention to the janitor. Everyone has value.
>
> PRINCIPLE 8: Use the power of silence. Calm your mind and listen.

Here are associated thoughts for each principle:

Dream It Simple, Say It Strong

- Dare to dream
- Be passionate about what you seek to be and achieve
- Articulate a clear, simple vision for yourself or your organization
- Demonstrate both the vision and the values in all that you do

To Get to the Angels, Deal with the Devil

- Remember who your angels are
- Know your ethical line
- Evaluate every choice against your line
- Don't cross your line

Wait! Then Pick Your Moment

- Patience is required
- Persistence is mandatory
- Assess your readiness: emotionally, financially, operationally
- Go!

Embrace the Power of Doubt

- Embracing doubt can be very powerful
- Use doubt to gauge when to check in with your organization and yourself
- Express your doubt without communicating fear
- Embed the power of doubt in action

Discover the Joy of Discipline

- If it can be done now, do it now
- Practice discipline
- Take your work seriously, never yourself
- Seek joy in all you do

Communicate in a Language People Understand

- Be authentic
- Know your audience
- Listen and show empathy
- Adjust your communication style to the other person

Pay Attention to the Janitor

- Treat each person with respect
- Each of us wants to feel valued
- The title never matters, the person always does

Use the Power of Silence

- Silence is about stopping
- Stop your talking—listen
- Stop your mind—be thoughtful
- Silence your heart—love

"Kind words can be short and easy to speak, but their echoes are truly endless."

"Discipline is the bridge between goals and accomplishment."

Key Takeaways

- Leaders need to think big, yet also do the little things.
- Leaders should make connections, impacting one person at a time if necessary.
- Leaders need to talk less and do more.
- Leaders need a relentless focus on the core mission.
- Effective leaders need to keep it simple and say it strong.
- Leaders need to be pick their moments and be prepared to seize them.

Warren Buffett

August 30, 1930 -

"It's better to hang out with people better than you. Pick out associates whose behavior is better than yours and you'll drift in that direction."

Biography

In some ways, it would be easier to digest the immense success of American investor and philanthropist Warren Buffett by simply reading a laundry list of the professional achievements that led to his rare place of influence on a global level and his unfathomable wealth. Even a straightforward list could easily fill pages of a book on leadership, beginning with his childhood days as a pint-sized door-to-door salesman in his native Nebraska, and culminating in the estimated $28 billion he has given away to charitable causes.

But such a list, while impactful, might skip over some of the details of his life that helped him build a playbook for unprecedented investment savvy and a platform to advocate for personal causes in the particular way that only those with Buffett's drive, relentless pursuit of opportunity, and keen awareness of the power of entrepreneurism can hope to emulate.

Born in Omaha in 1930, Buffett's interest in business and finance was so strong that, after paper routes and a network of pinball machines in local businesses allowed him to purchase a 40-acre farm when he was only 14, Buffett didn't even feel the need to attend college. His father, a U.S. Congressman, disagreed, sending Buffett to first to Wharton and then to the University of Nebraska. Buffett graduated with a bachelor's degree in business administration at age 19, and completed a Master's in Economics from Columbia University in 1951 before enrolling in the New York Institute of Finance.

Buffet's audacious nature was an asset. In 1954, he took a job at the Wall Street partnership started by one of his Columbia professors, the British-American investor and economist Benjamin Graham. Buffett took advantage of Graham's place on the board of the insurance company GEICO to secure a meeting with the corporation's then-Vice President Lorimer Davidson, reportedly by arriving at GEICO headquarters unannounced and convincing a member of the building staff to let him in. Both Graham and Davidson became early mentors of Buffett's, and Graham convinced him to return to Omaha, leaving Wall Street behind and applying Graham's teachings of value investing—the practice of looking for investment opportunities in undervalued companies and capitalizing on the perceived difference.

In 1957, Buffett founded Buffett Partnership Ltd., seeking out strategic partnerships in Omaha to build his early fortune. By 1962, he was a millionaire.

Buffett soon began investing in the textile manufacturing firm Berkshire Hathaway by purchasing shares in the company from its then-owner and leading investments from his other partnerships. By 1965, the price of shares in Berkshire Hathaway had doubled, and Buffett took control of the company. Realizing that textile mills were not a place for long-term growth, Buffett guided Berkshire Hathaway into a period of expansion into the insurance sector—including buying shares in GEICO—and media interests like *The Washington Post,* among other businesses across a diverse set of industries. Buffett eventually dissolved

Buffett Partnership Ltd. and devoted his attention to Berkshire Hathaway full-time.

In the ensuing years, Buffett's Berkshire empire grew, as did his national prominence and scandals of varying degrees of intensity. The U.S. Securities and Exchange Commission opened an investigation on Berkshire in 1974 after it acquired the financial services company Wesco Financial due to a conflict of interest with *The Washington Post*; the charges were dropped. For a time in the late '80s, Buffett himself became chairman of Salomon, Inc., an investment bank in which he invested, after the previous CEO failed to remove an employee who violated Treasury rules regarding trade limits. Neither had much lasting effect on Buffett's continued success, or the powerhouse nature of Berkshire Hathaway.

In fact, effects proved to be quite the opposite, when Berkshire took a 7% stake of Coca-Cola in 1988, a wildly lucrative investment that helped set Buffett on the course to become a billionaire by 1990. Problems associated with such large-scale and entangled business interests didn't cease—Berkshire was involved in a 2005 fraud investigation into General Re and AIG, thanks to the company's acquisition of the former, and the 2007 economic crisis cast a negative light on certain practices in which Buffett, Berkshire, and many others in the financial sector had engaged for years—but Buffett became the richest man in the world in 2008. Berkshire recovered with record earnings by the mid-2010's.

Along with his contemporary Bill Gates—whose own wealth has surpassed Buffett's, and at times, fallen short of his benchmark—Buffett is publicly committed to giving away the bulk of his fortune. In 2006, he pledged to donate 83% of his money to the Bill and Melinda Gates Foundation via Berkshire shares given annually. Buffett has also supported the Glide Foundation, Girls, Inc., the Nuclear Threat Initiative, and voting programs in Nebraska. Buffett is a vocal participant in American politics, endorsing the Presidential campaigns of Barack Obama and Hillary Clinton, supporting tax and healthcare reform, and investing in renewable energy.

Buffett's accolades, like his professional achievements, are many; in brief, he has been named to countless lists of the world's most influential figures, is the subject of dozens of books, and received the Presidential Medal of Freedom from President Barack Obama in 2011.

Leadership Insights and Buffett

American business leader, noted, investor, speaker, and philanthropist, Buffett serves as the chairman and CEO of Berkshire Hathaway, which owns, outright or in part, more than 60 companies, including insurer GEICO, battery maker Duracell, and restaurant chain Dairy Queen.

He is considered one of the most successful investors in the world. Buffett has been the chairman and largest shareholder of Berkshire Hathaway since 1970, and he has been referred to as the "Wizard," "Oracle," or "Sage" of Omaha by global media outlets for his investment history and record. He is noted for his adherence to long-term, value investing and for his personal frugality despite his immense wealth. Buffett is a notable philanthropist, having pledged to give away 99 percent of his fortune to philanthropic causes, primarily via the Bill & Melinda Gates Foundation.

He is also noted for this writings—including his annual reports—and leadership insights, and is frequently recognized by communicators as a great story-teller.

Buffett credits many of his success to his voracious reading habit. He says he starts every morning by poring over several newspapers and estimates he spends as much as 80 percent of his day reading. When asked once about the key to success, Buffett pointed to a stack of books and said, "Read 500 pages like this every day. That's how knowledge works. It builds up, like compound interest. All of you can do it, but I guarantee not many of you will do it. I do more reading and thinking, and make less impulsive decisions than most people in business. I do it because I like this kind of life."

Snyder (2017) captures some key thoughts that Buffett is well known to espouse from an investment lens:

1. **"It is not necessary to do extraordinary things to get extraordinary results."**

   Buffett suggests that the best successes in the workplace can come from those who are consistent. Flashy ideas and grandiose plans only take you so far. In the end, the results speak for themselves.

2. **"It takes 20 years to build a reputation and five minutes to ruin it. If you think about that, you'll do things differently."**

   Here, Buffett says that anyone's reputation can quickly take a hit and to always act with integrity. Otherwise, a whole career can be ruined easily no matter the effort over the years.

3. **"The difference between successful people and really successful people is that really successful people say no to almost everything."**

   It's important to focus on tasks at hand and not get too bogged down in various projects. Otherwise, it's easier to end up doing nothing well at all.

4. **"Risk comes from not knowing what you're doing."**

   An investor should always do his or her homework before making decisions. It's a strong piece of advice that ties in nicely with the next quote.

5. **"Chains of habits are too light to be felt until they are too heavy to be broken."**

   The 86-year-old understands how habits can end up harming a business leader. He warns against getting too comfortable and suggests, instead, that those in charge remain open to change.

Monk (2017) offered more perspectives on these points:

1. **Go Against the Grain**

   Warren Buffett has made his success by sticking to his values and investing his money in areas that fly directly in the face of intense market pressures to follow the crowd.

2. **Face Failure Head-On**

   If any one of the his large stock purchases had truly gone south, the very size of the purchases compared to the rest of the capital under Warren Buffett's command could very well have caused a severe crisis of investor confidence. This could have led to the demise of Berkshire Hathaway.

   Luckily, the story ends happily.

   This does not mean that Warren Buffett's ability to pick winners has been perfect. In his letter to Berkshire Hathaway stockholders, he details the results of all investments made on behalf of the investors.

   He unabashedly discusses the good, the bad, and the ugly. This trait of sharing his failures openly and publicly is a sign of real strength and leadership qualities.

3. **Be Humble**

   In the late 1990's, Berkshire Hathaway was conspicuously absent from the tech sector where even unsophisticated day-traders were creating gigantic wealth almost overnight. When critics started to circulate the opinion that Warren Buffett was causing his investors to miss out on the wealth being created, he openly stated that he didn't "**invest in businesses he could not understand**" and he flat out admitted that he simply didn't understand high tech business models.

> It is unimaginable that anyone else with such a high public profile would have basically admitted to the world that he couldn't understand something, even if this was indeed the case.
>
> In conclusion, one can learn a great deal from observing the actions of Warren Buffett. In particular, his ability to examine, ignore, or discard popular public opinion if they do not agree with his values and principles are traits that define true leadership. The ability to stand pat in the face of unrelenting public criticism cannot be underestimated. Anyone who can do this will truly earn the title "Leader".

Colvin (2016), also commented:

> *He's optimistic.* What comes through most strongly, as it does almost every year, is a powerfully upbeat attitude. No one has ever answered the call of someone who says, "Our situation is hopeless. Follow me." Effective leaders have figured out how to be optimistic while simultaneously confronting reality, regardless of the circumstances.
>
> *He explains what he's doing so that anyone can understand it.* Trusting leaders is important, but we all feel more comfortable knowing what they're doing and why. Part of Buffett's genius has long been his ability to explain the financial workings of a massive conglomerate in language that real people use. This year he devotes most of the letter to explaining just how each of Berkshire's main businesses operates and how each performed. I defy anyone who reads those pages to come away confused. On the contrary, you come away thinking, "This guy knows what he's doing." Because he doesn't ask you to trust him, you trust him more.

-He admits mistakes and makes no attempt to sugarcoat them. I'm not aware of any other leader who every year acknowledges his errors as openly as Buffett does. Yet most leaders haven't learned that lesson.

"It's only when the tide goes out that you discover who's been swimming naked."

"Never test the depth of the water with both feet."

Key Takeaways

- Leaders need to be consistent in attitude, word, and actions.
- Leaders always act with integrity.
- Leaders learn the value of "no" and have the discipline of priorities.
- Leaders do their homework, are prepared and always learning.
- Effective leaders fight complacency.
- Effective leaders are bold, confident risk takers, but with a dose of humility.
- Effective leaders face failure head on, admit mistakes, and learn from them.

Fred Smith

August 11, 1944 -

"Leaders get out in front and stay there by raising the standards by which they judge themselves—and by which they are willing to be judged."

Biography

By 2019 estimates, the FedEX Corporation—the global shipping and courier service founded as the Federal Express Corporation by Frederick Smith in 1971—operates over 650 airplanes in its worldwide fleet. So, it makes a certain degree of sense to learn that aviation was an early passion of Smith's, who became an amateur pilot as a teen in Mississippi.

Despite his early achievements, Smith's childhood was marred by tragedy. His father passed away when he was still a toddler, and Smith suffered from Legg-Calvé-Perthes syndrome, a bone disease that threatened to leave him permanently disabled. He was able to fully recover physically, rebounding enough to play high school football before enrolling at Yale University in 1962.

Smith's initial idea for the business plan that would lead to his founding FedEx has become something of American business legend, springing from a term paper he drafted in an economics class at Yale that outlined the concept of an air delivery service that operated overnight. Smith himself admits the paper wasn't enough to garner a commendable mark—he muses he likely received a C—but the idea remained with him for years.

Upon graduation, Smith's love of aviation drew him to the U.S. Marine Corps in 1966, where he served as a forward air controller (although he did not become a pilot himself). During his time in the Marines, Smith was deployed to Vietnam twice and saw 200 combat missions, including an operation in 1968 for which he was awarded the Silver Star. By the time he was honorably discharged as a captain in 1969, Smith had also garnered two Purple Hearts and received the Bronze Star, as well.

Before his death, Smith's father had built a successful business that included the Smith Motor Coach Company and a chain of quick service restaurants. Smith's inheritance—a reported $4 million—would provide the seed money with which he would launch Federal Express in 1971 after a foray into jet trading via a controlling stake he had previously purchased in a jet maintenance company. Smith also successfully raised $91 million in investments to kick start his Federal Express venture.

Upon its launch out of Memphis two years later—after a disagreeable relationship with the local airport in Little Rock caused Smith to seek a more cooperative hub—Smith had designed FedEx to operate with an innovative integrated air-ground system of planes and trucks. The company began with capabilities in 25 different American cities. Smith's lofty aim, however, outpaced his finances, and FedEx hemorrhaged money from the start, to the tune of tens of millions of dollars. In a now-infamous act of desperation to cover operating costs, Smith traveled to Las Vegas with company cash in hand to try his luck at the blackjack table. His winnings helped stem some short-term losses, and further investment set him on a path toward reversing FedEx's early misfires.

By 1976, FedEx was profitable and was shipping nearly 20,000 packages each day. The company went public in 1978 and, in 1983, exceeded $1 billion in sales.

Not content with domestic success, Smith acquired the Asian air carrier Flying Tiger in the late '80s. The move was costly, however, mirroring some of FedEx's early challenges, now in a new market. It didn't pay off in full until FedEx was able to logistically execute overnight international shipping from the U.S. to Asia in 1998, coinciding with a rapidly globalizing business world that helped drive the company to a new revenue stream that far outpaced the earnings of the original domestic model. By the early 2000's, FedEx was shipping to and from over 200 countries.

Not all of Smith's outsized gambles paid off, even with the benefit of time—see a failed bid to include FedEx parcels on British Airways' Concorde jet for supersonic transatlantic delivery—but other big bets were fortuitous. In 2004, FedEx acquired the shipping and office management retail company Kinko's. It was part of a bid to address a diversified service offering provided by the United Parcel Service (UPS), a perennial competitor that had recently purchased the similar Mail Boxes, Etc. Rebranded FedEx Office in 2008, the division does an annual business of $2 billion.

Under Smith's guidance, the FedEx Corporation was an early adopter of online tracking in the mid-90s and was a pioneer of "drop box" methods of shipping dating back to the '70s that allows users access to convenient places to leave their parcels for pick-up without visiting a dedicated shipping center. Customer service-minded features like those have helped FedEx enjoy trusted, near-ubiquitous status in a wide-ranging expanse of industries worldwide, along with a 2018 net income of roughly $4.6 billion and a value of an estimated $65 billion.

Smith serves as Chairman and CEO of the FedEx Corporation, covering strategy for operating units that include FedEx Ground, Express, Freight, and Services. Also co-owner of the Washington Redskins professional football team, Smith was recognized as one of *Time* Magazine's 50 greatest leaders in the world in 2014. He was also inducted into the San Diego Air & Space Museum's Hall of Fame in 2000, has served on the board of both St. Jude Children's Research Hospital and the Mayo Foundation, and is a trustee for United States Council for International Business.

Smith was inducted into the Junior Achievement U.S. Business Hall of Fame in 1998, and to the SMEI Sales & Marketing Hall of Fame in 2000. His other awards include "CEO of the Year 2004" by Chief Executive Magazine and the 2008 Kellogg Award for Distinguished Leadership, presented by the Kellogg School of Management in May 2008. He was also awarded the 2008 Bower Award for Business Leadership from The Franklin Institute in Philadelphia, Pennsylvania. He was the 2011 recipient of the Tony Jannus Award for distinguished contributions to commercial aviation.

Leadership Insights and Smith

Fred Smith is the founder, chairman, and CEO of FedEx, originally known as Federal Express. His interest in aviation grew from his early childhood and he became a pilot at age 15. In 1962, while attending Yale, he wrote a paper for an economics class, outlining overnight delivery service in a computer information age. The paper became the idea of FedEx.

Chief Executive Magazine (2012) noted some leadership insights gleaned from Smith:

1. **Make reputational intelligence a priority.** Your reputation is different from your brand. Smith notes that FedEx sells trust (e.g. the promise that medical equipment will make it to

important destinations) and not just package delivery. You need to know what your brand is really about and emphasize it.

2. **Create a culture that is always striving for excellence.** FedEx employees have the Purple Promise in which they declare, "I will make every FedEx experience outstanding."
3. **Don't hide your failures, but use them to improve.** When a video went viral of a deliveryman throwing a computer screen over a fence, Smith didn't try to hide it. Instead, he talked about it openly and used it as a platform for learning and improving.
4. **Always look to improve your processes.** FedEx has never sacrificed service (even if it would be almost unnoticeable to customers) in order to add to its bottom line.
5. **Take advantage of unexpected areas for growth:** Did you know that FedEx repairs electronics like iPads and Nooks? The delivery company has the systems in place to transport items to a central repair shop and the technology to fix products. While not the core of its business, it's still a $15 billion market.

Dumaine (2012) interviewed Smith and noted these comments:

> "Well, what we call reputational intelligence is particularly important in our organization because at the end of the day we're essentially selling trust. People give us some of the most important things that they own. There's medical equipment that's going to a surgery this morning or a part that's going to determine whether the new 787 flies. So, reputation is an integral part of the brand, but it's separate and distinct from the brand. You have to put your money where your mouth is. There isn't a year that's gone by where we haven't invested an enormous amount into trying to make the service better. There have been some years when we could have taken the approach: 'You know what? We're not going to try to make the service better. Let's

> just dial it back by 2%. Most people won't notice that, and we can put another 2% to the bottom line.' We've never done that. But, it's also directly related to the culture we've tried to create."

Lohrenz (n.d.) captured Smith's thoughts as he learned them during his time in the U.S. Marine Corps:

> "The greatest leadership principle I learned in the Marine Corps was the necessity to take care of the troops in a high performance based organization."
>
> "The Marine Corps' strong emphasis on this overriding leadership requirement has been of inestimable importance to me in developing FedEx over the years. In the main, people want to be committed to an organization and to do a good job. The principles of leadership taught by the USMC, and based on two centuries of experience, will produce outstanding organizational results in any setting, *if those principles are studiously followed.* In short, FedEx owes its success to this simple truth."

DiGirolamo (n.d.) noted this of Smith:

> While other leaders sit back and point fingers or complain about problems, Fred Smith takes the time to discern the issues, dig deep into the heart of the matter, formulate a strategy, and then promote it both internally and externally. His energy is palpable.

"Leadership is simply the ability of an individual to coalesce the efforts of other individuals toward achieving common goals. It boils down to looking after your people and ensuring that, from top to bottom, everyone feels part of the team."

"Fear of failure must never be a reason not to try something."

Key Takeaways

- Leaders must be positive energy sources in organizations.
- Effective leaders know that reputational capital is based on earned trust.
- Leaders must face failure and use it to improve.
- Leaders need a relentless focus on improvement.
- Good leaders take "care of the troops."

SEPTEMBER LEADERS

For September, we will learn from Jack Ma, Elie Wiesel, and Malcolm Gladwell.

Jack Ma

September 10, 1964 -

"Today is cruel. Tomorrow is crueller. And the day after tomorrow is beautiful."

"A leader should have higher grit and tenacity, and be able to endure what the employees can't."

Biography

From his humble beginnings as an English teacher in eastern China, to his emergence as one of the world's wealthiest businessmen, Jack Ma's persistence and determination have driven his career to incredible heights.

Born Ma Yun on September 10, 1964 in Hangzhou, China, Ma began studying English when he was young; he later received the nickname Jack from a tourist visiting his hometown. Though he had plans to go to college and pursue a degree in English, he faced a setback when it came to the required entrance exam, failing his initial attempts at the test. He eventually succeeded and went on to study at Hangzhou Teacher's Institute, graduating with a degree from the school in 1988.

The early years of Ma's professional career were marked by a struggle to find his footing, with Ma himself explaining, "I failed a lot. [...] I applied to 30 different jobs and got rejected." He also once wryly noted that he was rejected from Harvard no less than ten times. Ma ultimately became an English teacher, which sparked an interest in education that would become a passion in his later life.

A pivotal turning point for Ma came in 1995, when he visited the United States and had his first experience using the internet. Despite the fact that he had no background in working with computers, he was inspired to create his own website, with the aim of catering specifically to the Chinese market. In April of the same year, China Pages was launched.

Ma's first foray into web-based businesses was short lived. In 1996, China Pages entered into a joint venture with a government-owned entity, and Ma left the company. He then spent some time working for a branch of the Chinese Ministry of Commerce, but left in 1999, ready to return to entrepreneurship and looking to start another internet-based company.

Famously launched with a group of friends from Ma's Hangzhou apartment in 1999, the site was called Alibaba.com and formed as an e-commerce marketplace for businesses. Unique within China at the time, they were quickly able to find their niche; in less than a year, Goldman Sachs and SoftBank had both invested in the company, providing $25 million in financing. By 2002, Alibaba was profitable.

In May 2003, Ma was ready to launch the Alibaba Group's second e-commerce company, called Taobao. This time, he focused the platform on consumer-to-consumer interactions. For several years, it competed directly with eBay for the largest market share in China, before ultimately emerging victorious as the country's C2C platform of choice.

Driven by the need for a payment solution that could help the group's businesses facilitate online international payments across various currencies, in 2004 Ma created Alibaba's third business, Alipay. Though it was initially created to solve a problem for Alibaba specifically, adoption of Alipay quickly grew and now, more than a decade later, it is China's largest mobile payment platform, and is also credited with helping to transform China from a cash-centric society into one that has fully embraced electronic payments.

By the mid-2000s, Alibaba had attracted considerable international attention and interest, with Yahoo! purchasing a 40% stake in the business in 2005. In 2014, an initial public offering on the New York Stock Exchange raised $21.8 billion, and in the process became the largest initial public offering in the Exchange's history.

Viewed as the driving force behind the Alibaba Group's successes and astronomical growth, Ma surprised the world when he announced in 2013 that he would be stepping down from his role as the group's CEO (though he would stay on as Executive Chairman). Nevertheless, this was followed by an announcement in 2018 that he would also step down from his chairmanship the next year, but would still remain involved in the board's activities.

Resigning from these roles would allow Ma to devote more time to charitable causes. A keen philanthropist, he created the Jack Ma Foundation in 2014, looking to improve educational opportunities and structures in rural China. He is also an ardent environmentalist who sits on The Nature Conservancy's global board.

Ma's leadership has been publicly recognized over the years, with a steady flow of honors from international organizations spotlighting his entrepreneurial achievements. Among the long list of accolades he has received, Ma has twice been included in the *Time* 100 list of most influential people (2009, 2014). In 2010 he was named by *Forbes Asia* as one of their Heroes of Philanthropy. His honors include: ranked as the 30th most powerful person in the world in an annual ranking published by *Forbes* in 2014. In 2015, Asian Award honored him with the Entrepreneur of the Year award. In 2017, he was named number two on *Fortune*'s World's 50 Greatest Leaders list. Also in 2017, a KPMG survey ranked Ma third in a global technology innovation visionary survey.

Leadership Insights and Ma

Ma is a Chinese business magnate, investor, and philanthropist. Ma has resigned (effective in 2019) from the position of the CEO of Alibaba Group and reportedly decided to focus on philanthropy and educational work.

Chan (n.d.) in an analysis of Ma noted:

> The evidence show that Ma is a highly emotionally intelligent individual, and this, coupled with an effective leadership style, creates a positive climate in Alibaba. Ma appears to employ predominately an authoritative style of leadership with occasional overlaps into the democratic, affiliative and coaching styles. Ma's authoritative style often is presented in company speeches and interviews where he speaks of a vision to enable small businesses to succeed and to the globalize E-Commerce. However, during tougher times, he is known to democratically involve his senior staff in important decisions, such as the founding of Taobao. His use of various leadership styles has inspired many colleagues to be *flexible.* The continual repetition of his vision makes it clear to employees of their mission as well as his infectious commitment to the cause.

Driscoll, S. (2018) captured some career lessons from Ma that also can apply to leadership.

- Being rejected is not always bad.
- Hire people who are smarter than you.
- Do what you have to do to get started. And big things could come.
- Don't believe you've made it.
- Make your fancy ideas reality.

Birdsong, (n.d.) captured some more Ma perspectives on leadership:

1. **Develop one valuable skill that sets you apart from everybody.**

   Jack Ma distinguished himself early by learning one important skill: speaking English.

   He was quoted as saying: "English helps me a lot. It makes me understand the world better, helps me to meet the best CEOs and leaders in the world, and makes me understand the distance between China and the world."

   Learning English was the one skill that set him apart which eventually lead him to the U.S. years later — on that trip, he first discovered the internet.

2. **Embrace your shortcomings.**

   On paper, Jack Ma should not have ascended to one of China's most successful businessmen. No Ivy League education, little connections, and minimal mathematical proficiency were just a few of the setbacks. Yet, Jack embraced these setbacks, acknowledged them, and wears them as badges of honor.

   Here's how Jack embraces his shortcomings:

   Jack brags: "I don't have a rich or powerful father, not even a powerful uncle." He goes on: "Even today, I still don't understand what coding is all about. I still don't understand the technology behind the Internet."

   Jack has made a career out of being underestimated: 'I am a very simple guy, I am not smart. Everyone thinks that Jack Ma is a very smart guy. I might have a smart face, but I've got very stupid brains.'"

   Jack brags that he applied to Harvard 10 times and got rejected every time. He might as well wear a lapel, proud that of 24 people who applied at KFC, only 1 did not get the job: him. Jack Ma never worked at KFC, but he did end up buying a piece of it. He also never was accepted into Harvard, but he does end speak there on many occasions.

3. **Never give up. It's never too late to start.**

   Jack started two failed businesses before Alibaba: Hope Translation and China Pages. There was also a time when he worked for the government in Beijing. In 1999, he started Alibaba after a period where he felt he was "too late" to be an internet pioneer. After early traction as a company focusing on Business to Business, their goal was to help thousands of Chinese factories find an outlet overseas for their goods. Their progress was good... then the bubble crashed.

   In his darker moments, he took to comparing his struggles to those of the revolutionary Mao Zedong after the Long March, even calling for a 'rectification movement' to set Alibaba on a new course: 'Once many well-known managers in America came to Alibaba to be vice presidents. Each of them had their own opinions...It was like a zoo at the time. Some were good at talking while other were quiet. Therefore, we think the most important purpose of the rectification movement is to decide a shared purpose of Alibaba, and determine our value.'

   This was when they decided to pivot.

   Two years later Jack recalled the scene as he invited a half dozen, hand-picked employees to his office. Our COO, CFO, the vice president of HR, and I were all there. We talked to them one by one: 'The company has decided to send you to do a project, but you are required to leave your home, and you must not tell your parents or your boyfriend or girlfriend. Do you agree?' Holed up in the small apartment, the team got to work.'

4. **Create a clear, lengthy, purposeful vision, and promote your values.**

   Jack's vision for Alibaba is to survive for 102 years.

   In addition to his inspiring vision, Jack set's a clear set of values for his company. He branded the sum of value into what he calls the "Six Vein Spirit Sword." These values focus on building up one's own internal strengths in order to defeat any opponent.

   The Six Veins:

   - Customers First
   - Teamwork
   - Embrace Change
   - Integrity
   - Passion
   - Commitment

   Jack holds these values with very serious regard.

5. **Develop personal mantras and heartfelt stories.**

   Jack has a set of beliefs as stated above. In order to reiterate those values, Jack has a long list of mantras and stories that reinforce those values. Below are some favorites:

   "Believe in your dream and believe in yourself."

   "Learn from others the tactics and the skills, but don't change your dream."

   "If there are nine rabbits on the ground, if you want to catch one, just focus on one. Change your tactics, but don't change the rabbit."

   "Customers first, employees second, and shareholders third."

'Today is brutal, tomorrow is more brutal, but the day after tomorrow is beautiful. However, the majority of people will die tomorrow night."

"Work happily but live seriously."

"eBay may be a shark in the ocean, but I am a crocodile in the Yangtze River. If we fight in the ocean, we lose, but if we fight in the river, we win."

6. **Have an obsessive focus on the customer, not revenue or share price.**

   After the IPO, Alibaba went through major growing pains. The stock price was falling and pressure was mounting. Alibaba CEO, David Wei (Ma was the president) in turn thought he would receive a lot of pressure from Jack. He's quoted as saying 'Jack never picked up the phone or came to see me about the share price. Never once. He never talked about profit growth.' There was one occasion where Wei felt the wrath of Ma. Wei continued: 'The only time he ever called me after midnight was when our team changed the website a little bit. He was shouting, the only time he ever yelled at me. I had never heard him so angry. 'Are you crazy?" Jack did not yell at him for the stock price, instead he was irate that Wei and team moved a long-standing discussion forum set up for traders to chat *with one another. Jack demanded it be moved back the next day.*

"30% of all people will never believe you. Do not allow your colleagues and employees to work for you. Instead, let them work for a common goal."

"If you don't give up, you still have a chance. Giving up is the greatest failure."

Key Takeaways

- Effective leaders create positive and participative climates.
- Leaders need to learn from rejection and keep moving forward.
- Leaders must create and live a compelling and purposeful vision.
- Leaders cannot get complacent.
- Leaders need to persist and persevere.
- Leaders need an obsessive focus on the customer.
- Effective leaders hire the best staff, find talent smarter than them, and listen to them.
- Leaders must embrace their shortcomings and find staff to compliment or fill in gaps. Effective leaders are always learning.

Elie Wiesel

(September 30, 1928 – July 2, 2016)

"Words can sometimes, in moments of grace, attain the quality of deeds."

Biography

After experiencing firsthand the horrors of the Holocaust, author Eliezer "Elie" Wiesel would go on to become one of the most famous figureheads of that era and a tireless campaigner against global injustice and suffering.

Born on September 30, 1928 in Sighet, Romania—now referred to as Sighetu Marmației—to a Jewish family, Wiesel grew up immersed in both secular and religious studies and was deeply connected to his faith.

By 1940, the part of Romania where Wiesel lived had been annexed by Hungary, and in March 1944, the German occupation of Hungary began. As a result, by the time he was 15 years old, Wiesel and his family were forced into a Jewish ghetto in their town. In May 1944, the family was sent to Auschwitz, the most notorious concentration camp of World War II. It was here that Wiesel would acquire a tattoo with his unique identifying number: A-7713.

Wiesel suffered tremendously during the war. In addition to the physical and psychological terrors he was subjected to during his time at Auschwitz, he lost his mother Sarah and younger sister Tzipora; they were killed upon arrival. In total, more than one million people are estimated to have died at Auschwitz alone. Wiesel was later sent to Buchenwald, another concentration camp, with his father Shlomo, who died before the camp was liberated by the United States Army on April 11, 1945.

After the end of the war, Wiesel travelled to France and spent time living there, initially residing in a home with other children survivors from Buchenwald; he would later be reunited with his two older sisters Beatrice and Hilda, who had also survived the atrocities of the Holocaust. He learned French, and from 1948 to 1951, studied at the Sorbonne in Paris. He also became more active in journalism and writing during this time.

Wiesel moved to the United States in 1955 and would become a naturalized citizen by 1963. His first job was writing as the foreign correspondent for the Israeli newspaper *Yediot Ahronot.*

Still traumatized by what he had had lived through, it took ten years for Wiesel to open up about everything he had seen and experienced during the Holocaust. A key confidant in his decision to do so was his friend François Mauriac, a Nobel Laureate author and member of the French Resistance during World War II who encouraged Wiesel to write about the subject.

Weisel's written work about his experience during the Holocaust underwent several periods of revision and different iterations, starting as a long Yiddish manuscript entitled *Un di Velt Hot Geshvign* ("And the World Remained Silent"), before being pared down and published as a shorter book in France in 1958 under the title *La Nuit.* In 1960, it was published in the United States as *Night,* and became known as Wiesel's seminal work. The book speaks to Wiesel's time as a teenager in both Auschwitz and Buchenwald and explores notions of humanity and faith and how his experiences in the camps affected his belief in both.

Wiesel would go on to have a prolific career as an author, with *Night* serving as the first in a trilogy, followed by *Dawn* (1961) and *Dusk* (1962). He would eventually publish more than 50 books. His first volume of memoirs was released in 1994 (*All Rivers Run to the Sea*), followed by a second volume in 1999 (*And the Sea is Never Full*).

The Holocaust remained a central theme in Wiesel's work for the rest of his life, and he continued to speak and write about the subject at length, ensuring that the legacy of those who lost their lives would never be forgotten; he famously wrote in *Night* that "to forget the dead would be akin to killing them a second time."[1] From 1978 to 1986, he served as the Chairman of the Presidential Commission on the Holocaust, and was involved in the foundation of the United States Holocaust Memorial Museum in Washington, D.C.

Wiesel was also a vocal critic of tyranny and oppression in other countries in the 20th and 21st centuries, and was ultimately awarded the Nobel Peace Prize in 1986 for his work. At the time, the Norwegian Nobel Committee described him as "one of the most important spiritual leaders and guides in an age when violence, repression, and racism continue to characterize the world."[2] Other key awards that Wiesel received include the Presidential Medal of Freedom, an honorary knighthood in the United Kingdom, the Grand Cross in the French Legion of Honor, and his election to the American Academy of Arts and Letters.

Outside of his writing, Wiesel maintained a keen interest in education, and at different points throughout his career, he held key positions at various universities in the United States, including Distinguished Professor at the City University of New York, Andrew Mellon Professor of Humanities at Boston University, Henry Luce Visiting Scholar in the Humanities and Social Thought at Yale University, and Ingeborg Rennert Visiting Professor of Judaic Studies at Barnard College, part of Columbia University.

Wiesel passed away at age 87 on July 2, 2016 in Manhattan, having devoted his life's work to speaking out against inequality and injustice. A survivor who refused to stay silent and instead called upon the world to bear witness to the tragedy of the Holocaust, his legacy lives on in his many publications and in the Elie Wiesel Foundation for Humanity, which he founded in 1986 after winning the Nobel Prize for Peace.

Leadership Insights and Wiesel

Wiesel was a Romanian-born American Jewish writer, professor, political activist, Nobel Laureate, and Holocaust survivor. He authored 57 books, written mostly in French and English, including *Night*, a work based on his experiences as a prisoner in the Auschwitz and Buchenwald concentration camps.

Along with writing, he was a professor of the humanities at Boston University, which created the Elie Wiesel Center for Jewish Studies in his honor. He remained involved with Jewish causes throughout his life and helped establish the United States Holocaust Memorial Museum in Washington, D. C. Wiesel was awarded the Nobel Peace Prize in 1986, at which time the Norwegian Nobel Committee called him a "messenger to mankind."

Citterman (2016) highlighted some leadership attributes of Wiesel:

> Conviction is what makes leaders powerful, and there is much to learn from a man like Elie Wiesel. Here are three quotes from Wiesel that provide us lessons on leadership and conviction:
>
> **Develop clarity.**
>
> *"There may be times when we are powerless to prevent injustice, but there must never be a time when we fail to protest."*
>
> Clarity comes from self-awareness and from understanding what are the very few things that matter most—the things you're willing to fight for. We may not always win the fight, but a leader must use his or her voice, power and influence to try.
>
> **Inspire conviction.**
>
> *"We must take sides. Neutrality helps the oppressor, never the victim. Silence encourages the tormentor, never the tormented."*

As leaders, part of our job is to inspire confidence in others to express their point of view. If we want to work collectively with people who have the confidence to be decisive, who will constructively disagree and confront difficult situations, show leadership by listening, by asking good questions, and by challenging the thinking of others to draw out their conviction.

Show gratitude.

"When a person doesn't have gratitude, something is missing in his or her humanity."

There are few things a leader can do that have more impact than showing gratitude. Yet, so many leaders colossally fail because they're too busy or too focused on other things. It takes very little effort to say thank you, to give credit, or show appreciation. The best leaders do it frequently, and it pays dividends.

Elie Wiesel was a man of clear conviction, and there is much to be learned from a life lived with such purpose. As a leader or aspiring leader, I challenge you to define what you stand for and decide how you will show it every day using clarity, conviction and gratitude.

Popova (n.d.) captured Wiesel thoughts on the loneliness of leaders:

> He considers the peculiar kind of loneliness inherent to leadership:
>
> > Naturally, a true leader cannot function without those whom he or she leads. By the same token, the leader cannot work or live in their midst as one of them. Hence the ambivalence of his or her position. There must be some distance between the leader and those being led; otherwise the leader will be neither respected nor obeyed. A certain mystique must surround the leader, isolating

> him or her from those whose servant he or she is called upon to be or has been elected to be. Is there a leader, here or anywhere, who does not find time to complain about the terrible solitude at moments of decision?
>
> Wiesel points to Moses—"a man who had endured trials and upheavals, challenges and tragedies"—as a testament to another essential element of leadership: the willingness to not only proactively take the responsibilities that appeal to one's ambitions, but to accept and rise to the responsibilities that fall on one by unwilled or unwelcome circumstance.
>
> He writes:
>
> "Here is Moses's singularity. A man of the situation, he was always there when needed, and then he gave himself completely to his task. He had no ambition to become a prophet, but once he became one, he was the greatest. He did not seek the role of political or military leader, but once he took it on, he was the best. Philosophers would say that if a human being is what he or she becomes, Moses was a human being par excellence.
>
> And yet, Wiesel suggests, the most lonely-making of the prophet's trials is how God tends to leave most of his questions unanswered.
>
> He considers the possible moral of Moses's story:
>
> Could it be … that questions are more important than answers? … Could it be that questions are the remedy for solitude? After all, we have learned from history that people are united by questions. It is the answers that divide them."

According to the Elie Wiesel Foundation (n.d.), when Elie Wiesel is asked by students or readers what they should take away from his books or classrooms, he answers—as he has done for the last ten years or more—quite simply: "Think higher and feel deeper."

Former President Clinton (*The Guardian*, n.d.) noted: "In words and deeds, he bore witness and built a monument to memory to teach the living and generations to come the perils of human indifference. As he often said, one person of integrity can make a difference."

"Be careful with words, they're dangerous. Be wary of them. They begat either demons or angels. It's up to you to give life to one or the other. Be careful, I tell you, nothing is as dangerous as giving free rein to words."

Key Takeaways

- Leaders need courage of conviction. They need to "think higher and feel deeper."
- Leaders accept and rise to their responsibilities.
- Effective leaders show gratitude.
- Leaders need to lead with consistent integrity.
- Leaders need to have clarity of purpose.

Malcolm Gladwell

September 3, 1963 -

"Shallow communities are relatively easy to build."

Biography

During his career as a journalist and author, Malcolm Gladwell has established himself as a key thinker and voice within the sphere of popular culture. By combining an interest in big movements and moments in society with research from sociology and social psychology, Gladwell has painted a compelling picture of the world that encourages us to think outside of the box and explore trends we might not have otherwise considered.

Born in England in September 1963 to a black Jamaican mother and a white English father, Gladwell and his family emigrated to Canada when he was six, where he was raised in the midst of a Mennonite community in Ontario. Gladwell was a successful competitive runner in high school, but his most marked characteristic was his innate sense of curiosity and his ambition. As a youth, those around him—including his own father, a professor of mathematics—often commented on these traits, which demonstrably carried over into his career as a writer, driving him to explore a diverse selection of topics and themes in his work.

When he finished high school, Gladwell headed to Trinity College, Toronto (part of the University of Toronto) graduating with a history degree in 1984. As a student, he spent time in Washington, D.C. participating in the National Journalism Center's summer program. Initially interested in enrolling in a graduate degree, Gladwell's grades—by his own admission—were not high enough to warrant admission, so he changed course with subsequent plans to pursue a career in advertising. He faced difficulty in this as well, however, and after experiencing a lack of success in the industry, he pivoted back to pursuing a career in journalism, ultimately landing a job at *The American Spectator* in Indiana.

In 1987, Gladwell's national profile rose significantly when he joined *The Washington Post*, making a name for himself covering business and science, and, beginning in 1993, serving as the paper's New York correspondent.

In 1996, Gladwell moved to *The New Yorker* (where he remains a staff writer to this day), a key progression in his experience and exposure as a writer that would shape later developments in his career. Gladwell's early work at the magazine helped establish his particular voice as an intellectually-minded author for a new audience, and provided the inspiration for his first book *The Tipping Point*, published in 2000. The book was a hit, and Gladwell would go on to publish three more original titles (*Blink*, 2005; *Outliers*, 2008; *David and Goliath*, 2013), as well as a 2009 collection of articles previously published in *The New Yorker*, entitled *What the Dog Saw: And Other Adventures*.

A key skill of Gladwell's that has contributed to his popularity and commercial success as a writer is his ability to identify specific topics and themes that evoke curiosity at a broad level, and then explore them through patterns present across seemingly unrelated people and events within popular culture.

Tipping Point was originally inspired by Gladwell's investigation of lowered crime rates in New York in the 1990s relative to other decades, and ended up becoming an exploration of how little things can build up to form a powerful momentum; in the book, Gladwell used the television show *Sesame Street* and the novel *Divine Secrets of the Ya-Ya Sisterhood* as other illustrations to prove his points. In *Outliers,* Gladwell focused on cases of extraordinary success achieved by individuals or groups—naming Bill Gates and the Beatles as examples—and asked what external factors might have helped to shape and contribute to their experiences. In the process, he popularized the theory that 10,000 hours of practice is the amount of time required to become an expert in a specific field or skill. (It's important to note, however, that this idea was initially rooted in a 1993 paper written by Professor Anders Ericsson.)

Gladwell certainly wasn't the first to wonder why certain people are more successful than others, why we make the choices we do, or why things suddenly spike in popularity or influence, but the way in which he has chosen to approach these questions, with his special blend of popular culture and social psychology, struck a chord with mainstream audiences in a big way. Though his work has been criticized at times for being overly simplistic or too reliant on anecdotal evidence as opposed to pure scientific fact, Gladwell's use of easily understood cultural touchstones to illustrate and explain societal trends has spread his writing further than most academic texts could hope to resonate.

In addition to his work as a journalist and author, Gladwell has also made a name for himself as a popular public speaker, often booked to speak at colleges and universities, business conferences and high-profile events like TED Talks. While he continues to write, he has also turned his attention to podcasting, starting his own show in 2016 entitled *Revisionist History,* with each episode devoted to a different topic from the past that Gladwell explores and re-examines.

Gladwell was named to *Time*'s list of The 100 Most Influential People in 2005, *Foreign Policy*'s Top 100 Global Thinkers list in 2008, 2009, and 2010, and, in 2001, received the Order of Canada.

Leadership Insights and Gladwell

Gladwell is a Canadian journalist, author, and public speaker. He has written five books, three of which have interesting perspectives for leaders: *The Tipping Point: How Little Things Can Make a Big Difference* (2000), *Blink: The Power of Thinking Without Thinking* (2005), *Outliers: The Story of Success* (2008). *The Tipping Point* was named as one of the best books of the decade by Amazon.com customers. *Fortune* described *The Tipping Point* as "a fascinating book that makes you see the world in a different way." *Blink* was named to *Fast Company*'s list of the best business books of 2005.

Antonio (n.d.) captured key quotes from Gladwell which speak to various dimensions of leadership:

> "The key to good decision making is not knowledge. It is understanding. We are swimming in the former. We are desperately lacking in the latter."
>
> *Knowing is not enough. Understanding how 'it' fits within the context of what you're doing, how it applies—is the key. It's great to know, but seek to understand and apply.*
>
> "Truly successful decision-making relies on a balance between deliberate and instinctive thinking."
>
> *Find the balance between making a well-informed, strategic decision, and going with your gut. I've been wrong many, many times. On a daily basis even! However, my gut has never steered me wrong, even when I don't know all the facts.*
>
> "Our world requires that decisions be sourced and footnoted, and if we say how we feel, we must also be prepared to elaborate on why we feel that way...We need to respect the fact that it is possible to know without knowing why we know and accept that—sometimes—we're better off that way."

"We have, as human beings, a storytelling problem. We're a bit too quick to come up with explanations for things we don't really have an explanation for."

As mentioned, seek to understand. When we think we know without properly understanding, we can rush to judgments, explanations, and conclusions that are not appropriate. Sometimes, we don't need an immediate explanation. We have to wait until there is more information, or a different perspective, to get a better grip of what we just heard, learned, or saw.

"Emotion is contagious."

Whether it's with your family, in the workplace, in your school, or organization, be the most enthusiastic person you know. People may not tell you, but you never know who you're inspiring.

"Hard work is a prison sentence only if it does not have meaning."

In the midst of your hard work, make sure you're working on the right things. Work hard on tasks that give meaning, purpose, and the desired results for your life or current project.

"Insight is not a light bulb that goes off inside our heads. It is a flickering candle that can easily be snuffed out."

Insight comes from asking, 'why did this happen?'. Our insight is so delicate because it's very easy to accept events, people, and information at face value. It's easy to NOT connect the dots. It's easy to not ask why, and believe that's just the way it is. It's easy to be on autopilot – and there is absolutely no insight there!

"Success is not a random act. It arises out of a predictable and powerful set of circumstances and opportunities."

Redrup (2015), noted that Gladwell posits that leaders need to be disrupters at times. He offers three attributes of leaders as disrupters:

1. **Creative**

   To solve a major problem, you have to be creative.

   "People who transform the world...do not place much stock in what people say about them."

2. **Conscientious**

   Creativity in itself doesn't make a disrupter. Leaders reframe the problem.

   According to Mr. Gladwell, it is also a conscientious attitude which leads to success.

3. **Disagreeable**

   Above all, disrupters are disagreeable. Gladwell told the audience the story of American businessman and radio pioneer David Sarnoff.

   In the 1920s, Mr. Sarnoff was one of the few people who realized the potential of radio to do more than just communicate the news.

   He went to his bosses at RCA Wireless with a plan to live broadcast the 1921 boxing match between Jack Dempsey and Georges Carpentier. This event went on to kick start the popularity of radio in the U.S.

   "The board of directors say it's the stupidest thing they've ever heard. He comes back the next day and the next and they say he can do it, but he has to do it on his own," Mr. Gladwell said.

   "A rebellious activity is something that leads to success... that kind of courage lies at the heart of what it means to be disruptive."

"The key to good decision making is not knowledge.
It is understanding. We are swimming in the former.
We are desperately lacking in the latter."

"Insight is not a light bulb that goes off inside our heads.
It is a flickering candle that can easily be snuffed out."

"...If you work hard enough and assert yourself,
and use your mind and imagination, you can
shape the world to your desires."

Key Takeaways

- Leaders need to strive for understanding, often probing deeper to locate the root cause.
- Leaders need to be enthusiastic and to provide meaning.
- Leaders do the right things, eliminating the less important.
- Leaders need to balance rigor in decision making with gut instincts.
- Leaders need to be willing to be rebellious and disruptive.

OCTOBER LEADERS

For October, we will learn from Theodore Roosevelt, Bill Gates, and Indra Nooyi.

Theodore Roosevelt

(October 27, 1858 – January 6, 1919)

"Keep your eyes on the stars, and your feet on the ground."

Biography

In few positions is one's ability to lead and inspire the masses more scrutinized than in the office of the President of the United States. Of the dozens that have held that office since its establishment, even fewer have managed to enter it with as much vigor and exit it with as enduring a legacy as Theodore Roosevelt.

Born to a prominent family in New York City in 1858, Roosevelt showed intellectual promise as a child, but debilitating health conditions, including severe asthma, forced him to receive much of his education at home. He idolized his father, who inspired in him a love for travel, culture, nature and exercise—the latter of which significantly mitigated the effects of his asthma.

Roosevelt enrolled at Harvard shortly before the sudden death of his father, which devastated him, but he recommitted to his studies and graduated magna cum laude in 1880. He attended law school briefly, but realized that his true ambitions lied in "the governing class," and he was elected to the New York State Assembly in 1882.

Undeterred by his junior status (he was just 24 years old at the time of his election), Roosevelt undertook an aggressive anti-corruption crusade, which helped him earn landslide reelection victories in 1883 and 1884. After unsuccessfully campaigning for George Edmunds for the 1884 Republican Presidential nomination, however, Roosevelt moved west to take up residence in a cabin in the North Dakota badlands.

He returned to New York City just two years later, losing a mayoral election before accepting a job in the U.S. Civil Service Commission, where he remained for a decade. By 1898, war had broken out in the Caribbean and Pacific between the U.S. and Spain, and Roosevelt, who had been named Assistant Secretary of the Navy, resigned from that post and headed to Cuba to fight alongside the Rough Riders, a volunteer cavalry raised to support the understaffed U.S. Army in combat.

It was in Cuba that Roosevelt's talent for leading was truly put on display, galvanizing the roughly 1,000 men in his command to victories at Las Guasimas and Kettle Hill. 80 years after his death, Roosevelt was given the Medal of Honor for his actions.

He returned to New York a national hero, winning a narrow election to become Governor of New York just three months after his arrival from Cuba, following a tireless campaign. He spent much of his two-year term gaining an education in the business of politics and pushing back against the influence of trusts and political bosses.

Though he did not seek the Vice-Presidential nomination, backroom maneuvering saw Roosevelt added to the 1900 Republican ticket as William McKinley's running mate. This tenure, too, was short-lived, as McKinley succumbed to a gunshot wound in September, 1901, and Roosevelt was sworn in as the 26th President of the United States.

As President, Roosevelt's main priorities were trust busting, conservation, and foreign policy. He successfully split the nation's largest railroad monopoly into three separate companies, regulated Standard

Oil, which controlled 70 percent of the nation's fuel production, and lobbied Congress to enact the creation of the Department of Commerce and Labor.

His work in conservation was unparalleled by any President before or since, establishing the United States Forest Service and preserving five national parks, 18 national monuments, and 150 national forests, often by power of executive order.

Abroad, Roosevelt had generally softened his earlier imperialist views before entering federal office, but looked for opportunities to assert American authority in Central America and the Caribbean. He invested heavily in expanding the U.S. Navy, and leveraged that military might to ensure the completion of the Panama Canal, which would enrich the U.S. for decades. He won election to a full term in 1904, and was awarded the Nobel Peace Prize in 1906 for helping to mediate the end of the Russo-Japanese War.

Roosevelt was only 50 years old at the end of his term, but declined to run again and endorsed William Howard Taft, who would succeed him as President in the election of 1908. He traveled to Africa and Europe, but returned in 1912 to unsuccessfully challenge Taft, his former protégé, for the Republican Presidential nomination. He formed his own, progressive, "Bull Moose" party. He survived an assassination attempt at a campaign stop in Milwaukee, but both he and Taft lost the election to Woodrow Wilson, a Democrat from New Jersey.

Roosevelt traveled again, this time to South America, but an infected injury, tropical fever, and the bullet still lodged in his chest caused his health to decline. He remained in public life for the next five years, urging American support for the Allies at the outset of World War I, before dying in early 1919, at age 60.

His legacy is manifested not only in the physical, such as his iconic place in the pantheon of great Presidents atop Mount Rushmore, but also the metaphysical, a larger-than-life presence that shaped American ideals of the Presidency and patriotism itself.

Leadership Insights and Roosevelt

Roosevelt served in an array of leadership roles that formed his perspectives: State Assemblyman, Civil Service Commissioner, NYC Police Commissioner, Assistant Secretary of the Navy, Colonel in the military, Governor of New York, Vice President, and President.

Historians credit Roosevelt for changing the nation's political system by permanently placing the Presidency at center stage and making character as important as the issues. Dalton (2002) says, "Today, he is heralded as the architect of the modern Presidency, as a world leader who boldly reshaped the office to meet the needs of the new century and redefined America's place in the world."

Strock (2017) offered these leadership lessons from Roosevelt:

1. **Leaders are created, not born.** Roosevelt's life and work is an enduring answer to the eternal question: Are leaders born—or are leaders made?

   Roosevelt believed that leadership is an ongoing project of self-creation. He offered his life as a template for anyone who would seek to re-create themselves into an effective leader.

   "If I have anything at all resembling genius, it is in the gift for leadership.... To tell the truth, I like to believe that, by what I have accomplished without great gifts, I may be a source of encouragement to Americans."

2. **Courage is the foundational virtue.** Theodore Roosevelt was a warrior. His virtues and shortcomings are best evaluated with an eye toward the world in which he lived. Death was a constant companion.

   In his world, courage was paramount. Physical courage was prized. Moral courage, perhaps even more rare, was necessary for enduring service.

Roosevelt overcame a weak physical endowment and corresponding temperament. He aimed for his example to stir others—indeed the nation as a whole–to undertake the same transformation.

"There were all kinds of things of which I was afraid at first, ranging from grizzly bears to 'mean' horses and gun fighters; but by acting as if I was not afraid I gradually ceased to be afraid."

3. **Action, action, and still more action.** Theodore Roosevelt had a consistent bias for action. He believed in the initiative. He was never comfortable or effective on defense, responding to a state of affairs set by others.

   Whether it was the construction of the Panama Canal, taking on J.P. Morgan, or any number of other memorable challenges, Roosevelt took the risks of action, over the greater (if sometimes less evident) risks of inaction or delay.

   "Whatever I think is right for me to do, I do. I do the things that I believe ought to be done. And when I make up my mind to do a thing, I act."

4. **Put your team ahead of yourself.** One of Roosevelt's formative real-time leadership experiences was leading his regiment in the Spanish-American War.

   Roosevelt led from the front. He placed himself into undeniable danger, remaining on horseback while facing a rain of steel.

   He placed those he was serving before himself. As a result, many of the Rough Riders remained committed to him for the remainder of their lives.

   No man has a right to ask or accept any service unless under changed conditions he would feel that he could keep his entire self-respect while rendering.

5. **Leaders are learners.** From youth, Roosevelt was a voracious reader: "Reading is a disease with me."

   Roosevelt's curiosity, his ceaseless learning, never abated. The book, the classroom, formal education, these were far from the only venues for learning. They produced many of those he called the "educated in-effectives."

   Roosevelt's example, combining the life of ideas and the life of action, was central to his project of self-creation as a leader.

   As soon as any man has ceased to be able to learn, his usefulness as a teacher is at an end. When he himself can't learn, he has reached the stage where other people can't learn from him.

6. **Bring history to life, create the future.** Roosevelt was first among equals, a practicing politician who was also an accomplished historian. He, along with intimates such as Senator Henry Cabot Lodge of Massachusetts, would frequently turn to historical exemplars as they dealt with contemporary problems.

   There is nothing cheaper than to sneer at and belittle the great men and great deeds and great thoughts of a bygone time—unless it is to magnify them and ascribe preposterous and impossible virtues to the period.

7. **Maintain open channels with adversaries.** Many people think in all-or-nothing terms: Either you're for me, or you're against me. That can be appropriate in some circumstances, but, at least as often, it's not.

   Roosevelt's focus on results, on outputs, rendered him flexible as to means. He would, he said, "work with the tools at hand."

   Roosevelt, as governor of New York, met regularly with his frequent adversary and uneasy ally, the "Easy Boss," Senator Thomas Collier Platt. This prompted some criticism from critics who feared that such meetings would necessarily compromise Roosevelt or his positions on vital matters.

Roosevelt nonetheless maintained regular meetings and communications with Platt and other nettlesome personages:

"If my virtue ever becomes so frail that it will not stand meeting men of whom I thoroughly disapprove, but who are active in official life and whom I must encounter, why I shall go out of politics and become an anchorite. Whether I see these men or do not see them, if I do for them anything improper then I am legitimately subject to criticism; but only a fool will criticize me because I see them."

8. **Keep commitments.** Roosevelt was notable in striving to meet commitments. He would meet commitments to his children to play, even if it meant that meetings of state would have to end.

   Memorably, he declined numerous entreaties to walk back his commitment, made impulsively on election night in 1904, not to seek re-election in 1908.

   In Roosevelt's reckoning, holding to his word was vital to earning and maintaining the trust of those he served:

9. **Be authentic: Live your values.** Roosevelt was authentic in the true sense: He was the author of his character. He strove to live his demanding values, the better to serve a nation that could advance by the same values.

   Most of all, I believe whatever value my service may have, comes even more from what I am than from what I may do.

Strock (2003) further offered this list of leadership attributes inspired by Roosevelt:

- Begin hard and fast.
- Seize—and hold—the initiative.
- Continually communicate your vision to members of the organization.

- Make the welfare of your team your foremost responsibility.
- Hire people more talented than yourself.
- Ceaselessly search for new talent.
- Recognize strong performers.
- Acknowledge and forgive acceptable mistakes—including your own.
- Overlook "minor differences."
- Ruthlessly replace individuals who do not meet the standards of the enterprise.
- Develop leaders.
- Demonstrate faith in your team by delegation of authority.
- Delegation, though extensive, should be bounded by clear standards.
- Fortify delegation with selective intervention.
- Manage by wandering around.
- Back up your team.
- Create an "inner circle" of leadership.
- Continually convey loyalty and gratitude to your team—even after it has been disbanded or leadership has been transferred.
- Serve as a continual agent of change.
- Become the author of yourself

Nobody cares how much you know, until they know how much you care."

"The best executive is one who has sense enough to pick good people to do what he wants done, and self-restraint enough to keep from meddling with them while they do it."

Key Takeaways

- Leaders need to be life-long learners and engage in "ongoing self-creation."
- Leaders need to have courage of conviction.
- Leaders must be willing to take action.
- Leaders need a "team first" orientation.
- Leaders create the future.
- Leaders need to be authentic and keep commitments.

Bill Gates

October 28, 1955 -

"We all need people who will give us feedback.
That's how we improve."

Biography

Great industrialists like the Carnegies, Fords, or Rockefellers—those who amassed vast personal fortunes in pursuit of the American Dream while laying the foundation for the nation's rise to global superpower—seem to occupy a place in the national lore second only to the Founding Fathers themselves. Unlike these historical capitalists, who were also frequently branded with the less-flattering epithet "robber barons," contemporary billionaires and business magnates are expected to wield their wealth responsibly, ensuring that the corporations they lead contribute positively to society and reinvesting their profits in philanthropy.

And while he was explicitly influenced by the examples of predecessors like Rockefeller, much of that modern expectation of charitable giving has been driven by Bill Gates, the founder of Microsoft and—in terms of financial donations—the most charitable businessman of the 21st century.

Gates' interest in software—the business that would make him a billionaire—began in his early prep school years, when he was exposed to a teletype machine purchased for the students and wrote his first software program at age 13. After scoring a 1590 on his SAT, Gates enrolled at Harvard in 1973, studying pre-law but spending much of his time in the university's computer labs.

After encountering an article in a 1975 issue of *Popular Electronics* that described the Altair 8800, a computer based on the new Intel 8080 microprocessor, Gates and an old classmate, Paul Allen, sensed an opportunity. Gates dropped out of Harvard and the pair launched a new company, intending to adapt the BASIC programming language for use on the computer.

Fresh off their first success, the new venture, called Micro-Soft, piqued the interest of decisionmakers at IBM, who approached the team about creating an operating system for IBM's upcoming foray into the personal computer market. The ultimate success of the IBM PC was a windfall for Microsoft, which licensed the operating system to other computer manufacturers, and within three years, nearly one-third of the world's computers were running the company's software.

1985 saw the release of the first commercially available version of Microsoft Windows, the line of operating systems that would revolutionize personal computing and come to dominate 90% of the global market. A ruthless competitor and demanding leader, Gates spent much of the 1990s fighting antitrust litigation; accused of anti-competitive practices and unfair deals, he and Microsoft emerged mostly unscathed.

Foreseeing the impact that the rise of widespread internet access would have on society, Gates focused much of Microsoft's resources and manpower on developing software solutions for the world wide web, introducing numerous innovations and catalyzing another period of explosive growth for the company.

Gates stepped down as CEO of Microsoft in 2000 after 25 years, but remained as chairman until 2014, gradually transitioning out of day-to-day operations to focus on his charitable initiatives.

Since becoming a billionaire after Microsoft went public in 1986, Gates has given at least $35 billion to charity through the Bill and Melinda Gates Foundation, formed in 2000 to improve healthcare, fight poverty and open access to education. Gates has stated that he intends to devote 95% of his personal wealth to philanthropy over his lifetime, and has encouraged other wealthy people to do the same. In 2010, Gates and Warren Buffet formed The Giving Pledge, whose more than 150 signatories have pledged to donate a majority of their fortunes to charity.

He was named *Time* magazine's person of the year in 2005, alongside Melinda and Bono, for their collective efforts to help end poverty and disease. He was made an Honorary Knight Commander of the Order of the British Empire by Queen Elizabeth II in the same year, and later received both the Presidential Medal of Freedom and France's highest order of merit, the Legion D'Honneur. In 2017, Gates was surpassed as the richest person in the world by Amazon founder Jeff Bezos, in large part because he had already given one-third of his personal fortune away.

Leadership Insights and Gates

Gates is an American business magnate, investor, author, philanthropist, and humanitarian. He is best known as the principal founder of Microsoft Corporation. During his career at Microsoft, Gates held the positions of chairman, CEO and chief software architect, while also being the largest individual shareholder until May 2014.

Time magazine named Gates one of the 100 people who most influenced the 20th century, as well as one of the 100 most influential people of 2004, 2005, and 2006. Gates was listed in the *Sunday Times* power list in 1999, named CEO of the year by *Chief Executive Officers magazine* in 1994, ranked number one in the "Top 50 Cyber Elite" by *Time* in 1998, ranked number two in the *Upside* Elite 100 in 1999, and was included in *The Guardian* as one of the "Top 100 influential people in media" in 2001.

Chris (2015) offers these qualities of Gates that can be activated by other leaders:

1. *He follows a long-term approach.*

   He doesn't limit himself to the here and now, but looks beyond the present. When the rest of the world was content with the way things are going, he was quick to understand the impact of the internet and market conditions on Microsoft.

2. *He stays focused.*

   A lot of people think they are qualified to become leaders because they know plenty of things, and are equipped with several skills. Bill Gates, on the other hand, focused on the one thing that he has mastery over—software. All throughout his professional life, he stuck with it and worked hard to dominate over it. For him, clarity of thought and proper execution take precedence over everything else. He also understood that if he moves into unfamiliar territories, he could be risking it all. So, he focused on software.

3. *He thinks big.*

   Bill Gates is a visionary to begin with, which encourages him to dream big not only for himself, but also for his company. He then goes out to pursue his dream with single-minded determination and confidence in his abilities and that of his team. This led to great success in everything that he does. Being intelligent and aggressive greatly helped as well.

4. *He puts passion in whatever he does.*

   From a Thank You note to innovating an existing product, Bill Gates handles all of them with excellence and passion. When something is worth doing, then it is worth his time, energy and money. His passion is evident on Microsoft products—they are constantly evolving to suit the needs of users.

5. *He stimulates intellect and creativity.*

   The success of Microsoft would not have been possible without the amazing people working alongside Bill Gates. But without his charisma and his convincing abilities, none of his staff would probably have the drive and motivation to help him realize his visions. He empowers people, encourages creativity, and creates opportunities for people to explore new ways of doing things.

6. *He considers learning as a life-long process.*

   He may be focused on software, but Bill Gates continued to learn and develop something new so he can provide something better. It is no surprise then that he dominated on the software world. Most households all over the world use Microsoft products, after all. Forbes has also highlighted his efforts to improve on his skills in communication and public speaking. It also helps that he has a different way of looking at the world, according to Warren Buffett.

7. *He cares about people.*

   It is often hard to separate the billionaire from the philanthropist and humanitarian when you are talking about Bill Gates. He simply cared, which extends to the less privileged in other parts of the world. He was one of the 1% that gave away a majority of their wealth for a good cause. In a note he wrote to the Harvard community members, he made it clear that he wished for people to emulate what he is championing so that when they look back, they will not only have their professional achievements to be proud of, but "how well you work to address the world's deepest inequities, on how well you treat people a world away who have nothing in common with you but their humanity."

Kiplinger (2107) captured other leadership insights from Gates:

- **Maintain steely focus**. Easy to say, tough to do—especially when your organization is under fire. Gates prioritized well and kept his team riveted on producing results.
- **Tolerate—and welcome—failure.** Innovation rarely unfolds smoothly. Gates knew that any breakthrough flows from trial-and-error, and mostly from error. Rather than fear failure and try to avoid it, extract lessons from it and move on.
- **Fight complacency.** Success doesn't necessarily breed more success. Gates understood that even the most profitable company needs to stay one step ahead of trends and keep reinventing itself to continue to dominate in a hotly competitive industry.
- **Think in threes.** A master of reducing complex concepts into simple thoughts, Gates prefers to cluster ideas in groups of three. By mapping out your thoughts in a succinct, easy-to-remember list, you maximize your persuasive power.
- **Grow and evolve**. Gates was not a born leader with boundless charisma. Over the years, he steadily improved his communication skills.
- **Provoke healthy debate**. Some leaders crave harmony. Not Gates. In his early years running Microsoft, he loved to trigger intense arguments with his team—flinging criticisms and demands at them. Heated debates were commonplace. You'll discover how to make conflict a positive force rather than a destructive one.
- Power (2017) offers these insights from Gates and Steve Ballmer on leadership and working as a team:

Start with strong leadership.

Neither Gates nor Ballmer could be accused of weakness as leaders. Strong leaders exemplify the qualities they want in employees. That's why it's critical to not only hire executives whose values align with your own, but to also invest in your personal development as a leader and in the development of those around you.

When your team members view you as someone they want to emulate, they're more dedicated to the company and to each other. If you expect your employees to work hard and commit themselves to your company while you fail to show the same dedication, expect turnover rates to skyrocket and work quality to plummet.

Be intentional about open communication.

Ongoing communication is critical to any relationship—something Gates and Ballmer struggled with in the later years of their relationship

Show recognition and gratitude to your team.

Showing gratitude is key to building loyalty and trust in any relationship. In fact, it's so important that U.S. organizations spend more than $77 billion each year on incentive programs to motivate and reward employees. Recognizing the contributions of all the members of your team—and the time and energy that third-party vendors and consultants put into their relationships with you—will help you build bonds that last beyond the terms of a contract or the length of a project.

Handle conflict immediately.

Conflict is inevitable, no matter how strong a partnership is—in fact, 85 percent of employees said they have experienced conflict in the workplace. But it can be anticipated and minimized. Ballmer has emphasized the importance of respect in communication between himself and Gates, stating that they had "a brotherly relationship in the good parts and the bad parts."

"Patience is a key element of success."

"As we look ahead into the next century, leaders will be those who empower others."

Key Takeaways

- Effective leaders provoke healthy debate.
- Leaders need to think big and long-term.
- Leaders need "steely focus."
- Leaders need to be passionate and engaged.
- Leaders need to be intentional communicators.
- Leaders need to welcome failure and use them as learning opportunities.
- Leaders need to constantly confront and fight complacency.
- Leaders need to encourage and drive creativity.

Indra Nooyi

October 28, 1955 –

"I'm very honest—brutally honest. I always look at things
from their point of view as well as mine.
And I know when to walk away."

Biography

A major transition among business leaders in the 21st century has been a widespread sense of acceptance that executives must answer not only to their own fiduciary interests, but to the long-term impact of the companies they run on the future of an increasingly globalized world.

Before many of the world's most influential executives realized that social responsibility was beneficial to their bottom lines, Indra Nooyi's leadership at PepsiCo was becoming a case study in the dual pursuit of profit growth and a positive impact on society.

In 12 years as CEO of PepsiCo, Nooyi grew the company's revenues by more than 80 percent, significantly expanded its international footprint, and executed key acquisitions to ensure its future, from Gatorade and Quaker Oats, to Pepsi Bottling and SodaStream. At the same time, she foresaw early key market trends, redirecting the company's focus toward healthier alternatives, including in its soda and snack food offerings, and working to lessen the company's impact on environmentally-distressed areas of the world.

She accomplished all of this against the added scrutiny of being a woman of color at the helm of a Fortune 500 corporation, fending off leadership challenges and activist investors to pursue her vision for the company and its role in the world.

Born in the Indian city of Madras (now called Chennai) in 1955, Nooyi described herself as a rebellious child in a conservative, middle-class family, but has said she learned from her mother that she could accomplish anything with the proper attitude and work ethic.

After receiving an MBA from the Indian Institute of Management Calcutta in 1976, Nooyi emigrated to the United States—a risky move at the time for an unmarried woman in a conservative family—to pursue further graduate study at the Yale School of Management. She spent time at Boston Consulting Group, Motorola, and ABB Group in the 1980s before arriving at PepsiCo as Senior VP of Corporate Strategy and Development, in 1994.

Nooyi took on a major role in the company's strategic decision-making, lobbying successfully for the spinoff of the company's fast food business, as well as the ensuing acquisitions of Tropicana, Quaker Oats, and Gatorade from 1998 to 2001—each of which proved successful for the company. She rose to CFO in 2000 and led a difficult integration of the acquisitions in the following years, exceeding sales goals by the end of 2002 and meeting the company's synergy targets by 2004.

When Nooyi was named CEO in 2006, she was one of just 11 female chief executives on the Fortune 500 list. Fortune named her the "Most Powerful Woman in Business" for five consecutive years from 2006 to 2010, and apart from her renowned strategic vision, Nooyi gained a reputation for devotion to her work, sometimes putting in as many as 20 hours a day, seven days a week.

In 2018, Nooyi signaled her intent to step down as chairman and CEO of PepsiCo after 24 years with the company, in part to spend more time with her family, including her 86-year-old mother.

While Nooyi's results in evolving the company and growing its earnings and shareholder returns speak for themselves, on a deeper level, she stands as living proof of the enduring value of hard work, perspective, and the American dream.

Leadership Insights and Nooyi

Nooyi is a business executive, serving as chairperson of PepsiCo, the second largest food and beverage business in the world by net revenue, and as CEO for 13 years from 2006 to 2019. Nooyi was PepsiCo's first female chief executive and boosted revenue 80 percent during her tenure.

She has consistently ranked among the world's 100 most powerful women. In 2018, Nooyi was named one of the "Best CEOs In The World" by the *CEOWORLD magazine.*

The Yale School of Management will name its deanship in honor of Nooyi, as she gifted an undisclosed amount, becoming the school's biggest alumni donor and the first woman to endow a deanship at a top business school.

Hedayati (2014) offers these leadership qualities of Nooyi:

Communication

Indra Nooyi lists communication skills as one of the Five C's of Leadership. She has explained that competence, courage, confidence, and a strong moral compass go to waste without strong communication skills. What does it matter if someone is innovative on a subject if they can't clearly discuss it? In Indra's words, "You cannot over-invest in communication skills." In addition to listing communication as a key skill for leadership, Indra has received communication training to improve her abilities and flexes those communication muscles every time she makes a public appearance, meets with her C-Suite, and deals with a customer. In fact, communication is so valuable to Indra, that she maintains a blog at Pepsi where she talks to her employees via posts every other week.

Relationship Building

Indra goes beyond writing blog posts every other week to maintain a relationship with employees. She writes letters to their parents to thank them for their children. If that's not a CEO building strong relationships, what is? In regards to relationships, Indra has said, "If you only want people to help you when you need them and not have an ongoing relationship with them, they don't know you, they don't know where you come from, and they are doubtful whether you really are interested in the issue, or are you just trying to skate over a current problem?" In maintaining a company relationship with the public, Indra has been in tune with consumers needs for healthier snack and drink options, which has led to transformation in Pepsi's product line. Relationship-building may not be part of Indra's Five C's of Leadership, but it is certainly one of her strengths.

A Moral Compass

Indra lives by moral codes and she feels every corporation owes society care. Indra points out that many companies are bigger than small countries. Organizations need to help society reach goals and solve problems. When discussing the choice to face the challenges at Pepsi during the economic collapse, rather than slash prices and bolt quickly, Indra explained, "Look, this is my company, this is my living, my livelihood. And 300,000 people in PepsiCo depend on PepsiCo for their life and their livelihoods. There are pensioners and investors out there who are hoping PepsiCo will remain a successful entity forever." This is just one of many examples where Indra has turned to her moral compass and exercised strong emotional intelligence in making leadership decisions.

Indra herself had confessed that leadership is not easy. "Leadership is hard to define and good leadership even harder. But if

> you can get people to follow you to the ends of the earth, you are a great leader." The returns on building a better world are certainly worth the struggle. Like Indra, leaders who take the time to analyze methods of leadership and build communication skills are on a track for success.

Snyder (2015) offered these points:

> She's a perfectionist, a quality she brings to her leadership: "We ought to keep pushing the boundaries to get to flawless execution. Flawless is the ultimate goal."
>
> She even has a slogan: "Performance with purpose." And while she's demanding, she's realistic: "I wouldn't ask anyone to do anything I wouldn't do myself."

Chris (2015) captured a comprehensive set of leadership style rules of Nooyi:

She holds on to an immigrant mentality.

Being a naturalized American citizen, Nooyi said that she keeps this in mind to remind her that whatever position she has, it can always be taken away from her.

She uses inductive thinking.

Nooyi mentioned about the significance of what she learned being a strategic consultant at Boston Consulting Group (BCG) and how it contributed to her leadership style. With inductive thinking, she is able to zoom in to a problem and see little details, look at it from a bigger picture then seeing it again in micro terms. This way, she gets to understand it from different perspectives.

She keeps herself aware of the demands of being a leader.

When she became the president of PepsiCo, she told herself that it was just a piece of cake, given that she have worked with different companies and held important positions. However, when she became a CEO, it was different. Nooyi said that despite one's job being close to the top, as COO and CFO, there is nothing more challenging than being a CEO and having the expertise and experience in previous jobs will not suffice.

She believes in the importance of continuous learning.

One of the secrets of Nooyi as a leader is the advice she once got: "The distance between number one and number two is always a constant. If you want to improve the organization, you have to improve yourself and the organization gets pulled up with you. That is a big lesson. I cannot just expect the organization to improve if I don't improve myself and lift the organization, because that distance is a constant." She continuously looks for ways to improve herself, learn and what approach is best for the organization.

She both practices micro and macro management.

Unlike some CEOs and tycoons who are so held up with meetings, business travels, acquisitions, and mergers, Nooyi takes being a CEO a notch higher. Of course, she was the one behind the acquisitions and associations with ancillary businesses. She runs the company not only by looking at the big picture but she is also into details. Nooyi goes to stores and checks how their products are doing, from how they are displayed in shelves to the print quality of the logos. If she sees not enough products are catered to a particular market in a location or demographic, she takes note of this and does something about it.

She does not forget she is human and so are her employees.

Despite her achievements and power, she remains grounded. She said that this is important and that her family members are the ones responsible for keeping her feet on the ground. She cares about the well-being of her employees and her sincerity about this was shown when she wrote letters to her top executive employees' parents telling them they should be proud that their children are doing great at their jobs. This motivated them more and also made her connect deeper to her team.

She thinks global, but acts local.

PepsiCo sells to over 200 countries and this means different types of customers, a variety of preferences and cultures. Having been born and raised in India helped the CEO to look at how the market reacts from other parts of the world. By looking at it from the point of view of a local, she said that they will be able to cater according to the preferences of their target market.

She is open to changes.

One piece of advice she shares is the need for a leader to be able to adapt to new things and changes. She said that leaders should be open to debates and opposition from the people around them. When she pushed for healthier products for the company, not all were confident about it. Years later, they were proven wrong. Nooyi was not afraid to take a quantum leap for the company and it was a success.

She believes in the importance of private and public partnerships.

As a leader, she is a believer that both private and public sectors should treat each other as allies and not enemies. She has observed that there is some sort of conflict between private companies and NGOs. She advocates for both sectors to work together.

She encourages being comfortable and true to one's self.

Nooyi still walks barefoot and attends to phone calls from family members in the middle of meetings. She still wears a Sari at work some times, sings and does not forget her heritage despite being at the helm of PepsiCo. This also includes treating her employees as extended families and allowing a more informal atmosphere at the workplace.

She balances short and long term goals.

Unlike other leaders who concentrate on the quarterly figures, Nooyi believes in the importance of both short and long term goals. She claims that a true leader works hard to achieve short term goals and at the same time see to it that these goals lead also to meeting long term goals.

"Just because you are the CEO, don't think you have landed. You must continually increase your learning, the way you think, and the way you approach the organization. I've never forgotten that."

"Leadership is hard to define and good leadership even harder. But if you can get people to follow you to the ends of the earth, you are a great leader.'

Key Takeaways

- Leaders need to be effective communicators in all modalities.
- Effective leaders forge and leverage relationships and partnerships.
- Leaders must have consistent moral compass and be true to themselves.
- Effective leaders strive for flawless execution.
- Effective leaders are inductive thinkers.
- Leaders need to be able to seamlessly navigate between the short and long term and micro and macro management.
- Leaders need to be adaptable and effective change agents.

NOVEMBER LEADERS

For November, we will learn from Winston Churchill, Jack Welch, Indira Gandhi, and Condoleezza Rice.

Winston Churchill

November 30, 1874 – January 24, 1965

"If you're going through hell, keep going."

Biography

Few in history have possessed skills and convictions more ideally suited to their particular time and place than Winston Churchill. An inspiring leader and gifted director, skilled orator and tenacious patriot above all else, the course of history was irreversibly altered in World War II, when Churchill raised up a nation to counter the seemingly unstoppable spread of fascism through Europe and the world.

Born in Oxfordshire to an American mother and English father descended from Dukes of Marlborough, Winston's childhood was one of privilege, but also by most accounts characterized by parental neglect, save for Elizabeth Everest, his beloved nanny. After requiring three attempts to pass his entrance examination, he was sent to the Royal Military College before graduating in 1894, aged 21, and joining the 4th Queen's Hussars, a cavalry regiment, which would see him travel to the

United States and Cuba as both a soldier and journalist covering the Cuban War of Independence.

Soldiering and writing, either in conjunction or alternation, would become a common theme throughout Churchill's adult life. His regiment traveled to British India in 1896, where Churchill spent over a year attempting to address perceived gaps in his own education with a rigorous reading and self-education program. While in India, he began writing regular dispatches from the Northwest Front for *The Daily Telegraph.*

Envisioning a path by applying his reading, writing, and rhetorical inclinations to politics, he ran for Parliament as a Conservative, losing narrowly, before landing a job reporting on the South African War for *The Daily Mail* and *The Morning Post.* He was taken prisoner following an ambush by the Boers, but escaped the POW camp by stowing aboard freight trains, returning to London with a degree of fame.

He again ran for Parliament in 1900, this time winning by a narrow margin, and gained notoriety for his rhetorical skills, despite a speech impediment, as a 25-year-old MP. Defecting to the Labour party in 1904 on the basis of his support for free trade, he came to be influenced by more senior MP's such as David Lloyd George. He won reelection in 1906, married, and successfully helped take on the House of Lords to affect a series of social reforms.

The outbreak of World War I, in 1914, saw Churchill—then serving as First Lord of the Admiralty—take on his first wartime leadership role. Failures in the Dardanelles and Gallipoli, however, saw Churchill's political stock plunge to an all-time low. In 1922, after suffering from appendicitis during the campaign, he suffered a decisive electoral defeat, leaving him isolated entirely from the British government.

Churchill resumed writing, at which he procured himself a considerable income and achieved another short-lived tenure in Parliament as a Conservative, before reaching a political impasse. He was viewed with suspicion by both major parties, distrusted, and considered to have poor judgment despite his abilities and intelligence. By the early 1930's, he began to grow increasingly wary of Hitler's Germany, issuing grave public warnings about the need to take the threat seriously.

Churchill's warnings were mostly ignored, but he began to develop a following as Germany began to exert its influence in Central Europe. As the Nazi threat loomed larger, Prime Minister Neville Chamberlain placed Churchill in charge of the Admiralty again before resigning after the German push into France. Widely perceived as the sole figure who could lead Britain to victory in the impending war, Churchill was asked by King George VI to succeed Chamberlain as Prime Minister. It was here that Churchill came into his element as a leader. He formed a coalition government, bringing together disparate factions on both sides of the political spectrum, and instilling the idea that Britain had but one, solitary goal as a nation: the defeat of Hitler.

Addressing the House of Commons, he offered the iconic, "I have nothing to offer but blood, toil, tears, and sweat," wholly devoting himself to the war effort and regarding no task as too minor for his attentiveness. His emphasis on unity and inclusion of Parliament in national decision-making allowed Britain to avoid many of the internal political conflicts it endured during World War I. The nation began to see him as an icon of British strength, smoking cigars on the front lines of war and honoring victims and consoling survivors of the German blitz on London.

A lifelong proponent of transatlantic unity between the United States and Britain, Churchill nonetheless rushed to the Soviets' defense when Hitler invaded in 1941, before traveling at once to Washington after the Japanese attack on Pearl Harbor in December. Through these actions he formed an integral glue of the "grand alliance" between the three nations. Military successes abroad begot political problems at home, and with victory imminent, Britain voted the Labour party into office in 1945, forcing Churchill out as Prime Minister. A better leader than politician, Churchill was stunned by the voters' denial.

Out of power but still in politics, he continued ever forward to focus on the nation's next perceived threat: the "iron curtain" of the Soviet

Union. Learning from his prior mistakes, he helped the Conservatives to a general election victory in 1950, just five years after losing power, and once again assumed the role of Prime Minister.

By this time, Britain had, in many ways, moved on from war and security, but Churchill could not. He focused on further strengthening the U.S.-U.K. relationship and rallying support for a European union of nations. In 1953, along with the coronation of a new Queen, Churchill was named a Knight of the Garter and awarded the Nobel Prize in Literature. In declining health, he resigned in 1955 to expressions of adulation from across the political spectrum, but remained an MP.

He was given honorary citizenship by a vote of the United States Congress in 1963, and died in 1965, at age 90, receiving the largest state funeral in world history at the time at the behest of Queen Elizabeth II.

Leadership Insights and Churchill

Churchill was a British politician, army officer, and writer, who was Prime Minister of the United Kingdom from 1940 to 1945 and again from 1951 to 1955. As Prime Minister, Churchill led Britain to victory in Europe in the Second World War. Widely considered one of the 20th century's most significant figures, Churchill remains popular in the UK and Western World, where he is seen as a victorious wartime leader who played an important role in defending liberal democracy from the spread of fascism. Churchill is also praised as a social reformer and writer. Among his many awards was the Nobel Prize in Literature.

The historian Robert Rhodes James stated that Churchill had lived an "exceptionally long, complex, and controversial life," one which—in the realm of British parliamentary politics—was comparable only to Gladstone's in its "length, drama and incident."

Churchill's reputation among the general British public remains high; he was voted number one in a 2002 BBC poll of the 100 Greatest Britons of all time.

Strock (2018) offered these leadership lessons from Churchill:

Leaders are self-created. Winston Churchill was anything but a "self-made man." He was born to the aristocracy at Blenheim Palace. Nonetheless, as much as anyone could be, he was *self-created.* He transcended numerous limitations—from an unprepossessing physical endowment to a distracting speech impediment—transforming himself into the heroic mold conjured in his romantic imagination.

This process of self-creation never ended. He was continually evolving in significant ways, not held back by the needs for predictability and consistency that limit so many others. This also enabled him to recover from setbacks that most would have accepted as career-ending.

Churchill was, to a marked extent, forcing himself to go against his own inner nature: a man who was neither naturally strong, nor naturally particularly courageous, but who made himself both in spite of his temperamental and physical endowment. The more one examines Winston Churchill as a person, the more one is forced to the conclusion that his aggressiveness, his courage, and his dominance were not rooted in his inheritance, but were the product of deliberate decision and iron will.

Courage is the first virtue. If people were asked to describe Churchill in one word, who can doubt that *courage* would be the anticipated response.

In common with many other effective leaders, he exhibited courage in numerous ways. His career intertwined service as a soldier, a writer, and a politician. The disparate strands were braided tightly in his ultimate contribution, as warlord of the British Empire in the Second World War. His courage continued through his final premiership, in the 1950s, when he sought to broker improved relations between the United States and Soviet Union.

All of his accomplishments can be comprehended as arising from a shared root of courage—advanced through a related trait: audacity.

He once said, "Courage is rightly esteemed the first of human qualities because it is the quality that guarantees all others."

Insight is superior to intellect. Winston Churchill stands as an irrefutable monument to the power of Albert Einstein's dictum:

> The intuitive mind is a sacred gift and the rational mind is a faithful servant. We have created a society that honors the servant and has forgotten the gift.

Churchill was not university educated. He was nonetheless highly learned, largely self-directed. As a result, his thought processes were not limited by convention. His boundless curiosity and capacity for fascination were not wrested into compliance and conventionality by pedants.

He was notably gifted with insight. His variety of worldly experiences expanded it. His temperament, fortified with the assurance of an aristocrat who reached adulthood during the apogee of the British Empire, impelled him to express his often unexpected points of view.

Judgment is a fine thing: but it is not all that uncommon. Deep insight is much rarer. Churchill had flashes of that kind of insight, dug up form his own nature, independent of influences, owing nothing to anyone outside himself. Sometimes it is a better guide than judgment: in the ultimate crisis when he came to power, there were times when judgment itself could, though it did not need to, become a source of weakness.

When Hitler came to power Churchill did not use judgment but one of his deep insights. This was absolute danger, there was no easy way round. *That* was what we needed. It was a unique occasion in history. It had to be grasped by a nationalist leader. Plenty of people on the left could see the danger: but they did not know how the country had to be seized and unified.

Apply history to illuminate the present and future. Like Theodore Roosevelt (whom he resembled in many ways), Churchill was obsessed with history. He frequently turned to historical events and characters as if they were at his side. In fact, one might well say that they *were* at his side, coursing through the currents of his preternaturally active mind and imagination. Even as the emerging destiny of Churchill's political project—protecting the survival of the British Empire—stirred his forebodings, his immersion in history enabled him to see far into the future. It made him relentlessly adaptive and innovative–qualities not generally associated with a fundamentally conservative vision.

History, for Churchill, was not a subject like geography or mathematics. It was a part of his temperament, as much a part of his being as his social class and, indeed, closely allied to it.

Mr. Churchill's dominant category, the single, central, organizing principle of the moral and intellectual universe, is an historical imagination so strong, so comprehensive, as to encase the whole of the present and the whole of the future in a framework of a rich and multicolored past. Such an approach is dominated by a desire–and a capacity–to find fixed moral and intellectual bearings to give shape and character, color and direction and coherence, to the stream of events.

Everyone can recognize history when it happens. Everyone can recognize history after it has happened; but it is only the wise person who knows at the moment what is vital and permanent, what is lasting and memorable. –Churchill

"History will be kind for me, for I intend to write it," Churchill once said.

Master the written word. Churchill's early encounters with formal education were in large part unsatisfactory. Nonetheless, it soon emerged that he had gifts of memorization and writing–when his interest and passion were engaged.

His project of self-education included exposure to great English writers. Churchill's recognizable writing style at once reflected his thinking, refined it–and, at times, may have hijacked it toward unexpected destinations.

Churchill noted, "Writing a book is an adventure. To begin with it is a toy and an amusement. Then it becomes a mistress, then it becomes a master, then it becomes a tyrant. The last phase is that just as you are about to be reconciled to your servitude, you kill the monster and fling him to the public."

Master the spoken word. It is as a speaker that Churchill achieved his greatest leadership influence. As President Kennedy said, Churchill "mobilized the English language and sent it into battle."

Churchill acknowledged that he was not an orator. He meant that he was not a speaker, such as David Lloyd George, who could connect deeply with a live audience, receiving and responding to their rising emotions. One wonders if this was a lingering result of his hard-earned triumph over a distracting lisp and the concomitant self-consciousness it inevitably engendered.

By contrast, Churchill prepared extensively, speaking to his audiences with methodically crafted ideas and writing. Many of his legendary witticisms turn out, on inspection, to have been premeditated rather than impromptu. The value was created largely in the interplay of Churchill's evolving thoughts and words as he drafted the speech, rather than in the interplay of his relationship with an audience during presentation.

He customarily dictated his writing. He referred to this as living "from mouth to hand."

He said, "It was my ambition, all my life, to be a master of the spoken word. That was my only ambition."

Not only was the content of his speeches wise and right, but they were prepared with that infinite capacity for taking pains which is said to be genius. So was his appearance; his attitudes and gestures, his use of all the artifices to get his way, from wooing and cajolery, through powerful advocacy, to bluff bullying—all were carefully adjusted to the need. To call this acting is quite inadequate. What we are speaking of is transformation, a growth and permanent change of personality.

Summon unconquerable grit in oneself—as a prelude to inspiring others. One might be think of resilience as a notable aspect of Churchill's life and work, though one imagines that he might incline toward a simple, clear, onomatopoetic descriptor such as *grit.*

Churchill's journey of self-creation and self-assertion was marked by ever-greater examples of determination against all odds, against polite and expert opinion—sometimes in the face of rationality itself. The trials and errors might well have been viewed as constituting a failed career–had not fate summoned him to formal leadership in the struggle against Hitler in 1940.

Some quotes from Churchill for leaders to consider:

"If you're going through hell, keep going."

"Success is not final, failure is not fatal; it is the courage to continue that counts."

"Continuous effort—not strength or intelligence —is the key to unlocking our potential."

"Never, never, give up."

Embrace exuberance. Churchill battled depressive episodes throughout his life. According to Anthony Storr and others, this was an impetus for his ceaseless activity. Idleness was to be avoided at all costs.

He embraced exuberance as a fuel for his enthusiasm, which could then be transmitted to others.

In the struggle against Hitler, Churchill was able to combine the bracing realism of the pessimist with the indomitable optimism required to rouse the dispirited, demoralized people he served. His was not the easy optimism of one who had never known failure or misfortune. Rather, it was the hard-earned optimism of one who had proven that he could take a devastating punch–and, against all odds, pull himself off the mat.

Hedayati, F. (2014) offered these three insights into Churchill's leadership:

Honest

Churchill often argued that "to shrink from stating the true facts to the public" was a mistake. He recognized that that without transparency, there is no trust. Letting his feelings show in an appropriate capacity, he was emotionally intelligent and didn't hold back. His ability to seek truth and stick by the truth earned him dedication of the public. Churchill also said "The truth is incontrovertible. Malice may attack it, ignorance may deride it, but in the end, there it is." It's one thing to speak about honesty, but quite another to live honestly.

Decisive

Amy Woodson-Boulton, Professor of History at Loyola Marymount University, explains in a mini Churchill Biography that he was known for clear decision making. It was clear from his first time spent in British government that Churchill was wary of Stalin and Nazi Germany. And though it wasn't popular, he stuck to that assessment, even when it made him an outcast. And when Britain began to realize he was right and called him back to service, Churchill quickly came to aid. He decisively decided to defy the world's oppressors. The ability to stick to one's gut and step up to make decisions, rather than wait for others to take charge, is a trait of a successful leader.

Persistent

"Each night before I go to bed, I try myself by Court Martial to see if I have done something really effective during the day – I don't mean merely pawing the ground, anyone can go through the motions, but something really effective." And if his own words weren't proof enough of his persistence, it can be seen in his early reporting career when he escaped from the Boers in South Africa or his service to his country through the end of World War 2. Even in the first gloomy days of his British leadership when it seemed the war was already lost, he told the people "we shall fight on the seas and oceans, we shall fight with growing confidence and growing strength in the air, we shall defend our island, whatever the cost may be, we shall fight on the beaches, we shall fight on the landing grounds, we shall fight in the fields and in the streets, we shall fight in the hills; we shall never surrender."

Three qualities that may seem like every day traits enabled Churchill to change the fate of nations and save lives. But these qualities were not words he spoke to describe himself, or words he wore written in jewelry. They were core values that were integrated into his decisions every day. His ability to cause change in the world sprouted from his choices on a regular basis to look at the world with clear eyes, be transparent and stand for what is right. Without the decisions of "everyday Churchill," the accomplishments of "textbook Churchill" that changed the world would never have existed.

"A pessimist sees the difficulty in every opportunity: an optimist sees the opportunity in every difficulty."

"Success is not final, failure is not fatal. It is the courage to continue that counts."

Key Takeaways

- Leaders must be continually evolving.
- Leaders need to be exuberant and committed.
- Leaders need to faithfully transmit their vision.
- Leaders need to have courage of conviction and be decisive.
- Exceptional leaders have "deep insight."
- Effective leaders are masters of communication, both written and verbal.
- Leaders need to have grit and be resilient; they persist.

Jack Welch

November 19, 1935 -

"Good business leaders create a vision, articulate the vision, passionately own the vision, and relentlessly drive it to completion."

Biography

In the tradition of visionary leaders who emerged in the American corporate ranks in the late 20th century, few if any have had a greater influence on other managers than Jack Welch, who spent the latter half of his 41-year General Electric career as the company's CEO.

While many of his management tactics have been called into question by modern business leaders, and Welch himself stated that his legacy as a leader should be judged by the success of his successors (his immediate replacement, it turns out, oversaw a 16-year period that was far less prosperous for the company), one cannot deny Welch's impact in growing GE's revenues in exponential terms, diversifying it into television and financial services, and leaving it the largest and most valuable company in the world.

Born and raised in working class suburbs north of Boston, Welch took on a range of summer jobs through his childhood, from caddying at a country club to selling shoes and operating a drill press at a board-game manufacturer, before earning a B.S. in chemical engineering from UMass Amherst in 1957. Three years later, after completing his PhD at the University of Illinois, he arrived at GE as a chemical engineer in the company's Massachusetts-based plastics division.

Eager to help build a plastics division in a company that was primarily focused on aviation, energy and electronics, Welch was nearly fired early in his term in 1963 with the company when the roof exploded off of a plant under his management. He was given a second chance by the company brass in New York, and by the early 1970s had assumed leadership of multiple divisions as the company's youngest VP. In 1973, Welch was promoted to head of strategic planning, a position that brought him to GE's corporate headquarters permanently.

Still, Welch at times felt dissatisfied and undervalued at GE, blaming what he saw as an inefficient and silo-heavy corporate structure. When he emerged as a leading candidate to succeed Reginald Jones in 1981, it meant a chance to aggressively streamline the organization, and Welch immediately got to work.

By the mid-1980s, Welch had gained a reputation for the zeal with which he attacked GE's bureaucratic structure, eliminating one-quarter of the company's employees as part of a mandate that GE must be either first or second in each of the sectors in which it did business, or exit that industry. His system involved incentivizing top-performing 20 percent of employees with bonuses, promotions, and stock options, while regularly letting go of the bottom 10 percent, across the board.

Despite encouraging ruthless competition, Welch also championed openness and informality, attempting to eliminate internal barriers and lessen reliance on formal channels of communication—part of a vision Welch described as a "boundaryless" organization.

Welch used the savings and proceeds from the sales of various business lines to fund the major purchase of RCA in 1986, mainly to acquire its subsidiary, NBC, as well as RCA's headquarters at 30 Rockefeller Plaza. In the 1990s, Welch's business strategy evolved to adopt the Six Sigma approach to quality control, developed at Motorola in the 1980s, which became central to GE's culture. By the late '90s, he became increasingly focused on succession planning, and underwent a lengthy search for GE's next CEO. Out of three final candidates, Welch selected Jeffrey Immelt, a GE veteran in charge of the company's healthcare division, before retiring in 2001.

He was named Manager of the Century by *Fortune* magazine, received a nine-figure retirement package, and spent the following decade in various consulting and advisory roles, public speaking, and teaching a leadership course at the MIT Sloan School of Management. He founded the Jack Welch Management Institute, an online executive MBA program at Strayer University, in 2009, and took on an active role in planning its curriculum.

In the years since his retirement, Welch's legacy at GE and the long-term effectiveness of his strategies has remained a subject of debate. Although Welch argues that company's subsequent decline under his handpicked successor was driven by the economic downturns of the early and late 2000s, the corporate framework Welch laid down over his tenure bore a significant share of the blame. But contemporary assessments notwithstanding, the culture and organizational ideals Welch instilled remain intrinsic to GE's fabric nearly two decades into the 21st century, and emulated within corporations large and small around the globe.

Leadership Insights and Welch

Jack Welch is an American business executive, author, and chemical engineer. He was chairman and CEO of General Electric between 1981 and 2001. He instilled an organizational behavior that he called "boundaryless." He defined it as the removal of barriers between traditional functions, and finding great ideas, anywhere within the organization, or from outside the organization, and sharing them with everyone in the company.

At GE, Welch became known for his teaching and growing leaders. He has taught at MIT's Sloan School of Management and teaches seminars to CEOs all over the globe. More than 35 CEOs at today's top companies were trained under Jack Welch. In 2009, Welch founded the Jack Welch Management Institute (JWMI), a program now at Strayer University that offers an online executive MBA. He serves as Executive Chairman.

In celebration of its 100th anniversary (2017), Forbes magazine listed the most influential business leaders around the world (*The World's 100 Greatest Business Minds*) and included Welch. The magazine celebrated people who had either created something with a lasting impact on the world or innovated in a way that transcends their given field.

Welch offered his "4 Es" of Leadership (Bryce, 2005):

Energy

Individuals with energy love to "go, go, go." These people possess boundless energy and get up every day ready to attack the job at hand. High energy people move at 95 miles-per-hour in a 55 mile-per-hour world.

The first E: Positive *E*nergy

This characteristic means the ability to thrive on action and relish change. People with positive energy are generally extroverted and optimistic. They make conversation and friends easily. They start the day with enthusiasm and usually end it that way too, rarely seeming to tire in the middle. They don't complain about working hard; they love to work.

They also love to play. People with positive energy just love life.

Energizers

Leaders know how to spark others to perform. They outline a vision and get people to carry it out. Energizers know how to get people excited about a cause or a crusade. They are selfless in giving others the credit when things go right, but quick to accept responsibility when things go awry.

The second E: The ability to *E*nergize others (Welch & Welch. n.d.)

Positive energy is the ability to get other people revved up. People who energize can inspire their team to take on the impossible — and enjoy the hell out of doing it. In fact, people would arm wrestle for the chance to work with them. Now, energizing others is not just about giving Patton-esque speeches. It takes a deep knowledge of your business and strong persuasion skills to make a case that will galvanize others.

From having an edge to possessing the ability to execute plans, learn what one of the top businessmen in the world uses to evaluate employees...

Edge – Those with edge are competitive types. They know how to make the really difficult decisions, such as hiring, firing and promoting, never allowing the degree of difficulty to stand in their way.

The third E: *E*dge, the courage to make tough decisions (Welch & Welch. n.d.)

Look, the world is filled with gray. Anyone can look at an issue from every different angle. Some smart people can — and will — analyze angles indefinitely. But effective people know when to stop assessing and make a tough call, even without total information.

Little is worse than a manager at any level who can't cut bait, the type that always says, "Bring it back in a month and we'll take a good, hard look at it again," or that awful type that says yes to you, but then someone else comes into the room and changes his mind. We called these wishy-washy types "last-one-out-the-door bosses."

Some of the smartest people that I've hired over the years — many of them from consulting — had real difficulty with edge, especially when they were put into operations. In every situation they always saw too many options, which inhibited them from taking action. That indecisiveness kept their organizations in limbo. In the end, for several of them, that was a fatal flaw.

Execute

The key to the entire model. Without measurable results, the other "E's" are of little use. Executers recognize that activity and productivity are not the same and are capable of converting energy and edge into action and results.

The fourth E: *E*xecution, the ability to get the job done (Welch & Welch. n.d.)

Maybe this fourth E seems obvious, but for a few years, there were just the first three Es. Thinking these traits were more than sufficient, we evaluated hundreds of people and labeled a slew of them "high-potentials," and moved many of them into managerial roles.

In that period, I traveled to personnel review sessions in the field with GE's head of HR, Bill Conaty. At the review sessions, we would refer to a single page that had each manager's photo on it, along with his or her boss's performance review and three circles, one for each E we were using at the time. Each one of these Es would be colored in to represent how well the individual was doing. For instance, a person could have half a circle of Energy, a full circle of Energize, and a quarter circle of Edge.

Then one Friday night after a week-long trip to our Midwestern businesses, Bill and I were flying back to headquarters looking over page after page of high-potentials with three solidly colored-in circles. Bill turned to me. "You know, Jack, we're missing something," he said. "We have all these great people, but some of their results stink." What was missing was Execution.

It turns out you can have positive energy, energize everyone around you, make hard calls, and still not get over the finish line. Being able to execute is a special and distinct skill. It means a person knows how to put decisions into action and push them forward to completion, through resistance, chaos, or unexpected obstacles. People who can execute know that winning is about results.

The final P: *P*assion (Welch & Welch. n.d.)

If a candidate has the four Es, then you look for that final P: passion. By passion, I mean a heartfelt, deep, and authentic excitement about work. People with passion care—really care in their bones—about colleagues, employees and friends winning. They love to learn and grow, and they get a huge kick when the people around them do the same.

The funny thing about people with passion, though, is that they aren't excited just about work. They tend to be passionate about everything. They're sports nuts or they're fanatical supporters of their alma mater or they're political junkies.

Whatever—they just have juice for life in their veins.

Severson, D. (2017) noted:

Leadership is best taught by example. Follow these eight indisputable rules directly from the playbook of the former head of GE, Jack Welch. Leadership is all about growing others. It's about your team and its welfare. It's about your direct reports and their performance.

> Leadership is a tough act. It's a daily balancing act. As a leader, you're expected to use your insight, experience, and rigor to balance the conflicting demands of short- and long-term results.

Severson (n.d.) captured these eight lessons of leadership shaped by Welch:

1. **Leaders relentlessly upgrade their team, using every encounter as an opportunity to evaluate, coach, and build self-confidence.**

   The team with the best players wins--and leaders should expend their energy and time in evaluating, coaching, and building the self-confidence of team members.

   "People development," Welch writes, "should be a daily event, integrated into every aspect of your regular goings-on."

   As a leader, it's important to recognize and acknowledge the good work of your team in order to continue to encourage peak performance, why instilling confidence.

2. **Leaders make sure people not only see the vision, but they also live and breathe it.**

   Good leaders cast the vision of the future and motivate people to buy into it. They constantly talk about their vision and reinforce it with rewards, which may be in the form of a salary, bonus, or significant recognition of some sort.

   Even without the rewards, just sharing your vision as a leader can in itself bring about the motivation your team needs to accomplish the most difficult of assignments.

3. **Leaders get into everyone's skin, exuding positive energy and optimism.**

   Effective leaders fight the negative forces of life and encourage their teams with a high level of optimism that keeps members upbeat.

Welch says they do not allow a bad economy or brutal competition to put them down to the extent that their team catches the bug.

Why? "Unhappy tribes have a tough time winning," Welch writes.

Nothing brings down the morale of a team more than an unenthusiastic or disengaged leader. Your job is to be part coach and part cheerleader.

4. **Leaders establish trust with candor, transparency, and credit.**

   Welch decries a situation where leaders hoard information that could benefit direct reports in the performance of their duties. This, he says, drains trust right out of a team. And that, "trust happens when leaders are transparent, candid, and keep their word."

   Leaders, he also says, establish trust by giving credit where it is due. They detest a situation where they'll take credit for someone else's idea or work.

   If you want your team to be transparent with you, you need to lead by example.

5. **Leaders have the courage to make unpopular decisions and gut calls.**

   Effective leaders listen to their gut, Welch says, regardless of what team members think.

   "Obviously," he writes, "tough calls spawn complaints and resistance. Your job is to listen and explain yourself clearly but move forward. Do not dwell or cajole."

   Decision making is ultimately what you'll be judged on as a leader, as your choices could determine the overall success of the organization. With transparency, trust and a clear vision, you'll find that your team will stand behind your decisions (right or wrong).

6. **Leaders probe and push with a curiosity that borders on skepticism, making sure their questions are answered with action.**

   To get bigger and better solutions, Welch says leaders probe proposals and presentations by asking questions and stirring up a healthy debate.

   He writes:

   "When you're a leader, your job is to have all the questions. You have to be incredibly comfortable looking like the dumbest person in the room. Every conversation you have about a decision, a proposal, or a piece of market information has to be filled with you saying, 'What if?' and 'Why not?' and 'How come?'"

   Challenging your employees is an art, not a science. Each individual requires a unique approach. It's your job as a leader to get their best without diminishing their productivity.

7. **Leaders inspire risk taking and learning by setting the example.**

   "Winning companies," Welch writes, "embrace risk-taking and learning." Leaders set the example and encourage team members to experiment without being afraid of making mistakes.

   Experimentation is a major key to growth. Make sure your team feels confident in making mistakes.

8. **Leaders celebrate**

   While noting that leaders don't celebrate enough, the former GE boss advocates that leaders make a big deal out of small wins because "celebrating makes people feel like winners and creates an atmosphere of recognition and positive energy."

   Don't be afraid in celebrating early and often. Far too many leaders believe celebrating small victories leads to complacency. Nothing could be further from the truth.

"Because you are a leader, success is all about growing yourself. When you become a leader, success is all about growing others."

"If you're a leader and you're the smartest guy in the world - in the room, you've got real problems."

Key Takeaways

- Leaders are energizers; they create positive energy to mobilize the organization.
- Leaders have to have the courage to make the tough decisions.
- Leaders convert positive energy into action and results.
- Leaders have to have a deep and authentic passion and enthusiasm for the business.
- Leaders must set and live as exemplars.

Indira Gandhi

(November 19, 1917 – October 31, 1984)

"Have a bias toward action - let's see something happen now. You can break that big plan into small steps and take the first step right away."

Biography

A trailblazer, reformer, hero of the poor, and to many, a ruthless dictator, Indira Gandhi's legacy is as complicated as it is intertwined in the history of India's often-turbulent 20th century.

The only child of Jawaharlal Nehru, the Republic of India's first and longest-serving prime minister and a hero of the country's movement for independence from Great Britain, Indira Gandhi was destined for a life in public service from her birth in 1917, though she spent little of her childhood with her father, who was often incarcerated for acts of civil disobedience against the British Raj. Her mother, who was frequently ill, died of tuberculosis when Gandhi was 17.

She was educated in Switzerland and Britain, and in 1942, she married Feroze Gandhi, a fellow member of the Congress Party along with Indira and her father. She gave birth to two children, but was frequently away from her husband, accompanying her father when he took office as Prime Minister following the Partition of India in 1947.

Gandhi took on increasingly important roles in her father's government throughout the 1950s, and was appointed to the upper house of the Indian Parliament after his death in 1964. When Nehru's successor, Lal Bahadur Shastri, died two years into his term as Prime Minister, Indira was elected the Congress Party's new leader as a compromise between two disparate factions—in part because her status as India's first female Prime Minister brought with it the perception that she might be easily controlled once elected.

Infighting led to an attempt at expelling her from the Congress Party early in her term, an attempt which Gandhi survived, forming her own faction within the party and maintaining control of the government. Gandhi then pursued a series of anti-poverty reforms in the early 1970s—including nationalizing the banks and abolishing the Privy Purse system that benefited princely families—pragmatic moves that lent her a base of popular support among the poor throughout the nation.

On the foreign policy front, Gandhi was an early and ardent supporter of Bangladesh in its liberation war with Pakistan. The success of Bangladesh in gaining independence from Pakistan in 1971 was a victory for Gandhi, but was not enough to overcome a ruling by the Allahabad High Court, in 1975, that her 1971 election to Parliament as part of a landslide general election victory was the consequence of electoral fraud.

In response to the ruling, which would have removed her from public office, Gandhi proclaimed a state of emergency. In the darkest period of Gandhi's first term as Prime Minister, her political opponents were imprisoned, newspapers were censored, and controversial measures were undertaken by Gandhi's son, Sanjay, to curtail civil rights, including the forced sterilization of certain populations of males as a means of population control.

The two years of emergency rule destroyed Gandhi's popularity, and the Congress party was soundly defeated when national elections were finally held in 1977. She lost her seat in Parliament, and was briefly jailed in 1977 and 1978, before corruption charges against her were withdrawn in 1979. The Congress Party gradually regained the sympathy of the Indian public, aided by infighting in the ruling Janata Party, and a victory in the 1980 general election returned Indira to the office of Prime Minister, just three years after her removal from power.

Gandhi's second term faced a separatist challenge from Sikhs in the northern Punjab region, and her forceful attempt to preserve political control once again proved ill-fated. In 1984, Gandhi carried out Operation Blue Star, which authorized the Indian Army to attack the Golden Temple, a Sikh stronghold, in order to remove the Sikh leader Jarnail Singh Bhindranwale. Fighting lasted for four days, leaving nearly 500 dead, including hundreds of civilians, and outraging Sikhs throughout India.

Five months later, Gandhi was assassinated by two Sikh bodyguards in retaliation, setting off a wave of riots that saw thousands more Sikhs killed, to the widespread indifference of the government. Gandhi was 66 at the time of her death.

Leadership Insights and Gandhi

Gandhi was an Indian politician, stateswoman and a central figure of the Indian National Congress. She was the first and, to date, the only female Prime Minister of India. Indira Gandhi was the daughter of Jawaharlal Nehru, the first prime minister of India. As Prime Minister, Gandhi was known for her political intransigency and unprecedented centralization of power. Being at the forefront of Indian politics for decades, Gandhi left a powerful, but controversial legacy on Indian politics.

In 1999, Indira Gandhi was named "Woman of the Millennium" in an online poll organized by the BBC.

Clarke (2015) noted this about Gandhi:

> Nevertheless, Gandhi's unyielding pragmatism and cunningness undoubtedly led to the positive advances enjoyed by India that saw the country play its part on the global stage.

"You can't shake hands with a clenched fist."

On her ability to cope with the demands of leading one of the world's largest nations, she offered a characteristically rational analysis, "I think the only reason I'm able to survive this with equanimity is that I'm just myself, regardless of the situation in the country.

Gupta (2016) remembered Gandhi with:

We take a look at leadership qualities that Indira Gandhi embodied:

1. Her **independent decision-making quality** set her apart from her contemporaries in a major way. She was known for centralization of power during her regime and led India during its war with Pakistan that led to the liberation of Bangladesh. She had set her own rules regarding her approach towards Indian politics and the world in general. She chose to follow her father's non-alignment policy, trying to avoid succumbing to either the American or Soviet pressures on certain specific issues.
2. She was **outspoken** at a time when women were still struggling to even move freely out of their houses. At that time, she came across as a role model and showed that women could—and must—raise their voices and be heard.
3. **Strong-willed**, she addressed the challenges of a developing country. "Her decisions and timings were applauded and hailed as perfect. As Henry Kissinger admits in his memoirs, Indira Gandhi outclassed and out-maneuvered Nixon and Kissinger," as reported by the Mainstream Weekly.
4. Undoubtedly **a strong leader,** the vigor and the zeal with which Indira Gandhi performed during her term as Prime Minister of India have been widely praised.

Rajamani (2009) offered these insights into Gandhi:

> The qualities of fearlessness, courtesy, humor, wide interests and wisdom, deep commitment to Indian science and technology, passion for the environment, objectivity and the ability to see many things through not only a national but also an international prism -- these were some aspects of her life and personality which come out in the episodic narrative I have chosen to adopt.
>
> **Fearlessness**
>
> I single this out as the strongest trait -- fearlessness to do what she thought was in the national interest and fearlessness in the personal sense; physical and mental courage in adverse circumstances. This was translated into courage which infected others.
>
> One example in her life was when the door opened in the aircraft where she was sitting alone in the front cabin soon after take-off. The advice from the cockpit asking her to go to the back section was not heeded and when we tried to persuade her to come back she gave only a disarming smile which radiated her fearlessness. She did not leave the seat until we landed.
>
> Of course, one has read about the fearless way she handled the Bangladesh war and other similar situations, putting the national interest above those of personal safety.
>
> **Courtesy**
>
> As for courtesy, she had this in abundant measure and was the picture of friendliness with whomsoever, she interacted, whether it was a poor lady in a village in Medak district (of which was an MP) or a visiting dignitary from abroad.
>
> The manner in which she reciprocated Cuban President Fidel Castro's bear hug at the Non Aligned Summit is etched in

memory. She responded shyly, but without fuss, thus cementing a friendship.

The only occasion when I found her losing her cool was when we were in the Andaman islands, visiting the Onge tribe there. As the helicopter hovered above the settlement built for the Onges, she asked me to find out what the tin roofed structures were.

When we landed I found out these were hutments made for the Onges who normally lived in small huts on treetops and moved from place to place as their defecation mounds grew under the trees. This was ecologically sustainable as the land was nourished and they had a cooler micro-climate atop the trees.

When I reported this to her, I realized she was upset. To compound this, the Onges who were clad in multi-colored T-shirts were brought for dancing around her. When she asked the anthropologist present whether this was their usual mode of dress, he whispered they were not in the habit of wearing anything except a brief loin cloth and both men and women were bare-bodied.

On hearing this, she was in a rage and asked all the officers present if they realized what they had done this to these innocent people by locating them in hot tin sheds, away from their natural habitat and worse, making them wear ill-fitting and colorful clothes which they were not used to.

She thundered if they thought the prime minister of India would hesitate to talk to her people whether in their clothes or lack of it and how they had destroyed most of their values forever.

Humor

Indira Gandhi was not given to flippant humor, but showed flashes of mature humor on occasions.

Thus when the Indian Board for Wildlife was meeting and there were two consecutive items on the agenda, one relating to Save the Crocodile Project and the other to the scrapping of the Andhra Pradesh Preservation of the Elephants Act, I scribbled a note to her to say this was like the 'Gajendra Moksha' in reverse. She laughed heartily and read this out loudly to the members of the Board.

The other bit of humor was displayed by the prime minister when she came up to me sitting in the officer's box in Parliament. When I tried to stand up deferentially, she smiled and said, "Don't tower over me like that. Sit down" and let my tall frame go back into the chair and shaking in mirth!

"I suppose leadership at one time meant muscles; but today is means getting along with people."

"Opportunities are not offered. They must be wrested and worked for. And this calls for perseverance... and courage."

Key Takeaways

- Leaders have to be bold pragmatists.
- Leaders must be authentic and true to themselves.
- Leaders have to be willing to make decisions, sometimes standing alone.
- Leaders a certain fearlessness and courage of convictions.
- Leaders can be strong, bold and tough, but also respectful and courteous.

Bonus Addition – November

Condoleezza Rice

November 14, 1954 -

Biography

Condoleezza Rice's accomplishments as a trailblazer in public service—including her roles as the first woman of color to serve as Secretary of State and the first female National Security Advisor—are as renowned as the more controversial aspects of her legacy are notorious. Rice was, as recent history remembers, involved in leading the U.S. into an invasion of Iraq, and the abuses at Guantanamo Bay and in Abu Ghraib.

But beyond attempts to reckon with her legacy, an examination of Rice's life reveals a person of remarkable intelligence and wide-ranging talent who defied the odds to rise to the highest levels of government.

Born and raised in Jim Crow-era Alabama during the early years of the American Civil Rights Movement, Rice was the child of two educators, who instilled in her an early interest in language and fine arts—particularly music. Her parents attempted to shield her from discrimination in Birmingham, but violence was a constant threat.

Rice frequently missed school because of bomb scares, and when she was eight years-old, was just a few blocks away from bombing of a local church by white supremacists that killed one of her classmates. Despite the injustice around her, Rice's brilliance shined through. So adept was Rice at the piano, that at age 15, after relocating with her family to Colorado, she performed with the Denver Symphony Orchestra and planned to pursue a career as a professional pianist.

At the University of Denver, however, Rice's interest shifted toward international relations. She graduated cum laude with a B.A. in political science in 1974 at the age of 19. By 1981, at just 26, she had obtained a master's degree from Notre Dame and a PhD in political science from Denver, subsequently becoming a professor at Stanford University, where she remained into the early '90s.

In 1989, she took a brief leave to join the National Security Council, advising the George H. W. Bush Administration on dealings with the Soviet Union. Returning to Stanford, she was named Provost at just 38 years-old in 1993, which made her the first female, first African-American, and youngest Provost in the university's 100-year history. She took on additional work while at Stanford, serving on the boards of Chevron, Transamerica Corp., and Hewlett-Packard, before taking another leave in 1999 to serve as foreign policy advisor to the George W. Bush Presidential campaign.

After the younger Bush became President-elect, Rice stepped down from Stanford to become National Security Advisor. She entered unprecedented national prominence after the September 11, 2001 attacks, and spent much of 2003 urging both the American people and the international community to support a U.S.-led invasion of Iraq to counter Saddam Hussein. Rice became a primary target of public criticism against the Bush Administration when it became clear that Iraq did not have the weapons of mass destruction she had claimed. Still, she maintained her status within the administration and was appointed Secretary of State after Colin Powell's resignation at the end of Bush's first term.

As Secretary of State, Rice championed a policy of "Transformational Diplomacy," arguing that it was the duty of the United States to encourage the spread of democracy worldwide, particularly in the Middle East, as a matter of international security. She visited 83 countries, and helped broker the withdrawal of the Israeli army from the Gaza Strip in 2005, as well as a ceasefire in the 2006 Lebanon War that temporarily suspended hostilities between Israel and Lebanon.

Rice earned a final, long-sought victory late in her tenure as Secretary of State with the signing of the U.S.-India Civil Nuclear Agreement, a complex effort that took three years and numerous state visits to bring to fruition.

After the Bush Administration, Rice joined the Council on Foreign Relations, spent three years on the College Football Playoff Selection Committee, and became one of the first two women accepted as members of Augusta National Golf Club in its 80-year history.

Like many modern leaders, Rice's legacy is a mixed bag—and any current assessments of her ultimate influence on the status of democracy in the world are deeply premature. That alone does not preclude others from finding inspiration in her emergence—through ability, hard work, and an unwillingness to be intimidated—to a place of vital leadership in an age of international upheaval, pursuing her idea of the common good.

Leadership Insights and Rice

Rice is a Scholar, American political scientist and diplomat. She has had an array of leadership experiences. Her other leadership experiences include Provost at Stanford University, Fellow at the Hoover Institution, several Boards of Directors and the College Football Playoff Selection Committee. She also has been active in non-profits, including her work with The Center for New Generation, an after-school program created to raise the high school graduation numbers.

Rice is a Fellow of the American Academy of Arts and Sciences and has been awarded eleven honorary doctorates. She has authored and co-authored numerous books, including two bestsellers, *No Higher Honor: A Memoir of My Years in Washington* (2011) and *Extraordinary, Ordinary People: A Memoir of Family* (2010).

Rice commented at Norwich University (Jackson, 2014):

> "I think a leader, first of all, has to have integrity," said Rice. "That means you never ask someone to do something you would never do. ... I think the most important thing a leader can do is recognize leadership qualities in others. Part of your responsibility is to not just say, 'Charge this hill with me,' but to make sure you are developing other people's skills as well."

Leadership Expert (n.d.) captured these characteristics that Rice considers most valuable in a leader, shared while speaking at the 2012 Annual Global Leadership Summit:

> **Vision**
>
> The key element, Rice said, is "a true leader never accepts the world as it is, but strives always to make the world as it should be." An effective leader must have a clear idea of where they are trying to lead the team or organization that they are leading. They will be willing to take risks and selfless action in order to reach this vision, which will inspire others to do the same."
>
> **Patience**
>
> A good leader understands that world-changing goals cannot be reached overnight. Rice has spent decades in public service, tirelessly working to make, not just the US but the world, a better place to live. While striving toward optimistic objectives, a leader must also have patience in order to stay positive and avoid discouragement. When others see these qualities, they will gain confidence as well.

Boldness

Rice has been unafraid to publicly speak on topics of disagreement with US foreign policy and the current administration. Placing her values and her vision for international relations above political correctness, she boldly calls out US leaders on their timidity and lack of action that she feels is detrimental to the nation.

Dedication

When speaking against the Obama administration, Rice called for greater dedication in US leadership, saying, "I fully understand the sense of weariness. I fully understand that we must think: 'Us, again?' I know that we've been through two wars. I know that we've been vigilant against terrorism. I know that it's hard. But leaders can't afford to get tired. Leaders can't afford to be weary."

Optimism

Though Rice was raised in segregated Alabama, she was instilled with the idea that her potential was unlimited. She believes in making the most of every opportunity and having confidence in your potential. Despite race, gender, or any other factor, Rice has refused to be intimidated or discouraged from her objective of leaving the world a better place than how she found it.

Schawbel (2018) captured Rice's perspectives on a leadership career:

Be willing to stretch to get the job you want.

Instead of waiting around to get your dream job, or a promotion, Rice says that you need to be willing to stretch to make it happen. She notes that this is particularly important for women. "Women in particular sometimes are not aware of how they can translate certain skills into other skills and they tend to say, 'Well, I'm not ready for that.'"

Be confident and willing to use your skills to reach for better jobs in order to advance in your career.

Find and nurture good mentors.

Rice says that mentorship can't be forced and must be organic. "Mentorship comes when a mentor and mentee realize that they have something in common," she says. Good mentors advocate for their mentees and mentees need to work hard to support their mentors in return.

Long-term successful mentoring relationships need to be mutually beneficially for both parties involved. When selecting a mentor, Rice suggests you find people who you admire and who have achieved what you're aiming to achieve.

Surround yourself with a diverse group of people.

"One thing that diversity does is it gives you people who have come from different backgrounds and different experiences," she says. That can help you prevent the group-think that can occur in many homogeneous organizations.

Aside from being able to solve problems more quickly, Rice says that an "inclusive environment is one that is healthier" because you're "dealing with people who are different than you are and it makes you a better person as a result."

Here's what she has to say about getting the job you want, finding good mentors, embracing diversity, making better decisions and using technology properly.

Gather information before making critical decisions.

In order to make the best decisions possible, especially under intense pressure, Rice suggests gathering as much information as you can. In order to do that, you need to ask a lot of questions, especially if you're not an expert on the subject matter.

After you gather that information, she suggests you ask yourself, "What is it we're trying to achieve here and how can I best achieve that given the limitations that are in our face?" By asking the right questions, you uncover enough data to make more informed decisions that lead to better outcomes.

Learn how to communicate using technology.

While technology can help you communicate effectively, Rice says it's key to pay attention to what message you are actually trying to send when you use it. "Technology has a lot of benefits, but it's not a panacea. You have to still craft messages, know when you're using technology, when you're not, and use it in an appropriate way."

Technology is not a solution in and of itself but a tool, one that must be used wisely.

Lastly, Spain (2017) offered these five takeaways for leaders from Rice:

1. **Mentors come in all shapes and sizes.** One of Rice's early mentors was Josef Korbel, a Jewish Czech-American diplomat, political scientist and professor, who also happened to be the father of former Secretary of State Madeleine Albright.

   Condoleezza Rice thought she was going to be a concert pianist. Then she discovered international politics.

   "Josef Korbel ... was the person whose class [at the University of Denver] took this failed piano major and made her decide to study international politics," Rice said. "For me, the lesson of that is, it's wonderful to have role models and mentors that look like you, but sometimes they don't. Sometimes they're just people who take an interest in you, and I was very fortunate to have people like that in my life. What you really want in a mentor is someone who sees things in you that you don't even see in yourself."

2. **Everyone's path will be different.** "I had studied piano from the age of three; it was my first passion," said Rice. "I was going to be a great concert pianist. ... Then at the end of my sophomore year in college I went to the Aspen Music Festival School and I met 12-year-olds who could play from sight what it had taken me all year to learn -- and I was 17. And I thought, 'I'm about to end up being one of those people who plays the piano while you shop in the department store. There's got to be something better in life.'

   "And I started the search. ... Junior year -- and it's now spring quarter -- and I'm getting those letters from the registrar, 'You cannot register again until you have a major.' I wandered into a course in international politics, it was taught by Josef Korbel. He was a Soviet specialist, and I knew what I wanted to be."

3. **Your passion is your passion.** "Most black girls from Birmingham, Alabama, don't end up Soviet specialists," Rice said. "But I knew that it was something I was passionate about. ... Your passion is your passion. It shouldn't be your passion because somebody else defines it for you. You should never let someone say, 'Well that can't be your passion. You don't look like somebody who should be interested in that.' Who knows why you become absolutely attached to something, but once you've found it, you really have found a lease on life that's extraordinary."

4. **Be honest with yourself about your flaws.** "At some point you have to have a talk with yourself about your greatest flaws," she said. "What is it that you're not good at doing? What is the one characteristic that's perhaps getting in your way of advancement? You know, it's very easy to blame others if you're

not advancing. Well, they don't like me because of my color. Or, they don't like me because I'm a woman. Yeah, maybe, but sometimes it's something with you. Sit down and have an honest conversation about what characteristics are holding you back, and address them."

5. **Don't be afraid to ask for help.** "If you're gonna stretch, there are going to be things that you do not know. And you can't be afraid to ask people to help you. ... There's nothing wrong with admitting you're in a new situation for the first time and that you need help and you need support. You still have to remember that it is your job, and you have to make those tough decisions.

   "One of the hardest things I found, as Provost [of Stanford] and then later Secretary [of State] --I'm an academic. Academics like to be able to go with deep knowledge of something. I once knew more about the Soviet general staff than they knew about themselves, because that's what I did as an academic. Well, now I'm making decisions that are broad. The more you progress upward in organizations, the more you're dealing with decisions where you don't have the deep expertise yourself. You have to learn how to ask the questions, you have to learn who you can trust."

"Truly remarkable leadership is not just about motivating others to follow, it's about inspiring them to become leaders themselves and setting the stage for even greater opportunities for future generations."

"The first step for a leader is to be right with yourself. Integrity is the basis of leadership."

Key Takeaways

- Leaders never ask followers to do something they would not do.
- Leaders need to display optimistic patience.
- Leaders need to be bold and make the most of every opportunity.
- Effective leaders embrace diversity.
- Leaders need to "stretch." Fail and learn. Confront weaknesses and not be afraid to ask for help.

DECEMBERS LEADERS

For December, we will learn from Grace Hopper, Alex Ferguson, and Walt Disney.

Grace Hopper

(December 9, 1906 – January 1, 1992)

"You manage things, you lead people. We went overboard on management and forgot about leadership."

Biography

Perseverance in and of itself does not make one a leader. Individuals persevere for a limitless variety of selfish or nefarious reasons. But it's perseverance in the service of a greater good, to build a better, more harmonized world for those who come after us, that forces history to remember forward-thinking leaders like Grace Hopper.

As is often the case, things didn't initially go as planned for Grace Hopper. Rejected from Vassar College at the age of 16, she earned admittance upon a second attempt the following year. In the 1920s, a time when most women who pursued undergraduate degrees studied nursing, education, or social work,

Instead, Hopper graduated Phi Beta Kappa from Vassar with degrees in mathematics and physics before moving on to Yale, where she earned a master's degree and a Ph.D. in mathematics—a rare accomplishment for anyone in 1934, man or woman.

Hopper then encountered another barrier when her attempt to enlist in the Navy following the attack on Pearl Harbor was initially rejected on account of both age and physical size. Again, Hopper persisted, and against the suggestions of both her then-employer, Vassar, and her prospective one, the Navy, she was granted both an exemption and a leave of absence, joining the U.S. Navy Reserve in 1943 and graduating first in her class from the Naval Reserve Midshipmen's School at Smith College.

It was at this time that Hopper's determination yielded the first of her most tangible contributions to the future of society; she was assigned to the Bureau of Ships Computation Project at Harvard University, where she worked alongside Howard Aiken to perform advanced calculations necessary for the war effort on the MARK I, one of the earliest electromechanical computers. One of a trio of programmers who were working most intimately with the computer.

Still, external pressures to sway Hopper from her convictions remained. A person with lesser resolve may have accepted the offer of a stable job, a full-professorship Vassar offered when the war ended in 1946 and the Navy again declined Hopper's request to transfer to a Regular commission on account of her age. Hopper instead opted to continue as a reservist, working on the subsequent MARK II and MARK III computers before receiving no offers of tenure or a permanent position at the end of her research fellowship in 1949.

Undeterred, Hopper moved into the private sector, joining Eckert-Mauchly Computer Corporation to develop the UNIVAC I, the country's first commercially-marketed computer. At Eckert-Mauchly—and later Remington Rand, which acquired it in 1950—Hopper continued to push against the boundaries of what was expected of her.

While often erroneously credited with inventing the dictum, "It is easier to ask forgiveness than it is to get permission," Hopper nonetheless promoted the saying and lived by it. When her idea to create a way to input English-language instructions to a computer program was met with immediate skepticism and dismissal, Hopper rallied support from outside the company, enlisting clients like U.S. Steel and Metropolitan Life to back the idea of English-language programs.

By the mid-1950's, her team at Eckert-Mauchly was running an English-language compiler known as the FLOW-MATIC, the integral framework of COBOL—developed in part by Hopper a few years later—which endured for decades as the dominant programming language of business computing.

Hopper not only lived by her words, she imparted them to others, encouraging her students and younger colleagues to try new ideas and never fear failure or take no for an answer—a pursuit she consistently stated was more important important than her pioneering work in computing.

She remained a reservist in the Navy until her forced retirement at age 60 in 1966, but returned to active service the following year as director of the Navy Programming Languages Group, leading a standardization of the Navy's computer programs.

Rising to the rank of Admiral in the mid-1980's, Hopper retired from the Navy at age 79, having received special approval from Congress to remain on active duty for several years past the mandatory retirement age. She was awarded the Defense Distinguished Service Medal, the highest non-combat military honor in the United States.

Hopper spent much of her retirement on the lecture circuit for the Digital Equipment Corporation, speaking frequently at universities and computing industry events, before passing away in her sleep on New Year's Day 1992.

She was buried with full military honors at Arlington National Cemetery, the first in a series of posthumous distinctions, including a Navy destroyer, the USS Hopper, named in her honor and launched in 1996, the Presidential Medal of Freedom—the United States' highest civilian honor—bestowed by President Barack Obama in 2016, and Hopper College, one of 14 residential colleges at Yale University, named after her in 2017.

Leadership Insights and Hopper

Admiral Hopper was an American computer scientist and United States Navy rear admiral. One of the first programmers of the Harvard Mark I computer, she was a pioneer of computer programming who invented one of the first compiler related tools. She popularized the idea of machine-independent programming languages, which led to the development of COBOL, an early high-level programming language still in use today. Owing to her accomplishments and her naval rank, she was sometimes referred to as "Amazing Grace." The U.S. Navy *Arleigh Burke*-class guided-missile destroyer USS *Hopper* was named for her, as was the Cray XE6 "Hopper" supercomputer at NERSC.

During her lifetime, Hopper was awarded 40 honorary degrees from universities across the world. A college at Yale University was renamed in her honor. In 1991, she received the National Medal of Technology. On November 22, 2016, she was posthumously awarded the Presidential Medal of Freedom by President Barack Obama.

Another indication of her influence is the Grace Hopper Celebration which is the world's largest gathering of women technologists. It is produced by AnitaB.org.

Throughout much of her later career, Hopper was much in demand as a speaker at various computer-related events. She was well known for her lively and irreverent speaking style, as well as a rich treasury of early war stories.

Duke (n.d.) starts off with this assessment of her ability to deliver resonant soundbites to carry her beliefs:

> She is often quoted. But, of all her recorded wisdom, I've always been compelled to better understand her clear division between management and leadership. "*You manage things, you lead people,*" she said. It's a simple rule that I've striven to obey throughout my military and civilian careers.

Champagne, J. (2016) added:

> "They come to me, you know, and say, 'Do you think we can do this?' I say, 'Try it.' And I back 'em up," she said. "They need that.

> I keep track of them as they get older and I stir 'em up at intervals so they don't forget to take chances."

She also highlighted these quotes from "Amazing Grace:"

> "I've always been more interested in the future than in the past."
>
> "Humans are allergic to change. They love to say, 'We've always done it this way.' I try to fight that. That's why I have a clock on my wall that runs counter-clockwise."
>
> "The glass is neither half empty nor half full. It's simply larger than it needs to be. It is easier to get forgiveness than permission."
>
> "A ship in port is safe, but that's not what ships are built for."

The Navy Times Archives captured several insights on Hopper's leadership:

> Fort (2018). Hopper mentored and inspired young women and men to look for innovative ways to serve. She had no time for complacency, stale thinking or laziness. And she and her teams always carefully assessed their performance to look for opportunities to improve processes and technology.
>
> Fuller (2017). Grace Hopper faced an extra-thick glass ceiling. Others held her back because of her gender or because of rigid thinking and lack of imagination. But, Grace Hopper prevailed. She demonstrated her forward-thinking vision and the drive and commitment to achieve her vision. She believed in science-based decision-making. And she demonstrated mental toughness.
>
> Doughty (2011) noted: Always unconventional in her thinking, Hopper scorned the customary and traditional, was impatient with the status quo, and approached problem solving with instinctive innovation.

Lastly, Albury (2013) offers:

> Grace Hopper was a creative teacher who made great efforts to ensure programmers she was teaching understood how to be lazy, by which she meant efficient, inquisitive and always looking for better ways to solve problems.
>
> This example encapsulates the genius of Grace Hopper; a serious point about software design delivered in a creative, memorable and humorous way. She was a great scientist and her tenaciousness and strength of will in the face of adversity (from misogyny to depression and alcoholism) show that with effort, humor and a dogged belief in the importance of shaping the future any of us can both inspire and be inspired by those around us.

"The most damaging phrase in the language is: "It's always been done this way."

"Leadership is a two-way street, loyalty up and loyalty down. Respect for one's superiors; care for one's crew."

Key Takeaways

- Leaders manage things and lead people.
- Leaders both "back up" and "stir up" their teams.
- Leaders expect loyalty up, but also reciprocate with loyalty down.
- Leaders take a "forgiveness vs permission" orientation.
- Leaders need to be innovative and to continuously challenge status quo.

Alex Ferguson

December 1941-

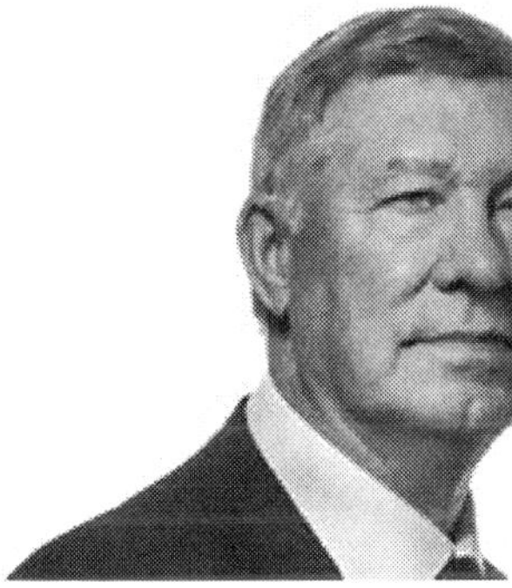

"Too many managers talk too much. The two most important words for a player, or for any human being, there is nothing better than hearing "Well done." And few reprimands are as powerful as silence."

Biography

Sir Alex Ferguson's half-century in English professional football was one of inherent contradictions. He remains simultaneously one of the most admired and vilified figures in the history of the sport, whose high-profile feuds, missteps, and controversies were outnumbered only by his successes on the pitch.

Oft-recounted anecdotes from his tenure managing the Scottish club Aberdeen F.C., where he first rose to fame, depict Ferguson fining a player for overtaking him on a roadway or attempting to kick an urn of hot tea at his squad after a poor first half.

But the prevailing commonality across each of Ferguson's career stops—beyond the "Furious Fergie" memes—are the ends: consistent, repeated success. In his second season at Aberdeen, he led the Dons to become the first team other than the "Old Firm" clubs—Celtic and Rangers—to win the Scottish League title in 15 years. To date, no club outside the Old Firm has achieved the feat since Ferguson left the league, in 1986.

A relatively young manager in his late 30's, Ferguson earned the respect of his players and acceptance of his disciplinarian tactics thanks in large part to said triumphs on the field. Even greater successes followed on the European stage, including the Cup Winner's Cup and European Super Cup in 1982 and 1983. Ferguson would add two additional league titles and three Scottish Cups to Aberdeen's trophy case before eventually heading south to Old Trafford in 1986 to accept the vacant manager position at Manchester United.

His accomplishments thereafter are mostly self-evident: five FA Cups, two Champions League wins, and 13 Premier League titles over 26 seasons—nearly double the amount the club had won in the 80 years preceding Ferguson's arrival. But his success at Manchester United didn't begin immediately. Inconsistent results in his early seasons at the helm of the Red Devils were met with widespread calls for his dismissal, until the club rallied for an FA Cup championship in 1990—a miracle run that saw Manchester United win each of its six rounds in the tournament on the road.

After two more seasons of improvement, Ferguson led Man U to dominate the Premiere League throughout the 1990s, earning seven league titles over nine seasons and cementing his place in the pantheon of all-time great managers. His early triumphs were intertwined with his efforts to affect cultural change in the organization upon arriving, demanding greater fitness and attempting to curb what he viewed as excessive drinking among his players. Ferguson's disciplinarian methods were occasionally met with resistance and, fairly or unfairly, were widely speculated to have precipitated the departures of popular players like Paul McGrath and Norman Whiteside.

But with more victories came more controversies: numerous temporary bans, accusations of intimidating behavior toward referees, and public feuds with his own players—most notably David Beckham, a relationship whose deterioration culminated in an infamous boot-kicking incident that left the star midfielder cut above the eye.

Evaluating Alex Ferguson's total legacy is not just about considering the line between passionate and untethered, but about whether the totality of the means justify their ends—not just his on-field success, but his impact as a leader. Among quarrels and hostilities, he developed teenagers like Beckham, Wayne Rooney into international superstars—Cristiano Ronaldo calls Ferguson his "father in sport"—and numerous others who played under him have moved onto long and distinguished managerial careers themselves.

His reputation for wrath and vindictive behavior is belied—or, depending on how you look at it, justified—by the contemporary praise and gratitude from stars like Beckham, McGrath, and Whiteside, all of whom had ostensibly left Ferguson's Manchester United on bad terms. Ferguson's Premiere League dominance continued into the new millennium, including six additional league titles from 2003 to 2013 on top of a second Champions League win in 2008, nine years after Man U's first. Off the field, he was appointed Commander of the British Empire in 1995, was later knighted as part of the Queen's Birthday Honors in 1999, and became the only active manager in the inaugural class of English Football Hall of Fame inductees in 2002.

After a 56-year association football career, Ferguson retired in 2013 as the most successful manager in British football history, earning one last Premiere League title in his final season. Upon retirement, he accepted a teaching position at Harvard Business School, imparting management wisdom on business leaders across an array of industries and sectors as part of the university's executive education program.

Leadership Insights and Ferguson

Ferguson is a football (soccer, for US readers) coaching icon. He is considered one of the greatest managers of all time. He was knighted in the

1999 Queen's Birthday Honours list, for his services to the game. When he retired in 2013, *The Guardian* announced it was the "end of an era," while UEFA president Michel Platini called Ferguson "a true visionary."

Mohamed (2016) offered these traits of successful leaders from Ferguson:

1. **Self-confidence**

   Leaders who are confident get the support of their team members because they exude a positive attitude. Sir Alex Ferguson was self-confident, and had the right knowledge and skills to run Manchester United. His past football and managerial experiences allowed him to lead the club, and he knew he was capable of doing so. Even though the club was doing badly and supporters were demanding his dismissal, "Ferguson had the support of United directors, and paid back their trust by leading United to an English FA Cup victory and European Cup Winners." Because of his self-confidence and drive, people followed and trusted him.

2. **Great communication skills**

   The ability to convey a message, inspire and influence people's attitudes and actions is crucial in attaining objectives. Leaders must be able to make use of verbal both and non-verbal communication, paying attention to such things as body language, to ensure the right message gets across efficiently. Sir Alex Ferguson is a great communicator. Individuals can get distracted easily, but he was always able to make sure that everyone stayed focused on the objectives. One example is how he used the 15-minute break between games to reconnect with the players and motivate them. "When that cup is going to be presented, just remember that you can't even touch it if you are the losers. You'll be walking past it with your loser's medals, knowing someone walking behind you is going to lift the cup." These words motivated Manchester United players in 1999 during their match against Bayern Munich, and allowed them to grab the victory after half-time.

3. **Team development and high standards**

   In order to succeed, businesses need to create and develop a strong foundation. The more employees know, the better they can affect a company. In the case of Manchester United, Sir Alex Ferguson always showed the drive to succeed by encouraging his team members mentally and physically. "By prioritizing youth player development, rebuilding the team, emphasizing attacking football, and bringing the best out of his players," he led Manchester United's come back to the top of the first division.

   Just as Sir Alex did, even in the non-football professional world, providing employees with "on-the-job" training has shown to increase job satisfaction and employee morale. Employees are often more motivated, since they appreciate the fact that the company invests in their professional development.

   In addition, in Sir Alex's case, everyone understood what was expected from them, and were held accountable for their actions. As Andy Cole said, "If you lose and Sir Alex believes you gave your best, it is not a problem... but if you lose in a limp way...then mind your ears!" Ferguson set high standards and used his creativity to tell inspirational stories to keep his troops motivated.

4. **Honesty and integrity**

   Being honest and having integrity in the workplace and in our working relationships is very important. Ferguson had these traits, which earned him respect and admiration from everyone around him. He was honest, and encouraged open communication with his players, where people felt valued. As a result, people considered him trustworthy and reliable.

5. **Emotional intelligence**

   Leaders with high emotional intelligence find it easier to influence people (Robbins, Judge, 2015). Leaders who demonstrate empathy, compassion and humility obtain greater commitment and a higher performance level from their employees. (Labier, 2015) Empathetic leaders can sense other people's needs, listen to what followers say, and read the reactions of others. Ferguson has been credited with spending time and being dedicated to his team members. When players needed to talk to him, the first thing he would do is turn his chair around. Ferguson communicated with all of his players privately, and took pride in the fact that he would sit with players and explaining privately the reasons behind his decisions. As he stated, "I have been dropped from a Cup final in Scotland as a player at ten past two, so I know what it feels like." By doing this, Ferguson showed concern for people around him, and his team members knew that he had their backs. When people feel valued and cared for, they push themselves to hit targets.

Snyder (2015) had his own five lessons from Ferguson:

Be consistent in imposing discipline.

Being consistent, says Ferguson, is the essence of being a leader. Discipline is an important aspect of management, and employees need to know who you are and trust that you are right when you impose rules. But don't be too quick to resort to severe sanctions. "Inexperienced, or insecure, leaders are often tempted to make any infraction a capital offense. That is all well and good—except, once you have hung the person, you are plumb out of options," he says.

Embrace your entire team.

Long before he became a coach, Ferguson was a player, and he still remembers the coach who didn't say good morning but would just walk by. "You must recognize that people are working for you. Knowing their names, saying good morning in the morning is critical," he says.

And every time you win a cup or a trophy, Ferguson says, you should bring every member of your staff into that canteen — "the laundry girls, the canteen staff, the groundsmen" — and pour the champagne for everyone because it's their trophy as much as the players'.

Firing is hard—do it right.

Firing people is never easy, says Ferguson, but once a manager realizes it needs to be done, "nothing beats honesty. I gradually learned that there was no point beating about the bush by taking somebody out for dinner or sending his wife a box of chocolates or flowers to try to soften the news. The gimmicks don't change the message."

Think long term.

I often get a measure of someone by listening to the questions they pose. It shows how they think.

Alex Ferguson

Having the time to establish a solid foundation and to gradually build toward long-term prosperity is not a luxury afforded most football managers or business leaders, Moritz says. The pressure to win or the need to produce quarterly earnings makes the quick fix almost irresistible, but the top management of Manchester United sheltered Ferguson from that pressure. "This freedom from the tyranny of immediate results enabled Sir Alex to constantly work on the composition of the club several years into the future, without worrying whether he would still be there if United had a bad losing streak," says Moritz.

Lean forward.

Body language is important: Someone who sits up properly and is leaning forward a little is showing that they are eager to start, says Ferguson. Asking questions at a job interview is crucial. "I often get a measure of someone by listening to the questions they pose. It shows how they think; offers a sense of their level of experience and degree of maturity," he says.

LeadershipGeeks (2016) added these:

The individual is not bigger than the organization.

Ferguson saw the importance of instilling humility in his players. He never allowed a single player to rise above the club.

Over the years, there were superstars whose egotistical behavior caused a detrimental effect on the whole team. While most managers might compromise in order to keep the star, Ferguson was ruthless in removing such people from the organization.

He understood that if one man's ego was allowed to be bigger than the club, the whole team would suffer. For example, he famously dropped superstar David Beckham for a crucial match against title rivals Leeds United in 2000.

In today's world, we exalt celebrity CEOs and some believe that changing and turning a company around takes just one man. However, the truth is that we need the entire team's cooperation to achieve organizational success.

The value of hard work, discipline and determination.

Ferguson was always the first on the training ground every morning. He expected extremely high standards of discipline and character from his players, whether they were rookies or superstars. He didn't just focus on their skills; he wanted to ensure they had the character and determination to maximize their talents.

To him, victory came not from talent, but from sustained, persistent effort and determination. Similarly, the success of your team or organization cannot merely rest on natural ability or talent; it's necessary to put in the work, be disciplined and stay determined on the road to reaching your goals. It's not enough to merely hire the best talent; you must also provide an environment that nurtures them and pushes them to be even better.

Finally, Elberse (2013) offered these leadership insights:

Start with the foundation.

Ferguson said:

> From the moment I got to Manchester United, I thought of only one thing: building a football club. I wanted to build right from the bottom. That was in order to create fluency and a continuity of supply to the first team. With this approach, the players all grow up together, producing a bond that, in turn, creates a spirit. Winning a game is only a short-term gain—you can lose the next game. Building a club brings stability and consistency. You don't ever want to take your eyes off the first team, but our youth development efforts ended up leading to our many successes in the 1990s and early 2000s. The young players really became the spirit of the club.

Dare to rebuild your team.

Even in times of great success, Ferguson worked to rebuild his team. He is credited with assembling five distinct league-winning squads during his time at the club and continuing to win trophies all the while. His decisions were driven by a keen sense of where his team stood in the cycle of rebuilding and by a similarly keen sense of players' life cycles—how much value the players were bringing to the team at any point in time. Managing the talent development process inevitably involved cutting players, including loyal veterans to whom Ferguson had a personal attachment. "He's never really looking at this moment, he's always looking into the future," Ryan Giggs told us. "Knowing what needs strengthening and what needs refreshing—he's got that knack."

Set high standards—and hold everyone to them.

Ferguson speaks passionately about wanting to instill values in his players. More than giving them technical skills, he wanted to inspire them to strive to do better and to never give up—in other words, to make them winners. Everything we did was about maintaining the standards we had set as a football club—this applied to all my team building and all my team preparation, motivational talks, and tactical talks.

I had to lift players' expectations. They should never give in. I said that to them all the time: "If you give in once, you'll give in twice." And the work ethic and energy I had seemed to spread throughout the club. I used to be the first to arrive in the morning. In my later years, a lot of my staff members would already be there when I got in at 7 AM. I think they understood why I came in early—they knew there was a job to be done. There was a feeling that "if he can do it, then I can do it."

Match the message to the moment.

When it came to communicating decisions to his players, Ferguson—perhaps surprisingly for a manager with a reputation for being tough and demanding—worked hard to tailor his words to the situation.

Observation is critical to management. The ability to see things is key—or, more specifically, the ability to see things you don't expect to see.

During training sessions in the run-up to games, Ferguson and his assistant coaches emphasized the positives. And although the media often portrayed him as favoring ferocious halftime and postgame talks, in fact he varied his approach. "You can't always come in shouting and screaming," he told us. "That doesn't work." The former player Andy Cole described it this way: "If you lose and Sir Alex believes you gave your best, it's not a problem. But if you lose [in a] limp way...then mind your ears!"

Generally, my pregame talks were about our expectations, the players' belief in themselves, and their trust in one another. I liked to refer to a working-class principle. Not all players come from a working-class background, but maybe their fathers do, or their grandfathers, and I found it useful to remind players how far they have come. I would tell them that having a work ethic is very important. It seemed to enhance their pride. I would remind them that it is trust in one another, not letting their mates down, that helps build the character of a team.

Prepare to win.

He *prepared* his team to win. He had players regularly practice how they should play if a goal was needed with 10, five, or three minutes remaining. "We practice for when the going gets tough, so we know what it takes to be successful in those situations," one of United's assistant coaches told us.

United practice sessions focused on repetition of skills and tactics. "We look at the training sessions as opportunities to learn and improve," Ferguson said. "Sometimes the players might think, 'Here we go again,' but it helps us win." There appears to be more to this approach than just the common belief that winning teams are rooted in habits—that they can execute certain plays almost automatically. There is also an underlying signal that you are never quite satisfied with where you are and are constantly looking for ways to improve. This is how Ferguson put it: "The message is simple: We cannot sit still at this club."

Winning is in my nature. I've set my standards over such a long period of time that there is no other option for me—I *have* to win. I expected to win every time we went out there.

I think all my teams had perseverance—they never gave in. So I didn't really need to worry about getting that message across. It's a fantastic characteristic to have, and it is amazing to see what can happen in the dying seconds of a match.

Never stop adapting.

Responding to change is never easy, and it is perhaps even harder when one is on top for so long. Yet evidence of Ferguson's willingness to change is everywhere. As David Gill described it to me, Ferguson has "demonstrated a tremendous capacity to adapt as the game has changed."

One of the things I've done well over the years is manage change. I believe that you control change by accepting it. That also means having confidence in the people you hire. The minute staff members are employed, you have to trust that they are doing their jobs. If you micromanage and tell people what to do, there is no point in hiring them. The most important thing is to not stagnate. I said to David Gill a few years ago, "The only way we can keep players at Manchester United is if we have the best training ground in Europe." That is when we kick-started the medical center. We can't sit still.

Most people with my kind of track record don't look to change. But I always felt I couldn't afford *not* to change. We had to be successful—there was no other option for me—and I would explore any means of improving. I continued to work hard. I treated every success as my first. My job was to give us the best possible chance of winning. That is what drove me.

"You can't aspire to be loved, because that isn't going to happen, nor do you want people to be frightened of you. Stay somewhere in the middle and have them respect and trust and see you as fair."

"The experience of defeat, or more particularly the manner in which a leader reacts to it, is an essential part of what makes a winner."

Key Takeaways

- Leaders are self-confident, persistent, and drivers.
- Leaders need to be consummate communicators, embracing an open approach.
- Leaders put their teams first.
- Leaders set high standards and live them.
- Leaders adapt and always lean forward.
- Leaders are consistent.
- Leaders are prepared; they do the work necessary.

Walt Disney

(December 5, 1901 – December 15, 1966)

"Times and conditions change so rapidly that we must keep our aim constantly focused on the future."

Biography

Any artist whose works attain such a level of cultural significance so as to endure for decades after his or her death will inevitably find themselves the subject of intense, posthumous personal scrutiny, and Walt Disney is no exception.

Although oft-repeated allegations of personal prejudice are denied by those who knew him, other criticisms are more nuanced. In creating numerous iconic and generationally cherished films, Walt Disney Studios has been consistently cited among the most effective postwar instruments of cultural imperialism—namely, the imposition of the American middle-class outlook and value system on the rest of the world, as demonstrated by the fact that Mickey Mouse remains as globally pervasive a brand icon as Levi's, McDonald's, or Coca-Cola.

The extent to which this was a conscious undertaking by Disney—and, similarly, the extent to which his activities within Hollywood's most politically conservative circles represented sympathy for either anti-Semitism or communist blacklisting—remains a subject of contemporary debate. What is not debatable is the way in which Disney rose to such a level of prominence that he earned his first of 12 Academy Awards—more than any other individual in history—before his 42nd birthday.

Known as a demanding leader, expecting excellence from those who worked for him and rarely offering outright praise, Disney's penchant for hard work was instilled at a young age, much like his interest in drawing. While living in Kansas City at age 10, Walt and his older brother Roy would arise before dawn to deliver the morning paper on a route their father had purchased, break to attend school, and then deliver the evening papers before dinner. Despite not being paid for the work, which continued into his teenage years, Walt found other ways of earning income, making deliveries along the route for a local pharmacy, or purchasing additional routes without his father's knowledge.

At 16, Walt lied about his age to find work in a post office, then lied about it again to follow Roy into World War I as an ambulance driver for the Red Cross (though he arrived after the Armistice of November, 1918).

Back in Kansas City after the war, Walt turned an interest in drawing into the Laugh-O-Gram Studio, his first major foray into professional cartooning, which saw brief success producing short animations before quickly going bankrupt. He reunited with Roy in Hollywood, where the pair founded the Disney Brothers Studio, initially with a single client worth $100 a month.

As the studio expanded, the brothers began to hire additional artists, including Lillian Bounds, whom Walt married in 1925. It was Bounds who suggested the name for a new character intended to star in a series of short cartoons: Mickey Mouse. Two series of early sound cartoons followed. One starred the eponymous mouse. The other was the musically-driven *Silly Symphonies,* which marked the debut of three-strip

Technicolor processing—a financially risky move that quickly paid off to the tune of numerous Academy Awards, including the first ever for an animated film. By 1933, the studio that Disney started from scratch ten years earlier had swelled to more than 200 employees.

In a bid to move beyond shorts and, according to some accounts, to take on a more active role in animation, Walt began production on the first feature-length animated film to use both full color and sound. Nicknamed "Disney's Folly" by some naysayers, the budget for *Snow White and the Seven Dwarfs* ballooned to nearly $1.5 million over four years in production, triple its original estimate and swelling beyond the amount of money than the studio was taking in. Again, Disney's knack for risk-taking and demand for thoroughness proved worthwhile; wildly enthusiastic audiences around the world propelled the film to more than $10 million in box office receipts over its initial run, by far the most successful sound film of its time.

Disney produced two additional features at the outset of World War II, *Pinocchio* and *Fantasia*, neither of which matched *Snow White*'s box office success. As such, the studio sank into debt. Cost-cutting measures proved unpopular, and a 1941 animators' strike gutted the studio and left Disney with life-long resentment for staffers by whom he felt betrayed.

Disney retreated from large-budget films for much of the 1940s, before he once again risked the future of his company on a fairy tale adaptation in 1950. Like *Snow White, Cinderella* was a major financial success, allowing Disney to move ahead with other projects like *Alice in Wonderland, Peter Pan,* and *Sleeping Beauty.*

By the mid-1950's, Disney turned his attention away from the company's animation division and towards other visions: primarily, developing a destination amusement park for children and their parents to visit and enjoy together. He eventually settled on a 160-acre site in Anaheim, California, at the time a rural area 25 miles southeast of Los Angeles consisting mostly of orange groves.

Difficulties funding the theme park spawned an innovative solution: a weekly television series promoting Disneyland on ABC, in exchange for ABC helping to finance construction. Despite early hiccups, Disneyland was instantly popular when it opened in 1956, attracting 3.6 million guests in its first year.

More films followed, including the highly acclaimed *Mary Poppins* in 1964, as well as the development of a second amusement park in Florida, called Walt Disney World—designed to be accompanied by a "city of tomorrow," a prototype community rooted in Walt's budding interest in city planning and concerns about the planet's future. He didn't live to see either plan come to fruition, succumbing to lung cancer in late 1966, shortly after his 65th birthday. The "city of tomorrow" concept would later be incorporated into Disney World's EPCOT theme park.

Disney's honors, both late in life and posthumous, included the enshrinement of seven of his films in the Library of Congress's National Film Registry, two separate stars on the Hollywood Walk of Fame, a Presidential Medal of Freedom, and the Congressional Gold Medal. The Walt Disney Company employs over 200,000 people today, with revenues well into the billions.

Leadership Insights and Disney

Disney was an American entrepreneur, animator, voice actor, film producer, and a pioneer of the American animation industry. As a film producer, Disney holds the record for most Academy Awards earned by an individual, having won 22 Oscars from 59 nominations. He was presented with two Golden Globe Special Achievement Awards and an Emmy Award. He was also one of the builders of the amusement park industry with Disneyland and Disneyworld. He was the founder of Disney Productions. His film work continues to be shown and adapted; his namesake studio and company maintains high standards in its production of popular entertainment, and the Disney amusement parks have grown in size and number to attract visitors around the world.

Disney remains the central figure in the history of animation. Through technological innovations and alliances with governments and corporations, he transformed a minor studio in a marginal form of communication into a multinational leisure industry giant. His vision of a modern, corporate utopia as an extension of traditional American values has possibly gained greater currency in the years after his death.

Disney was a shy, self-deprecating and insecure man in private, but adopted a warm and outgoing public persona. He had high standards and high expectations of those with whom he worked.

Pahl (2015) starts us off on the leadership insights of Disney:

> **Have vision.**
>
> Walt himself has explained his formula for having leadership vision as starting with one simple stepping stone, "I dream." If we don't dream or desire to have a vision for something better for ourselves or others, then what is it that gets us out of bed every morning? He then continues on by saying, "I test my dreams against my beliefs." In this case, he was making sure his dreams were consistent with everything he stood for, such as his beliefs, core values, and integrity. Next, he explains, "I dare to take risks." He would act boldly and bet on himself to win. There were a few times in Walt's life where he would bet his entire studio on producing an animated film and, due to his vision, charisma, and leadership style, he repeatedly came out on top. Lastly he said, "I execute my vision to make those dreams come true." Walter would focus all his time, talents, energy, and resources to make the dream a reality.
>
> **Become an animated leader.**
>
> To create memorable animated films and, later on, the first ever theme park, Walt had to emulate his legendary films and be

animated in the leadership sense. There have been stories told by some early Disney Studios employees explaining how Walt would demonstrate his ideas for a new animated film.

He would gather everyone together in the studio, then act out the entire movie sequence to personally show what he envisioned the story to be and give his artists direction. He brought the story to life and in doing so, he lit the path of creativity and opened his employees' minds to possibility.

We may not be illustrating for animated cartoons, but we can each be as lively, energetic, and enthusiastic about our work as Walt was. If you strive to bring positive energy into the work place and refuse to live in a watered-down, repetitive environment, then you're one step closer to being like Walt.

Be a salesman.

Walt was a salesman. Possibly one of the greatest salesman the world has ever known. You can have dream, but if you can't SELL the dream then it won't come true. Dreams take people, money, and resources, to become a reality. Fortunately for Walt, his incredible people skills allowed him to do just that.

One day Walt attended a board meeting for a company that he wanted to sponsor his Autopia attraction. He convinced the board that it was a great investment and they wrote him large check right then and there. After Walt had shaken hands and left, one board member, who had been so drawn to Walt's love and enthusiasm for the project, said, "I have a question. What did we just buy??" Scenes like this play over and over again throughout Walt's career.

Disney felt the top executive should be the lead salesperson and brand champion. Here are five great characteristics of a salesman that Walt shows us throughout his career:

Honesty

The best salesmen have integrity, honesty and live off repeat business. Imagineer Harriet Burns stated, "Walt's best sales technique was his absolute honesty."

Enthusiasm

All great salesmen are enthused about their product. Walt motivated his employees and was constantly encouraging them. "Walt's enthusiasm made over-achievers out of all of this." -Norman Palmer

Confidence

"Walt had the ability to inspire us by selling us on ourselves," said Disney Sculptor Blaine Gibson. Be the kind of leader that instills confidence in your employees. After all, Disney is famous for his quote. "It takes people to make the dream a reality."

Courage

"Walt was completely focused on his product and his goals, not on himself," said Disney historian Craig Hodgkins. It takes courage to look outside of yourself. One of the scariest things in life can be letting go of the image of yourself that is right in front of you and reaching for something further.

Persistence

Nothing that is worthwhile is easy. Disney biographer Bob Thomas has said, "Walt succeeded because he was persistent and determined. He didn't let rejection and criticism stop him. Walt was a finisher."

Build partnerships.

Walt and his brother Roy Disney were the perfect dynamic duo. Walt had the creative ideas and spent most of his time with the Disney Studio artists. In contrast, Roy was a well-educated financial advisor and preferred to spend his time with lawyers and accountants. Yet, these differences didn't hinder the Disney brothers; rather, they complimented each other. It was the way these brothers collaborated with each other that made them such a successful team. Every Walt needs a Roy and every Roy needs a Walt.

Serve others.

Above all, what truly makes a great leader is someone who is willing to serve. Walt served in countless ways. To name a few, he personally took a co-worker's reluctant paraplegic friend to Disneyland. He rolled out the red carpet and showed his guest all the attractions as well as front row seats to every show. All this just so a disabled friend could enjoy the park without feeling left out in his wheelchair.

A gardener at the Disney studios left some tools in an empty parking space and a producer chewed him out for it. Walter noticed this from his window, went down and said, "Don't you ever treat any of my employees like that! This man has been with me longer than you have, so you'd better be good to him!"

To his employees, Walt was not just a leader, he was their servant and defender. That's what separates leaders from bosses.

James (2018) noted these concepts embedded by Disney into the Disney Institute:

- **Vision and Values:** Every leader is telling a story about what he or she values. These values must be aligned with the vision for an organization or team. If a leader's personal values do not align with organizational values, it will be difficult to genuinely express a vision that motivate others.

- **Behaviors over Intentions**: Those within an organization will look to a leader as a model to develop their own behaviors and decisions. While people tend to judge themselves based on intentions, they judge others based on actions. As a leader, it is essential that your behaviors are authentic, and reflect your values and your vision. When rallying a team around a new initiative, it is crucial that you demonstrate its importance through your words and deeds. The best motivation can come from a leader's example every day.
- **Purpose before Task**: When assigning new projects to a team, it is important to discuss the purpose behind the task. Tasks that are isolated from the larger goal can become tedious and confusing, finding their way to the bottom of the priorities list. However, if a team understands the common purpose behind individual responsibilities, they will be more inspired to own the tasks as well as the goal.

Lastly from Sullivan (2017), these leadership qualities of Disney:

Resilient

"When you believe in a thing, believe in it all the way, implicitly and unquestionable."

Walt Disney, as a young man was fired from *Kansas City Star Newspaper* because his boss thought he lacked creativity. Many people have caved into failure after such a negative event in their life, but he was able to prove the newspaper wrong by building an empire based on creativity.

Not only was he able to prove he had creativity and resilience but later in life, Walt Disney demonstrated his ability to become a successful entrepreneur.

Ability to Accept Failure

"We did it Disneyland, in the knowledge that most of the people I talked to thought it would be a financial disaster—closed and forgotten within the first year."

One of his early ventures, called Laugh-o-gram Studios, went bankrupt. But his biggest failure was Oswald the Lucky Rabbit, in 1928, Charles Mintz took the rights of Oswald from Walt Disney and claimed Oswald as an official Universal Studios character.

On his train ride home after learning he lost Oswald, Walt created Mickey Mouse. The creator of Mickey and Minnie Mouse went on to be nominated for 59 Academy Awards, winning 32.

Constantly Improving

"Whenever I go on a ride, I'm always thinking of what's wrong with the thing and how it can be improved."

After Walt Disney proved his animation movie model was a raving success with movies like Cinderella and Alice in Wonderland, he set his eyes on new adventures. Disneyland! In 1955, Disneyland was opened and Walt would personally ride all the rides to make sure they met his expectations.

Also, he would walk the theme park and ask customers questions to make sure everyone was satisfied. Walter was constantly trying to improve the experience for his customers.

Tolerance for Risk

"It's no secret that we were sticking just about every nickel we had on the chance that people would really be interested in something totally new and unique in the field of entertainment."

When Walt Disney created Laugh-O-Gram he quit his job in order to create his own business.

Most people sneered at Snow White and the Seven Dwarfs, including his brother and his mother. Thanks to this risk money came flowing in and saved the company. Without this risk we also wouldn't have any of the well know Disney movies today.

Walt Disney had many businesses that failed, even the rights to Oswald pulled from underneath him. He persevered until he got a company that worked but his tolerance for risk were a huge part of his success.

"First, think. Second, believe. Third, dream. And finally, dare."

"When you believe in a thing, believe in it all the way, implicitly and unquestionably."

"The way to get started is to quit talking and begin doing."

Key Takeaways

- Leaders need vision and need to put purpose ahead of tasks.
- Leaders need a bit of fearlessness and be willing to risk.
- Leaders need to be animated positive energy sources.
- Leaders need to be evangelists for the organization.
- Leaders need to be resilient and learn from failure.
- Leaders need to first serve others.
- Leaders know they cannot go it alone; they forge partnerships.

BRINGING IT ALL TOGETHER

We hope you enjoyed this journey through the leadership insights of this eclectic compendium of leaders. We did not assemble this set of leaders with any underlying thematic intentions. We wanted to offer a diverse set of perspectives, experiences and insights and to discover any themes that emerged.

There are certainly unique perspectives given the context in which some of the leaders had their primary leadership impact. For example, the insights of Grace Hopper, largely formed from her background in mathematics, as a pioneer of the computer industry and as a woman rising to Rear Admiral in the US Navy. She reminds leaders; "*You manage things, you lead people.*"

We also learned from the insights of Elie Wiesel whose leadership perspectives were forged in the horrors of the Holocaust. He offered this simple, but powerful thought for leaders; "*Think higher and feel deeper.*"

Another leader from a unique perspective was Cesar Chavez, a union organizer for farm workers and migrant workers, whose leadership perspective was honed on dusty dirt farms and rural rally meetings. He highlights that leaders can do the improbable; *"Si se puede!" ("Yes, it can be done!").*

Mother Teresa, who led from the slums of Calcutta tells leaders *"you're never too small to think big"*, and *"dream it simple, say it strong."*

We also have the perspective of Tammy Duckworth, a veteran and double amputee from combat wounds she suffered during the Iraq War, and also the first woman with a known physical disability to be elected to Congress. She offers; *"And just forgetting about what other people are saying about how you should be and how you're supposed to be, just bring your own strengths to it."*

Finally, the leadership insights of Katharine Graham, an accidental leader thrust into the role through the death of her husband. She had to rise to the role through immersion. She trusted her instincts and intensified her understanding of the news business because she observed it as it happened, by listening, and by asking questions.

We were also pleased to see that despite the historical, cultural and professional differences amongst our 40 leaders, common themes emerged. There were ten themes that stood out, each of which had a minimum of twelve leaders who offered insights related to the theme.

We offer these in no specific order...

Effective Leaders are Talent Connoisseurs

"A great person attracts great people and knows how to hold them together."

Johann Wolfgan von Goethe

Effective leaders understand that talented people can be game changers and they surround themselves with the best talent they can find. There is a war for talent being waged globally, there is just not enough talent to meet the demand. A growing number of leaders face the harsh reality: talent acquisition is under siege. Nearly half of recently surveyed employers (46%) are highly concerned with attracting and retaining talent, and 93% are taking active steps to hire and keep qualified employees (Recruiting Daily, 2019). Wintrip (2017) quoted Kahan with: "leaders rely on people who know how to go beyond what they are asked, people who imagine what is possible and create results where they have not existed before."

Leaders know that talent is a "productivity kicker." Superior talent is up to eight times more productive. A recent study of more than 600,000 researchers, entertainers, politicians, and athletes found that high performers are 400 percent more productive than average ones. Steve Jobs of Apple summed up talent's importance with this advice: "Go after the cream of the cream. A small team of A+ players can run circles around a giant team of B and C players." (Keller & Meaney, 2017).

Given the demographic and workforce trends that suggests leaders are facing what I call a 'nomadic' workforce, they are essentially renting talent. The Bureau of Labor Statistics says that workers now stay at each job, on average, for 4.4 years, but the average expected tenure of the youngest workers is about half that. A recent Willis Towers Watson study noted that more than 50% of all organizations globally have difficulty retaining some of their most valued employee groups. Data from the US Bureau of Labor Statistics show that 3.5m employees leave their job every month (Dickson, n.d.). The best leaders find ways to attract, recruit, develop and retain talent longer than their rivals.

These leaders know they can create advantages by infusing different perspectives, experience and insights into the organization. It not just about the talent itself, but also as the fuel for energizing the organization, building a collaborative environment, driving innovation and as a means for self-growth. The best leaders surround themselves with talented people who will tell them what they need to hear versus want to hear.

Lincoln was an exceptional exemplar of this with his "team of rivals" (Kearns-Goodwin, 2006). As Coutu (2009) noted, Lincoln came to power when the nation was in peril, and he had the intelligence and the self-confidence to know that he needed the best people by his side—people who were leaders in their own right and who were acutely aware of their own strengths. He surrounded himself with people, including his rivals, who had strong egos and high ambitions; who felt free to question his authority; and who were unafraid to argue with him.

Kearns-Goodwin (2006) wrote:

> His success in dealing with the strong egos of the men in his cabinet suggests that in the hands of a truly great politician the qualities we generally associate with decency and morality—kindness, sensitivity, compassion, honesty, and empathy—can also be impressive political resources.

These skills are also critical leadership skills especially as they intersect with talent acquisition, deployment and retention.

Edison was called a 'player-coach' by Murphy (2018). He defined this as "an individual contributor who also manages the work of other employees." Edison surrounded himself with bright people, creating a collaborative culture that allowed him to innovate at a far faster pace than he ever could have achieved alone.

Sara Blakely once commented:

> Two lessons that just keep getting stronger and louder are: Hire your weaknesses, and stay in your lane. So, I encourage people to delegate and hire where you aren't strong. And realize that the self-awareness of *what are my strengths, and what are my weaknesses?* comes when you are quiet with yourself and you're listening, you're paying attention (Brody, 2018).

Steve Jobs once noted: "It doesn't make sense to hire smart people and then tell them what to do, We hire smart people so they can tell us what to do." He also noted that "Great things in business are never done by one person. They're done by a team of people"(Jobs, n.d.)

Leaders have to be adept talent scouts constantly trolling for new talent, both internally and externally. They have to be able to recognize talent in many different 'packages' and non-traditional sources. Once they find and deploy the best talent, they need to create a compelling Vision, set expectations, communicate clear boundaries and rules of engagement and then get out of the way and let the talent emerge, flourish and push the future.

Bistrisky (2019), captured this well: "Great leaders find people who are best at different things and get them all on the same team."

Effective Leaders Champion Creativity and Innovation

"Innovation distinguishes between a leader and a follower."

Steve Jobs

Creativity has always been at the heart of business, but the shift to a more intense innovation-driven economy has been somewhat abrupt. Today, effective leaders must foster greater creativity among their employees. "Employees are more likely to produce creative outcomes when they are aware that creativity is expected from them and is encouraged by their leaders" (Huang, Krasikova & Lui, 2016).

Barsh, Capozzi & Davidson of Mckinsey Research (2008) noted:

> As globalization tears down the geographic boundaries and market barriers that once kept businesses from achieving their potential, a company's ability to innovate—to tap the fresh value-creating ideas of its employees and those of its partners, customers, suppliers, and other parties beyond its own boundaries—is anything but faddish. In fact, innovation has become a core driver of growth, performance, and valuation. More than 70 percent of the senior executives in a survey we recently conducted say that innovation will be at least one of the top three drivers of growth for their companies in the next three to five years. Other executives see innovation as the most important way for companies to accelerate the pace of change in today's global business environment

While senior executives cite innovation as an important driver of growth, few of them explicitly lead and manage it. Steve Jobs is an example of those senior leaders who not only lead innovation, but championed it as a core organizational value. Jobs (n.d.) noted:

> "Sometimes when you innovate, you make mistakes. It is best to admit them quickly and get on with improving your other innovations."
>
> "I'm as proud of many of the things we haven't done as the things we have done. Innovation is saying no to a thousand things."

Several of our selected leaders evangelized the importance of innovation. Gates (2016) said:

> "The best leaders have the ability to do both the urgent things that demand attention today and at the same time lay the groundwork for innovation that will pay dividends for decades." He also said: "It's always innovation that get us out of just straight-line thinking of what problems look like."

Bezos (n.d.) offered three lessons for innovators: Disrupt your own business before someone else does, innovate in another field with your spare capacity and anticipate customer needs. He also said, "you have to be willing to be misunderstood if you are going to innovate."

Winder (2005) captured the need for innovative leaders as far back as Hamilton who believed leaders need to foster ideas, prize creativity, and be open to others' inputs.

An organization without ideas cannot move forward. Ideas are the stuff that makes us both what we are and what we will be. In any organization, it is an absolute necessity to have a core group of creative thinkers. Leaders must learn how to harness and direct creativity.

Edison was known as a prolific inventor, but it could be argued that his greatest contributions were his evangelization of a culture of innovation. He saw invention as a means to "do it better." His strong focus on innovation extended beyond just technology or products to include process, as well. Edison argued against falling to the trap of complacency, as evidenced by one of his most succinct mantras: "There's a way to do it better—find it." (Brox, 2012).

Champagne (2016) noted Hopper's focus on innovation and need to avoid complacency. "Humans are allergic to change. They love to say, 'We've always done it this way.' I try to fight that. That's why I have a clock on my wall that runs counter-clockwise."

Fort (2018) noted Hopper mentored and inspired young women and men to look for innovative ways to serve. She had no time for complacency, stale thinking or laziness. And she and her teams always carefully assessed their performance to look for opportunities to improve processes and technology.

The Center for Creative Leadership (2014) noted:

> Leaders must learn how to create an organizational climate where others apply innovative thinking to solve problems and develop new products and services. It is about growing a culture of innovation, not just hiring a few creative outliers.
>
> Innovative thinking is not reliant on past experience or known facts. It imagines a desired future state and figures out how to get there. It is intuitive and open to possibility. Rather than identifying right answers or wrong answers, the goal is to find a better way and explore multiple possibilities.
>
> Studies have shown that 20 percent to 67 percent of the variance on measures of the climate for creativity in organizations is directly attributable to leadership behavior. What this means is that leaders must act in ways that promote and support organizational innovation.

Graham-Leviss (2016) captured results of two studies:

> In Conference Board's 2015 CEO Challenge study, 943 CEOs ranked "human capital" and "innovation" as their top two long-term challenges to driving business growth.
>
> XBInsight has collected competency data on nearly 5,000 leaders across a wide range of industries. Analyses were done to identify the competencies that innovative leaders share:
>
> **Demonstrate Curiosity**
>
> Innovative leaders exhibit an underlying curiosity and desire to know more. These leaders will actively take the initiative to learn new information, which demonstrates engagement and loyalty to company goals.
>
> **Lead Courageously**
>
> Innovative leaders are proactive and lead with confidence and authority. They turn tough circumstances into prime opportunities to demonstrate their decisive capabilities and take responsibility for difficult decision making. These leaders are sure to engage and maintain audience attention in high-stakes meetings and discussions, and they do not avoid conflicts and differences of opinion.
>
> **Seize Opportunities**
>
> Innovative leaders are proactive and take initiative and ownership for success. These leaders anticipate potential obstacles before taking action, but avoid over-analysis.

Expedite (2019) helps sum up the need for leaders to champion creativity and innovation:

> According to an IBM survey of 1,500 chief executives around the world, creativity is the most sough-after trait in leaders today.

> One of the reasons creative leadership is becoming an increasingly essential attribute, is due to the positive impact such leaders have on the workforce. A large part of being a creative leader is being able to inspire people to generate and develop original and creative ideas. By facilitating creativity in employees, leaders can increase workplace satisfaction and build a team that works with enthusiasm and drive.

The best leaders know that innovation must come from an array of sources, both internally and externally. When people and their different points of view and experiences can be integrated and shared in a meaningful manner, they create the types of innovations that individuals could not have done or found alone.

Effective Leaders are 'Ever-Learning'

"Education is the mother of leadership."

Wendell Willkie

"Leadership is not merely a state of being,
it is an action; it is like a sport that must be
studied, practiced, and whittled down to an art!"

Tina O'Toole

Edward Paxton Hood (1852) noted, "Our whole life is an Education — we are 'ever-learning,' every moment of time, everywhere, under all circumstances something is being added to the stock of our previous attainments. Mind is always at work when once its operations commence. All men are learners, whatever their occupation, in the palace, in the cottage, in the park, and in the field. These are the laws stamped upon Humanity." (McKay & McKay, 2019).

This was the most common theme amongst our leaders, 18 of them emphasized the need for leaders to be life-long learners, open to input and feedback and to share knowledge.

Leidner (2017) saw Hamilton as an exemplar of the need to learn and share. He paraphrased Hamilton: *Be humble, keep learning, and share knowledge.*

Wikihow (n.d.) captured lessons on learning from Jefferson:

> *Broaden your knowledge.* A polymath by nature and experience, Jefferson spoke five languages, and was passionately interested in philosophy, science, religion, architecture, and invention. He was well read and always had a thirst for knowledge.

> Never assume that you are "above" digesting popular information sources as well. A leader should know the pulse of what the majority of the public is thinking and following by way of trends, fads and curiosities. Knowing what matters to the people you lead (whether it's a team or a company) will always help you to tailor your ideas and visions to make them resonate with those you're guiding. Be curious and genuine in your desire to understand what moves people.
>
> *Learn from others, even if it means you must follow for a while.* Great leaders learn skills by not just forging ahead without knowledge but by identifying mentors or guides, studying their strategies and molding their techniques to their advantage.

Kearns Goodwin (2005) captured Lincoln's focus on learning, "Life was a school to him and he was always studying and mastering every subject before him."

Churchill once said, "Personally I'm always ready to learn, although I do not always like being taught."

Klagsbrun (2017), noted we can learn from Meir's habit of quietly listening. Even at the height of power, Golda Meir would sit through hours of meetings hardly saying a word, but listening to every side of every argument before reaching a decision about what needed to be done. "Instead of throwing an idea at us," recalled a former staff member, "she would say, 'You tell me what to do,' allowing people to feel they had been heard and their views considered."

Strock (2017) noted Roosevelt's obsession with reading. From youth, Roosevelt was a voracious reader: "Reading is a disease with me." Roosevelt's curiosity, his ceaseless learning, never abated. The book, the classroom, formal education, these were far from his only venues for learning. They produced many of those he called the "educated ineffectives." Roosevelt's example, combining the life of ideas and the life of action, was central to his project of self-creation as a leader. "As soon as any man has ceased to be able to learn, his usefulness as a teacher is at an end. When he himself can't learn, he has reached the stage where other people can't learn from him."

Other leaders (Gates, Buffett, Cuban) have also argued that leaders should be avid readers.

Chris (2015) noted that Gates considers learning as a life-long process. Bill Gates continues to learn and develop something new so he can provide something better.

Gates says he reads about 50 books a year, which translates to about one per week. Gates noted:

> Reading is one of the chief ways that I learn, and has been since I was a kid. These days, I also get to visit interesting places, meet with scientists and watch a lot of lectures online. But reading is still the main way that I both learn new things and test my understanding.

Gates draws attention to the need to think when reading, as opposed to simply absorbing the words. When you take the time to ponder what you're reading, to see if and how it truly applies to your life (or the lives of others), the value of that material increases significantly.

Montag (2017) captured thoughts from Buffett and Cuban on reading and learning:

> Buffett devotes a large portion of his day to reading. He has said he reads six newspapers every day.
>
> > I still probably spend five or six hours a day reading. I like to sit and think. I spend a lot of time doing that and sometimes it is pretty unproductive, but I find it enjoyable to think about business or investment problems.
>
> He also said to students:
>
> > Read 500 pages every day. That's how knowledge works. It builds up, like compound interest. All of you can do it, but I guarantee not many of you will do it.

Mark Cuban has said,

> I read more than three hours almost every day. Most people won't put in the time to get a knowledge advantage. To this day, I feel like if I put in enough time consuming all the information available, particularly with the net making it so readily available, I can get an advantage in any technology business.

Gerard Seijts (2013) in *Good Leaders Learn* stated,

> Good leaders are really the product of a never-ending process of skill and character development. Good leaders develop through constant learning about their personalities, relationships and careers, not to mention the kind of leader they want to become. "Simply put, the leaders I met were all passionate about excelling and dedicated to doing it through continual learning."

A good way to capture this theme is through the words of Richard Branson (Bradt, 2014): "Listen out there. One of the keys to 'the way' we do things is nothing more complex than listening – listening intently to everyone. Ask why with a wide-angled lens."

Stay aware throughout your life that you don't always know everything, not even in your own field of expertise. Even seasoned leaders understand that always improving your knowledge is the real source of power––and that it is impossible to know everything.

Dyson captured this simply; *leaders must be willing to learn from others.*

Effective Leaders are Infused with Doses of Patience, Humility and Empathy

"He that can have patience can have what he will."

Benjamin Franklin

"Humility is not thinking less of yourself, it's thinking of yourself less."

C. S. Lewis

"I think we all have empathy. We may not have enough courage to display it."

Maya Angelou

There has been a raging debate for more than 100 years on the personality traits of effective leaders. The challenge has always been to find a comprehensive list of leadership traits that gains widespread acceptance. We often see lists developed by practitioners and scholars which are inevitably challenged about some inclusions and exclusions. We are not entering the debate with our own list from our included leaders. Instead we offer shared insights from many of our leaders who exemplified or who offered thoughts on the role of patience, humility and empathy in effective leadership.

The old saying that 'patience is a virtue' is certainly being tested in today's chaotic, 24x7, instant environment that leaders confront. There is systemic impatience across almost all stakeholders that leaders must navigate.

The business graveyard is filled with examples of leaders who fell prey to this impatience and didn't properly exercise patience. Expectations were unrealistic and leaders did too much, too soon.

Cassidy (2016) has said:

> If you want to be the best leader you can be, begin fostering the characteristic of patience. Slow down and be deliberate. Most leaders, ironically, are not patient people. The tendency is get it done and get it done now. But great leaders are patient and it reflects in their team members and productivity.

Moran (2002) strongly asserted:

> True leaders recognize that patience enables them to take stock of the situation, to understand what is required, and wait while they build the capacity to take appropriate and effective action. Patience requires composure and character (as discussed in earlier blogs). Societal pressures for action may cause others to criticize and condemn a leader's perceived inaction or lack of speed. People will first demand action. Then they will demand results. The greater the crisis, the greater the impatience.
>
> By demonstrating patience, leaders reinforce the importance of focusing on the long-term outcomes. Patience doesn't mean ignoring the interim milestones or short-term deliverable. It does mean keeping them in context.

I admire bold leaders, those willing to go first and have the courage of conviction to try. That said, I do not want arrogant, narcissistic, vain or prideful leaders who make it too much about them. I want a leader who is confident and bold, but with doses of humility, realism and pragmatism.

Hamilton had a challenge getting the balance right. As Winder (2005) noted:

> Hamilton's Achilles' heel was his pride, which prevented him from acknowledging his own fallibility. Compromise was extremely difficult for him to accept. In the early years of their time spent working together, Washington was able to check

> Hamilton's hubris and helped him avoid some tactical mistakes. Without Washington's mentoring, Hamilton repeatedly let his pride—and in some cases his arrogance—paint him into dangerous corners. Ultimately, it was this lack of humility that led to his death in a duel at the hands of the equally prideful Aaron Burr.

Pride and vanity are not prerequisites for leadership. Even the most brilliant leaders can benefit from considering and, when appropriate, implementing the views of others. If leader's pride will not permit let him/her accept input, they will likely find themselves on a slippery slope toward failure.

Though it is important to exhibit humility, it can be equally important not to give up on a good idea. Transformative ideas are often overlooked simply because timing was wrong. Effective leaders blend patience, humility and perseverance.

Dr. Seuss noted (Cocci, n.d.):

> Don't be a Yertle! Good old King Yertle was an extremely ambitious turtle who had no regard for the people he ruled. He expected his fellow turtles to do exactly what he said, without any disagreements, because he was far superior to them. He didn't listen to or care about the people he ruled, which were the people who created his throne.
>
> Leadership lesson: Don't be King Yertle. Instead, embrace humility as a leader and use your power to serve, rather than exploit, others (Spungin, 2017).

Clark (2016) offers this view of Glenn and the role of humility:

> During our discussions, he told me something that changed my life, and might change yours. He told me that whenever he arrived at a crossroads in his life—when it was time to decide

> whether to, say, return to NASA or run for public office—he would sit down with his wife and discuss: *"What is the best use of me?"*
>
> That approach to his role in life—always looking for the best use of his particular abilities and talents—was a revelation to me. I've tried to keep that, and his example of courage, humility and decency, foremost in my mind as I proceed through the years.

Effective leaders also tend to have a high level of emotional intelligence, particularly large doses of empathy.

Coutu (2009) noted,

> What Lincoln had, it seems to me, was an extraordinary amount of emotional intelligence. He was able to acknowledge his errors and learn from his mistakes to a remarkable degree. He was careful to put past hurts behind him and never allowed wounds to fester.

He also followed what Barker (2014) called the ability to "lead by being led." Lincoln always gave credit where credit was due and took responsibility when things went wrong.

Branson keeps it simple*: Be Approachable: Be someone others find it easy to be around. Be Real: Give up pretense and ditch the ego (Warrell, 2015).*

Gourguechon (2017) noted:

> No less a hard-muscled body than the U.S. Army, in its Army Field Manual on Leader Development insists repeatedly that empathy is essential for competent leadership. Empathy is the ability to understand another person's experience, perspective and feelings. Also called "vicarious introspection," it's commonly described as the ability to put yourself in another person's shoes. But make sure you are assessing how *they* would feel in their shoes, not how *you* would feel in their shoes.

Vicki C. (2018) noted that:

> Empathetic leaders are assets to organizations, in part, because they are able to effectively build and maintain relationships—a critical part of leading organizations anywhere in the world.
>
> Empathy is the way to connect with others in a very real, human way and lays the foundation to inspire, empower, influence and motivate them to, in the words of the U.S. Army, "accomplish the mission, improve the organization" as well as become their best selves to improve their world.

*Wie*sel (Citterman, 2016) offered these thoughts on gratitude:

> *Show gratitude.*
>
> When a person doesn't have gratitude, something is missing in his or her humanity. There are few things a leader can do that have more impact than showing gratitude. Yet, so many leaders colossally fail because they're too busy or too focused on other things. It takes very little effort to say thank you, to give credit, or show appreciation. The best leaders do it frequently, and it pays dividends.

Effective Leaders Model the Way

"A leader is one who knows the way, goes the way and shows the way."

John Maxwell

"We learn by emulating or copying those we want to be like, often subconsciously. If you want people to behave a certain way, don't tell them to do it. Model the way yourself."

Phil Dourado

Leaders today are under intense scrutiny from a host of stakeholders including: customers, suppliers, employees, regulators, community activists and governance officials. They are always on stage and someone is watching and judging. There are no 'private moments' for leaders. Lombardi (1997) dubbed this "The Spotlight Era" (p. 1).

Thomas (2018) quoted consultant Davia Temin "Reputational risk has increasingly become a top-line preoccupation of boards at least in part because the internet, fueled by social media, can turn an indiscretion into a viral bonfire in a heartbeat."

Winder (2005) offered this insight from the lessons learned from mistakes that Hamilton made in his personal life:

> Leaders are often susceptible to the belief that power gives them the right to misbehave. In truth, persons in leadership roles are under constant scrutiny from others. Leaders set the ethical standard for their organization. Far too often we see otherwise great people become victims of their own undoing. Leaders must be aware of their actions in both their professional and personal lives and how they affect not only themselves, but the

> people who work with and for them. Especially today with the dramatically increased access the general public has to intimate details of everyone's lives via social media, 'private moments' for leaders are fewer and further in between; in some instances, it is as though they are always on stage.

Thomas (2018) also shared:

> A study of 2,500 global companies by Strategy & Consultants concluded that 5.3 percent of CEO exits stemmed from ethical lapses from 2012 to 2016, up from 3.9 percent in the preceding five-year period. Lapses included fraud, bribery, insider trading, inflated resumes, and sexual indiscretions. The researchers said it was not because CEOs are less ethical today, but rather because the public is more vocal, regulators are more proactive and punitive, and because digital communications and the 24/7 news cycle spread word of the misconduct.

Because of this intense scrutiny, there is a greater need for leaders to be consistent. They need to be consistent in attitude, words and actions and any deviation is quickly seen, dissected and can become a distraction.

Leaders today are expected to model the way, be exemplars and consistently live and demonstrate the values they espouse. There is a continuum in play here. Expertise, experience, behaviors and position will drive leadership respect. Consistency will move to earned credibility. From there, consistency in values will embed trust. Followers will not believe in leadership messages unless they believe in the leader.

Baldoni (2019) sums this up nicely:

> Leaders are those who make good things happen. One of the best ways they do it is by giving people a reason to believe and to follow. That's simple and easy to say, but it takes a lifetime of trying to put into practice. There are no shortcuts, but there are signposts.

These "signposts" include consistency, values, integrity, honesty, conviction and actions.

Jefferson said: "In matter of style, swim with the current; in matters of principle, stand like a rock.

Hamilton himself offered: Exemplify Moral Integrity*:* Be honest with your followers, admit your own weaknesses, and develop an environment of trust (Leidner (2017).

Citterman (2016) cited Elie Wiesel as a man of clear conviction, and there is much to be learned from a life lived with such purpose. As a leader or aspiring leader, challenge yourself to define what you stand for and decide how you will show it every day using clarity, conviction and gratitude.

Cocci (n.d.) added from Dr. Seuss: *Be as honest as Horton.*

> Being honest and straightforward with employees is the quickest way to earn their respect. Even if you're delivering bad news, be honest and upfront about it. Trying to sugar-coat it will only cause decay in your relationships. It's not always easy striking a balance between transparency and honesty, but if you want to earn your employees' respect, it's absolutely necessary.
>
> It is extremely important for senior leaders to model their declared values – every day, with every interaction.

Too often senior leaders "manage by announcements," publishing a set of expectations or rules that they declare are to be embraced from that moment forward, yet they do not actively demonstrate those expectations themselves, measure how well others embrace those expectations, etc. No wonder leader credibility suffers in many organizations. Only when senior leaders model desired valued behaviors will the rest of the organization trust those leaders, follow those leaders, and model those desired valued behaviors themselves.

Buffett noted the importance of integrity. "We look for three things when we hire people. We look for intelligence, we look for initiative or energy, and we look for integrity." Jon Huntsman said, "the difference between the unsuccessful, the temporarily successful, and those who become and remain successful is *character*" (Schwantes, n.d.).

Marcus, L. (2014) also shared some leadership insights from Angelou:

> All of us knows not what is expedient, not what is going to make us popular, not what the policy is, or the company policy—but in truth, each of us knows what is the right thing to do. And that's how I am guided.

Klagsbrun (2017) noted that Meir was an example of integrity even out of office:

> Of the many leadership traits Golda Meir embodied, her integrity stands above everything. She devoted herself tirelessly to building a homeland for the Jewish people, never once seeking personal gain for herself or her family. And when out of office, she declined any perks, riding buses and shopping in the supermarket like anyone else. Her integrity gained her the respect of even her severest critics.

Rice commented at Norwich University (Jackson, 2014):

> I think a leader, first of all, has to have integrity," said Rice. "That means you never ask someone to do something you would never do. . . . I think the most important thing a leader can do is recognize leadership qualities in others. Part of your responsibility is to not just say, 'Charge this hill with me,' but to make sure you are developing other people's skills as well.

Rice also said: "The first step for a leader is to be right with yourself. Integrity is the basis of leadership."

Many of our selected leaders called out the need for leaders to model the way by going first, doing themselves what they expected of others and being consistent exemplars. These leaders understand the dangers embedded in an approach of "do as I say, not as I do."

Lombardi set the example and expectation:

> Instead of putting the responsibility of winning on the players, he assumed that duty himself. He communicated to his team his expectations on their commitment and hard work during training, but also outlined what he would be responsible for — teaching them and pushing them to maximize their potential.
>
> By taking on the burden of winning, Lombardi removed pressure from the players and allowed them to focus on being their best on the field. This also built trust between him and his team — trust that if both sides focused on their roles, they could achieve success.

Eikenberry (n.d.) commented on the old phrase, "lead by example:"

> The "lead by example" cliché is a cliché because it is true – people are influenced by our actions. Our life as a leader would be easier if we could say all the right things and know that those words would significantly influence our team. While that would be easier, it is also unrealistic. While our words matter, what we do matters far more. Put another way, others watch our feet more than our lips.

Schwantes (n.d.) stated:

> How would you feel if, every day, your colleague said what he meant, stayed true to himself, and behaved in accordance with this? Chances are you'd quickly trust the judgments and decisions of that person because his actions are consistent with his words.

We conclude this theme with these thoughts from Schrage (2016):

> Serious leaders understand that, both by design and default, they're always leading by example. Some want to "lead from the front" while others prefer "leading from behind." But everyone senses their success — and failure — at leading by example is integral to their "leadership brand."
>
> That's why inconsistency and hypocrisy so acutely matter. The executive who is always — always — unapologetically late to his own meetings evokes eye rolls when his lead-by-example stories stress "respect."
>
> The true lead-by-example test is who follows those examples and how.
>
> Do colleagues and clients see those examples as leadership?
>
> Are direct reports inspired to admire and emulate?
>
> When people describe "the right way" of getting the job done or getting the best out of people, is an example explicitly referenced?
>
> These questions aren't rhetorical; they're central to meaningful and measurable leadership exemplar behavior.

Effective Leaders Confront the Status Quo

"A leader who loves the status quo soon becomes a follower."

John Maxwell

"Success breeds complacency. Complacency breeds failure. Only the paranoid survive."

Andy Grove

Effective leaders are always facing forward and embracing progress. These leaders see the value in the 'status quo,' but do not succumb to it's appeal. This is not to say there isn't value in experience, effective processes or things that are working. The best leaders just do not live there for long, they fight the onset of complacency. They bring forward what is working while also looking for opportunities to do even better. They understand the point that Grace Hopper (1976) made when she said, "the most dangerous phrase is "we've always done it this way" (WADITW).

Nothing can stifle innovation or opportunity faster than a work environment that discourages looking for new ways to improve. Leaders must challenge the corrosive "We've always done it this way" mindset. They know that we can not mindlessly carry on with what has actually worked, but to build off them and take them further. They know to confront assumptions and test seeming limits.

Llopis (2014) called out leadership:

> More than ever, leadership has become an exercise in survival of the fittest – and as a consequence, those leaders who have grown

> more complacent, are finding it difficult to maintain their competitive edge and thought-leadership footing.
>
> Leadership in the 21st century requires mental toughness, stamina and patience. Being a market leader demands a new breed of leadership that can withstand the punishment of the daily grind and the people pressures along the way. It's easy for market leaders to grow complacent when they feel the alternative is to take two steps back before taking one step forward in an effort to find their footing in today's changing terrain
>
> He quoted Warren Bennis when it came to not giving in to the dangers of becoming a complacent leader: "The manager does things right and has their eye on the bottom line; the leader does the right thing and has their eye on the horizon."

Complacency is rampant in many of today's organizations mainly due to over-managed and under-led cultures (Gleeson, n.d.).

Torben Rick (2015) made the point:

> Complacency ignores opportunities, big and small. It turns a blind eye to serious and dangerous threats. It hushes innovative ideas. It stomps on energy, enthusiasm and anything new. It hangs on to the old ways of doing things with white, arthritic knuckles. It doesn't want to hear or see what is happening in the world. Learning new things is not up for discussion. It is of no concern to those who are complacent.
>
> Complacency almost always comes from a sense of success and lives long after the success that created it has disappeared. Organizations and individuals that are complacent do not look for new opportunities or hazards.

This image from Torben Rick captures a range of complacent phrasing often heard in organizations:

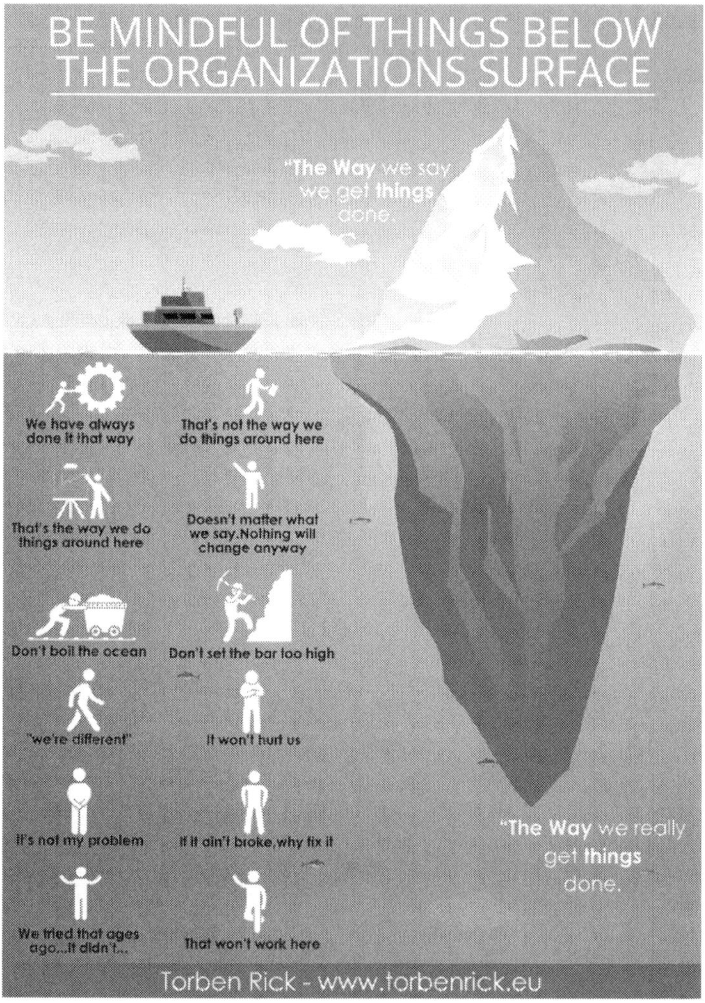

Below the organizations surface – Complacency is a dangerous culture – When the organizational culture needs to change

Gleeson (n.d.) further noted:

> Most organizations that continue to succeed and innovate have a culture poised for positive change and taking risk. They don't wait for the ship to spring a leak. They proactively and constantly set aggressive goals. They sometimes even intentionally develop a sense of urgency.

Smith (2016) offered this from Dr. King: *Be disruptive.* Dr. King's cause was fueled by his refusal to accept the status quo. By challenging yourself to step outside your comfort zone, you create opportunities for evolution and innovation.

Lynch (n.d.) added based on the insights of Dr. King: *Great leaders refuse to accept the status quo.* Dr. King refused to accept what was currently acceptable and instead, outlined a bold vision on what needed to be changed, why it needed to be changed, and how it would be changed. *Great leaders create a sense of urgency.* Leaders are impatient—in a good way. They refuse to sit by as change takes its natural course. They have a sense of urgency and communicate it. Dr. King reminded America of the "fierce urgency of now."

Toyoda championed the concept of *kaizen* derived from Toyoda's core values and has been a mandate for his successors to constantly improve performance. At the root of *kaizen* is the idea that nothing is perfect and everything can be improved. This is critical to the company, as every leader is taught to remember that the process is never perfect and that the company has never achieved the perfect "lean solution" (Liker & Convis, 2012).

Blakley stated: *Break the rules and be relentless.*

> Blakely has never asked permission to do things her own way. She also didn't like how masculine the traditional business environment felt, so she turned tradition on its head. This voice inside of my head just said, 'Do it differently. Take a different approach" (Briody, 2018).

Dyson also said: "You are just as likely to solve a problem by being unconventional and determined as by being brilliant. Be a bit whacko, and you shake people up...And we all need shaking up" (Gottlieb, 2004).

Gladwell said: "A rebellious activity is something that leads to success...that kind of courage lies at the heart of what it means to be disruptive" (Redrup, 2015).

To sum up this theme, we offer this from John Glenn: he always was striving and never completely arriving (Braden, 2016). Nooyi adds: "We ought to keep pushing the boundaries to get to flawless execution. Flawless is the ultimate goal" (Snyder, 2015).

Effective Leaders are Visionaries

"Leadership is the capacity to translate
vision into reality."

Warren Bennis

"Good business leaders create a vision, articulate
the vision, passionately own the vision,
and relentlessly drive it to completion."

Jack Welch

"The very essence of leadership is that you
have to have vision.
You can't blow an uncertain trumpet."

Theodore Hesburgh

Effective leader's time horizons tend to be more into the future. They do not ignore the present, they seamlessly move between now and later, but their primary focus is what to come. They see a future to pursue.

Leadership is all about seeing and creating a brighter and better future. It's about inventing, innovating, creating, building, improving, and transforming. A positive leader sees what's possible and then takes the next steps to rally and unite people to create it. (Gordon, 2017.)

Allan Mullaly, former Ford CEO, said:

> It's important to have a compelling vision and a comprehensive plan. Positive leadership — conveying the idea that there is always a way forward — is so important because that is what you are here for — to figure out how to move the organization forward.

Leaders today have a critical trifecta to deliver. They must be able to create a compelling Vision, communicate it to create broad and deep buy-in and then lead the execution to the expected outcomes. If you have been part of a Visioning process, you know it can be very challenging. Being able to deliver the trifecta, separates good leaders from average ones and leaders from managers.

Gordon noted also:

> The vision a positive leader creates and shares serves as a North Star that points and moves everyone in an organization in the right direction. The leader must continually point to this North Star and remind everyone that this is where we are going. Positives leader carry a telescope and a microscope. The telescope helps your team keep your eyes on your vision, North Star, and big picture. The microscope helps you zoom-focus on the things you must do in the short term to realize the vision in your telescope (2017).

Wroblewski (2019) pointed out several attributes of visionary leaders. These include:

> From Ray Dalio: He calls visionary leaders "shapers" – *people who bring shape to their vision, often after conquering the doubts and objections of others.*
>
> Visionary Leaders See Things Others Can't
> *They seem to see before others or can connect dots in the gray.*
>
> Visionary Leaders View the World Through a Dual Prism.
> *Visionary leaders can see – and commingle – micro and macro views of the world.*
>
> Visionary Leaders Formulate Mental Maps
> *These leaders can bring clarity to the vision and paint the picture.*
>
> Visionary Leaders Are Creative Yet Practical
> *They are bold, confident and will push the edges, but with doses of pragmatism.*

> Boldness Matters
> *The word likely to have the most staying power is "boldness" since visionary business leaders must be both daring and courageous as they take risks to realize their vision.*
>
> They may fear failure, but not nearly as much as they fear not going for it.

I like the way McLaughlin (2001) captures visionary leaders:

> Visionary leaders are the builders of a new dawn, working with imagination, insight, and boldness. They present a challenge that calls forth the best in people and brings them together around a shared sense of purpose. They work with the power of intentionality and alignment with a higher purpose. Their eyes are on the horizon, not just on the near at hand.

Many of our leaders in this compendium stressed the critical intersection of leadership and vision.

Smith (2016) shared this lesson from Dr. King:

> *See the bigger picture.*
>
> One trait that made Dr. King unique was his ability to see beyond the present situation. He had a vision and dream that was so much larger than the time in which he lived. Think about what your dream speech would be, and remain committed to your vision.

IFP (2017) captured this lesson from Bezos:

> *Ignore the peer pressure.*
>
> As Bezos once said, "*We are stubborn on vision. We are flexible on details." (Masnick, 2011).* The Amazon boss was confident about his approach to online retail and kept his eye on the prize. He was uncompromising, even though nearly everyone around

> him doubted his actions. Of course, you can change the details of how you're going to reach your overall goal, but it's important that you remain determined about the overall vision for your company.

Colin Powell offered one of his 'rules' on leadership related to vision:

> **Rule 11: Have A Vision and Be Demanding.**
>
> While leaders can be empowering and humbly serve those around them they also need to have a vision and be demanding on fulfilling it. This means holding people accountable, not accepting mediocrity, and expecting more out of everyone.

Bose & Faust (2011) captured eight leadership principles of Mother Theresa:

> PRINCIPLE 1: Dream it simple, say it strong. Create a vision that is simple. Say it strongly with words and actions at every possible moment.
>
> Jacobson (n.d.) added: One of Mother Teresa's great strengths was her relentless focus on the core mission of her organization: helping the poorest of the poor.

Pahl (2015) noted Disney's focus on vision:

> Walt himself has explained his formula for having leadership vision as starting with one simple stepping stone, "I dream." If we don't dream or desire to have a vision for something better for ourselves or others, then what is it that gets us out of bed every morning? He then continues on by saying, "I test my dreams against my beliefs." In this case, he was making sure his dreams were consistent with everything he stood for, such as his beliefs, core values, and integrity.

> Next, he explains, "I dare to take risks." He would act boldly and bet on himself to win. There were a few times in his life where he would bet his entire studio on producing an animated film and, due to his vision, charisma, and leadership style, he repeatedly came out on top.
>
> Lastly he said, "I execute my vision to make those dreams come true." He would focus all his time, talents, energy, and resources to make the dream a reality.

Visionary leaders by definition are forward facing and willing to go first. They have courage of conviction and are prudent risk takers. They have backbone and a strong sense of purpose. They are relentless in the pursuit of their envisioned future.

Effective Leaders are Master Communicators

"You can have brilliant ideas, but if you can't get them across, your ideas won't get you anywhere."

Lee Iacocca

"Developing excellent communication skills is absolutely essential to effective leadership. The leader must be able to share knowledge and ideas to transmit a sense of urgency and enthusiasm to others. If a leader can't get a message across clearly and motivate others to act on it, then having a message doesn't even matter."

Gilbert Amelio

Can we imagine an effective leader who is not an effective communicator?

Leaders today are expected to be adept at the three main communication modalities: one-to-one, one-to-many and the various 'e' forms (e.g. email, teleconferences, webcasts, blogs and others). They are also expected to be able to communicate effectively using various mediums in an authentic manner.

They need to be able to deliver compelling messages and make connections to move various stakeholders towards intended goals. They also have to navigate this array of internal and external stakeholders with consistent messages. They are always on stage and can not afford to create confusion or miscommunication in this fast paced environment with any inconsistency in attitude, words or actions.

The best leaders create connections, both formal and informal, across and down the organization to ensure active bi-directional feedback channels are in place. They purposely create connections and sources to tell them what they need to hear versus may want to hear. They keep a finger on the pulse and do what Tom Peters (1980) called 'management by walking around.' Lincoln practiced this extensively, often going to the front lines to see his Generals.

Hedayati (2014) offered this communication thought from Nooyi:

> Indra Nooyi lists communication skills as one of the Five C's of Leadership. She has explained that competence, courage, confidence, and a strong moral compass go to waste without strong communication skills. What does it matter if someone is innovative on a subject if they can't clearly discuss it?
>
> In Indra's words, "You cannot over-invest in communication skills." In addition to listing communication as a key skill for leadership, Indra has received communication training to improve her abilities and flexes those communication muscles every time she makes a public appearance, meets with her C-Suite, and deals with a customer. In fact, communication is so valuable to Indra, that she maintains a blog at Pepsi where she talks to her employees via posts every other week.

Using communication to create connections

Citterman (2016) captured Weisel

> As leaders, part of our job is to inspire confidence in others to express their point of view. If we want to work collectively with people who have the confidence to be decisive, who will constructively disagree and confront difficult situations, show leadership by listening, by asking good questions, and by challenging the thinking of others to draw out their conviction.

Strock (2018) commented on Churchill who some think is one of the historically best orators:

> Master the spoken word. It is as a speaker that Churchill achieved his greatest leadership influence. As President Kennedy said, Churchill "mobilized the English language and sent it into battle."
>
> Churchill acknowledged that he was not an orator. He meant that he was not a speaker, such as David Lloyd George, who could connect deeply with a live audience, receiving and responding to their rising emotions. One wonders if this was a lingering result of his hard-earned triumph over a distracting lisp and the concomitant self-consciousness it inevitably engendered.
>
> By contrast, Churchill prepared extensively, speaking to his audiences with methodically crafted ideas and writing. Many of his legendary witticisms turn out, on inspection, to have been premeditated rather than impromptu. The value was created largely in the interplay of Churchill's evolving thoughts and words as he drafted the speech, rather than in the interplay of his relationship with an audience during presentation.

Leaders are story tellers

Barker (2014) noted Lincoln's tendency to influence people through storytelling.

> Lincoln also had a wonderful gift for telling stories and intentionally used his quick and benign wit to soften wounded feelings and dispel anxieties.
>
> Lincoln stated, "They say I tell a great many stories. I reckon I do; but I have learned from long experience that plain people, take them as they run, are more easily influenced through

> the medium of a broad and humorous illustration than in any other way…"

Lynch (n.d.) made these points from Martin Luther King:

> *Great leaders engage the heart.*
>
> While logic may compel the mind, stories and metaphors move the heart. This is the difference between offering information and inspiration. Dr. King chose not to make a fact-based argument and instead decided to make a direct appeal to the hearts of the world. In so doing, he made history.
>
> *Great leaders paint a vivid picture of a better tomorrow.*
>
> Leaders can never grow weary of articulating their vision. They must be clear and concrete. They need to help their followers see what they see.

Ruggiero (n.d.) also noted Chávez's ability to connect and inspire, writing, "The standard of excellence that Chávez displayed was his ability to make it possible for members of all races and classes to relate to his cause and his struggle.

Marcus, L. (2014) also shared some leadership insights from Angelou:

> All of us knows not what is expedient, not what is going to make us popular, not what the policy is, or the company policy—but in truth, each of us knows what is the right thing to do. And that's how I am guided.
>
> Whatever you want to do, if you want to be great at it, you have to love it and be able to make sacrifices for it.
>
> Words mean more than what is set down on paper. *It takes the human voice to infuse them with deeper meaning.*

Schnall, M. (2018) also interviewed Angelou and offered these communication lessons:

> *Speak with confidence and power.*
>
> First off, there was her voice. Slow, thoughtful, deliberate, commanding, and so eloquent. She delivered each word thoughtfully, as though it was a gift—and it was. She did not speak off the top of her head, but from the depths of her soul. She knew who she was and stood firmly within her truth.
>
> Maya also taught me the importance of taking pride in who you are and talking with authority as an expert. This skill comes from within, not from someone else granting us this ability. She used her powerful voice (as we all can) to share her stories, to advocate for tolerance, justice and equality, and to move people to feel more beauty, peace and love.

Effective leaders actively practice the '7 Cs' of Communication especially clarity, conciseness and concreteness.

In our complex world, a key lesson we can learn from Einstein is to simplify. To him, the best solutions were the simple ones. Great leaders execute seamlessly because they avoid, when possible, complexity in the change they drive and in their communications. This makes it easy for everyone to be aligned (Thiran, 2018).

> Einstein highlights something you generally hear from great leaders—they know they don't know. And this drives them to keep learning. Einstein's insatiable curiosity and perseverance were driven by his belief that he lacked knowledge. So many times, we read Einstein's journals and letters stating he didn't know the answer, hence he had to keep learning.
>
> He goes further on to say that leaders like Einstein focus on 'simplicity.' Einstein claimed, "Any intelligent fool can make things

> bigger, more complex. It takes a touch of genius, and a lot of courage, to move in the opposite direction."

To help sum up this theme, Bose & Faust (2011) captured eight leadership principles of Mother Theresa, two of which speak to communication:

> PRINCIPLE 1: Dream it simple, say it strong. Create a vision that is simple. Say it strongly with words and actions at every possible moment.
>
> PRINCIPLE 6: Communicate in a language people understand.

Effective Leaders Eat Last

"And when a leader embraces their responsibility to care for people instead of caring for numbers, then people will follow, solve problems and see to it that that leader's vision comes to life the right way, a stable way and not the expedient way."

Simon Sinek

"In the past a leader was a boss. Today's leaders must be partners with their people... they no longer can lead solely based on positional power."

Ken Blanchard

"Nobody cares how much you know, until they know how much you care."

Theodore Roosevelt

In his work with organizations around the world, Simon Sinek noticed that some teams trust each other so deeply that they would literally put their lives on the line for each other. Other teams, no matter what incentives are offered, are doomed to infighting, fragmentation and failure. Why?

The answer became clear during a conversation with a Marine Corps general. "*Officers eat last*," he said. Sinek watched as the most junior Marines ate first while the most senior Marines took their place at the back of the line. What's symbolic in the chow hall is deadly serious on the battlefield: Great leaders sacrifice their own comfort--even their own survival--for the good of those in their care (Sinek, 2014).

The Center for Servant Leadership (n.d.) offers this view:

A servant-leader focuses primarily on the growth and well-being of people and the communities to which they belong. While traditional leadership generally involves the accumulation and exercise of power by one at the "top of the pyramid," servant leadership is different. The servant-leader shares power, puts the needs of others first and helps people develop and perform as highly as possible.

Long before the theory of 'servant leadership' emerged, several of the leaders in this compendium called out the need in invest in people and to have a deep caring for their development and support.

Crowly (n.d.) noted that Lincoln fundamentally cared about people and made every effort to demonstrate that to them. Through kind and encouraging words, and authentic gestures of exceptional thoughtfulness, he assured people of their individual significance. He was most essentially a human being who identified with the challenges people faced and the sacrifices they made.

Tye (2018) added about Nighingale:

> But one of the most remarkable—and most often overlooked—attributes of Nightingale's leadership was her intense and enduring loyalty to those she served and led. One of the greatest qualities of the greatest leaders is the way they earn the loyalty of those that they presume to lead. And as Nightingale's example shows, the best way to earn such loyalty is to give it. As was the case with Nightingale, a leader's loyalty is not just a mushy emotional attachment—it requires hard work and sacrifice on behalf of those one presumes to lead.

Murphy (2016) also commented on Powell:

> Powell's emphasis on humility and appreciation of the value of teamwork still stands as a model for public service, and indeed for all leaders. Powell understood that just as no man is an island,

> so too is no leader. Leaders serve as the heads of organizations, but are also still simply a part of the whole. Appreciating the contributions of all the parts to the whole makes the organization run better, which is the overarching goal. Powell understood this, and even when no one was watching, went above and beyond to ensure organizational success.

Powell himself commented (n.d. Military Transition):

> No matter what your job, you are there to serve. It makes no difference if it is government, military, business, or any other endeavor. Go in with a commitment to selfless service, never selfish service...get off the train before somebody throws you off, go sit in the shade with a drink, and take a look at the other tracks and trains out there. Spend a moment watching the old train disappear, then start a new journey on a new train.

Moore (2018) highlighted a core value of Graham with this story; Stand up for your employees:

> One Sunday afternoon Graham heard that the Chinese government ransacked the room of one of her foreign correspondents and held the woman for questioning. Graham did not pick up the telephone or ask for a letter of protest to be written. She put on her heels and single strand of pearls and drove to the Chinese embassy, marching up to the door and insisting on a justification. Her actions were not lost on her reporters.

Landking (2010) noted that elements of Puller's leadership style can apply to servant leadership:

> *Be visible.*
>
> Get out from behind the desk and make sure your people see you. The less you're hidden away in meetings, or at your computer,

> and the more you are engaging and encouraging your people, the better off you'll be.
>
> Schick (2015) noted: Chesty instinctively knew what his Marines wanted to hear—a confident commander who would stop at nothing to get the mission accomplished. That is why when his unit found itself surrounded by an enemy division in Korea, Chesty was able to reassure his Marines by explaining to them how this was, in fact, a blessing in disguise. As Chesty pointed out, "We've been looking for the enemy for several days now. [And] We've finally found them. We're surrounded. That simplifies our problem ..." As one battalion commander later recalled "[Chesty] kept building up our morale higher and higher, just by being there."
>
> *Make your team's welfare a priority* — Its possible to demand results while looking after the best interests of individuals.

Schick (2015) noted Chesty lived with his men. There were no officers' messes in Puller's outfit and he fell in line with the privates, carrying his own mess gear. In combat, he rigidly refused comforts unattainable for his men, and in training, he carried his own pack and bedding roll while marching at the head of his battalion.

Dhliwayo (2018) compiled seven reasons why Mandela was a great leader:

> He focused on the needs of others, not his own, listening to those who society had ignored and sought out those who society had cast away. He served the poor and the rich; he served the educated and the illiterate. There is no one Mandela did not care for. He saw everyone as his brother and sister—even his enemies. While rulers all over the world were busy empowering themselves and their friends, he was busy empowering his people.

Lohrenz (n.d.) captured Smith's thoughts as he learned them during his time in the U.S. Marine Corps:

> "The greatest leadership principle I learned in the Marine Corps was the necessity to take care of the troops in a high performance based organization."

Strock (2017) offered this related leadership lesson from Roosevelt:

> *Put your team ahead of yourself.* One of Roosevelt's formative real-time leadership experiences was leading his regiment in the Spanish-American War.
>
> Roosevelt led from the front. He placed himself into undeniable danger, remaining on horseback while facing a rain of steel.
>
> He placed those he was serving before himself. As a result, many of the Rough Riders remained committed to him for the remainder of their lives.
>
> No man has a right to ask or accept any service unless under changed conditions he would feel that he could keep his entire self-respect while rendering.

Chris (2015) on Nooyi:

> *She does not forget she is human and so are her employees.*
>
> Despite her achievements and power, she remains grounded. She said that this is important and that her family members are the ones responsible for keeping her feet on the ground. She cares about the well-being of her employees and her sincerity about this was shown when she wrote letters to her top executive employees' parents telling them they should be proud that their children are doing great at their jobs. This motivated them more and also made her connect deeper to her team.

Pahl (2015) helps us sum up this theme with the leadership insight of Disney:

> *Serve others.*
>
> Above all, what truly makes a great leader is someone who is willing to serve. Walt served in countless ways. To name a few, he personally took a co-worker's reluctant paraplegic friend to Disneyland. He rolled out the red carpet and showed his guest all the attractions as well as front row seats to every show. All this just so a disabled friend could enjoy the park without feeling left out in his wheelchair.
>
> A gardener at the Disney studios left some tools in an empty parking space and a producer chewed him out for it. Walter noticed this from his window, went down and said, "Don't you ever treat any of my employees like that! This man has been with me longer than you have, so you'd better be good to him!"
>
> To his employees, Walt was not just a leader, he was their servant and defender. That's what separates leaders from bosses.

Effective Leaders are Triple & Laser Focused

"Concentrate all your thoughts upon the work at hand. The sun's rays do not burn until brought into a focus."

Alexander Graham Bell

"It's only by saying "No" that you can concentrate on the things that are really important."

Steve Jobs

"The main thing is to keep the main thing a main thing."

Stephen R. Covey

To become a great leader, you need to be focused on achieving your vision, living your core values and accomplishing your goals (Stark, 2014). Leaders today are expected to be able to create a compelling Vision, communicate it in such a way to drive deep buy-in across and down the organization and lead the execution to the expected outcomes. They have to do all three at speed, with authenticity and grounded on a set of consistent core values. They have to be the face, voice and lead exemplar of the organization.

We highlighted how our selected leaders viewed how leaders and vision intersect in the Leaders as Visionaries section earlier. We also noted how they saw the leader as exemplar in the Modeling the Way theme. Our leaders take this further in saying leaders need to be determined, focused, and persistent. Stark (2014) noted that 'great leaders have a laser focus."

Leaders need the courage of conviction to persist and to stay focused on what matters most. Churchill captures this with "Never give in - never, never, never, never, in nothing great or small, large or petty, never give in except to convictions of honour and good sense."

Lynch highlighted how Martin Luther King did not sugar coat reality: Martin Luther King Jr. talked directly about the conflict and brutal reality facing the nation so that he could set the stage for his vision for overcoming these problems together.

Edison said leaders must maintain coherence. It's not unusual for any team to get distracted and lose momentum. The key is to inspire the team with the shared purpose to keep them engaged. Einstein called for perseverance; "If there is a single trait which could make you a true leader...I would have to call it 'Stick-to-it-ive-ness'—the ability to finish each job begun."

Bezos talks often about creating a 'culture of metrics." IFP (2017) captured this:

> In a world where defining workplace culture is crucial for many businesses, Bezos bucks the trend. Instead of employee happiness coming first, data does. He has described his company culture as "friendly, but intense" but "if push came to shove, it would be intense."
>
> What does the data say? This is the key influencer behind all the decisions made at Amazon. Whether it's a new website layout or the launch of a new product, if the data doesn't back it up then it will be swiftly changed.

Toyoda focused on constantly improving, never accepting the status quo:

> Now famous, the concept of *kaizen* derived from Toyoda's core values and has been a mandate for his successors to constantly improve performance. At the root of *kaizen* is the idea

> that nothing is perfect and everything can be improved. This is critical to the company, as every leader is taught to remember that the process is never perfect and that the company has never achieved the perfect "lean solution" (Liker & Convis, 2012).

Tye (2015) also commented on the need for continuous improvement with his Lesson 10 – Aspiration from Nightingale:

> She never rested on her laurels, but rather continuously raised the bar. After proving that a more professional approach to nursing care would improve clinical outcomes, she helped found the first visiting nurses association, chartered the first modern school of professional nursing, and through her writing, helped establish professional standards for hospital management.

Chris (2015) brought this forward from Nooyi:

> Unlike some CEOs and tycoons who are so held up with meetings, business travels, acquisitions, and mergers, Nooyi takes being a CEO a notch higher. Of course, she was the one behind the acquisitions and associations with ancillary businesses. She runs the company not only by looking at the big picture, but she is also into details. Nooyi goes to stores and checks how their products are doing, from how they are displayed in shelves to the print quality of the logos. If she sees not enough products are catered to a particular market in a location or demographic, she takes note of this and does something about it.

Gates said leaders need to maintain steely focus. Gates prioritized well and kept his team riveted on producing results. He focused on the one thing that he had mastery over—software. All throughout his professional life, he stuck with it and worked hard to dominate over it. For him, clarity of thought and proper execution take precedence over everything else.

Severson (n.d.) captured related lessons shaped by Welch:

> Leaders probe and push with a curiosity that borders on skepticism, making sure their questions are answered with action.
>
> To get bigger and better solutions, Welch says leaders probe proposals and presentations by asking questions and stirring up a healthy debate.

He writes:

> "When you're a leader, your job is to have all the questions. You have to be incredibly comfortable looking like the dumbest person in the room. Every conversation you have about a decision, a proposal, or a piece of market information has to be filled with you saying, 'What if?' and 'Why not?' and 'How come?'"
>
> Challenging your employees is an art, not a science. Each individual requires a unique approach. It's your job as a leader to get their best without diminishing their productivity.

Kofman (2018) identifies "transcendent leaders" who keep employees focused on a single overarching question: "Why are we here?" "The gravitational pull is always going to be toward each person's individual role," Kofman says. «The job of the leader is to defy gravity.»

Desko (2019) identifies "flashlight leadership" and "laser leadership." He notes:

> Even though a flashlight and a laser both use light, they differ in concentration and intensity. Leaders who want to have the most positive difference and make the greatest impact will strive towards being a laser rather than a flashlight. There is a significant link between leaders who focus their attention on what is most important for the organization and the organization being highly effective.

Goleman (2013) helps sum up this theme:

> A primary task of leadership is to direct attention. To do so, leaders must learn to focus their own attention. Grouping these modes of attention into three broad buckets—focusing on *yourself,* focusing on *others,* and focusing on *the wider world*—sheds new light on the practice of many essential leadership skills. Focusing inward and focusing constructively on others helps leaders cultivate the primary elements of emotional intelligence. A fuller understanding of how they focus on the wider world can improve their ability to devise strategy, innovate, and manage organizations.
>
> Every leader needs to cultivate this triad of awareness, in abundance and in the proper balance, because a failure to focus inward leaves you rudderless, a failure to focus on others renders you clueless, and a failure to focus outward may leave you blindsided.

Heemstra (2018) notes:

> There are very few things more important to a leader than focus. What do you actually spend your time doing? Unfortunately for most leaders, the answer is probably that you spend most of your time oiling the squeakiest wheel. It can't be that way. Your skills and abilities need to be applied where you can have the most impact. Too many leaders spend most of their careers doing things they're not very good at because they get pulled into it and can't get out. You can't let that happen.

To become a great leader, you need to be focused on achieving your vision, living your core values and accomplishing your goals. To be able to accomplish these ambitions and dreams, you need to have a laser focus on how you spend your time. If the task adds value to accomplishing your vision, living your core values or accomplishing your goals, that's exactly where you want to spend your time.

Laozi, the great Chinese philosopher was right. *To obtain wisdom, subtract things every day* (Stark, 2014).

These ten themes emerged from the insights of our 40 selected leaders, they are not meant to be THE list or even exhaustive. They are the ones most exemplified by our leaders or offered by them as specific leadership attributes. Deploying these themes in authentic and contextually appropriate ways likely will enhance your leadership brand and make you an even more effective leader.

References

100 Leaders in World History, n.d. (2018). Thomas Alva Edison. Retrieved January 18, 2018 from: https://100leaders.org/thomas-alva-edison

AIB (2015). Featured Business Leader: James Dyson. Retrieved June 8, 2018 from: https://www.aib.edu.au/blog/business-leaders/featured-business-leader-james-dyson/

Albury, S. (2013). Grace Hopper – the Lazy Programmer Who Changed the World. Retrieved August 14, 2018 from: https://blogs.it.ox.ac.uk/adalovelace/2013/10/11/grace-hopper-the-lazy-programmer-who-changed-the-world/

AllBusiness (2018). 4 Great Lessons In Entrepreneurship Everyone Can Learn From Spanx Founder Sara Blakely. Retrieved March 20, 2019 from: https://www.forbes.com/sites/allbusiness/2018/08/26/entrepreneurship-lessons-spanx-founder-sara-blakely/#7e8a4c7b69c2

Ambrose, J. (2015). The Vince Lombardi leadership secret every employee should start using. Retrieved September 26, 2018 from http://fortune.com/2015/10/11/vince-lombardi-leadership-secret-build-trust/

Anders, G. (2012). Jeff Bezo's Top 10 Leadership Lessons. Retrieved May 24, 2019 from: https://www.forbes.com/sites/georgeanders/2012/04/04/bezos-tips/#6b3a13672fce

Anderson K. (2015). Toyota Leadership Lessons. Retrieved February 11, 2018 from: https://kbjanderson.com/toyota-leadership-lessons-part-5-if-you-believe-you-are-perfect-you-wont-find-the-answer/

Antonio, C. (n.d.). 25 Malcolm Gladwell quotes on leadership, success, and 10,000 hours. Retrieved August 3, 2018 from: https://everydaypowerblog.com/malcolm-gladwell-quotes/

Athie, A. (2001). Alfred Athie, 73-year-old Construction Worker and César's bodyguard. Interviewed in Spanish (English translation available), August 2001 by Ruben Zepeda. California Department of Education César E. Chávez Website.

Axtell, C, Wall, T., Stride, C. & Pepper, C. (2002). Familiarity breeds content: The impact of exposure to change on employee openness and well being. *The Journal of Occupational & Organizational Psychology,* 217-231.

Baldoni, J. (2016). John Glenn: 'A Natural Public Servant.' Retrieved July21, 2018 from https://www.forbes.com/sites/johnbaldoni/2016/12/08/john-glenn-a-natural-public-servant/#78d592f37d14

Bariso, J. (2017). In just 3 words, Amazon's Jeff Bezos taught a brilliant lesson in leadership. Retrieved 12/27/2017 from: https://www.inc.com/justin-bariso/it-took-jeff-bezos-only-three-words-to-drop-the-best-advice-youll-hear-today.html

Barker, E. (2014). Lessons from Lincoln: 5 Leadership Tips History and Science Agree on. Retrieved January 29, 2018 from: http://time.com/37025/lessons-from-lincoln-5-leadership-tips-history-and-science-agree-on/

Barsh, J., Capozzi, M. & Davidson, J. (2008). Leadership and innovation (McKinsey Research). Retrieved August8, 2019 from https://www.mckinsey.com/business-functions/strategy-and-corporate-finance/our-insights/leadership-and-innovation

Bartleby.com (n.d.) Essay on Leadership Skills of Dr. Martin Luther King, Jr. Retrieved 12/27/2017 from: https://www.bartleby.com/essay/Leadership-Skills-of-Dr-Martin-Luther-King-F3LHUSYVJ

Bechard, R. & Pritchard, W. (1992). Changing the essence. San Francisco: Jossey-Bass.

Beinhocker, E. (1999). Robust adaptive strategies, *Sloan Management Review, 40*(3), 95-107.

Bezos, J. (n.d.) Innovation insights from Jeff Bezos and Amazon. Retrieved August 9, 2019 from https://www.destination-innovation.com/innovation-insights-from-jeff-bezos-and-amazon/

Birdsong, J. (n.d.). 6 Lessons for Leaders From Jack Ma, Founder of Alibaba. Retrieved August 2, 2018 from: https://wideangle.com/6-lessons-for-leaders-from-jack-ma/

Bistrisky,E.(2019)Empowerpeopleintheirroles.RetrievedAugust9,2019 from https://www.effectiveconsulting.ca/empower-people-in-their-roles/

Bose, R. & Faust III, L. (2011). Mother Teresa, CEO. San Francisco: Berrett-Koehler Publishers, Inc.

Braden, T. (2016). What Can John Glenn Teach Us about Serving Leadership? Retrieved July 22, 2018 from: https://www.trippbraden.com/2016/12/13/can-john-glenn-teach-us-leadership/

Bradt, G. (2014). The Virgin Way - Insights Into Richard Branson's Leadership. Retrieved July 21, 2018 from: https://www.forbes.com/sites/georgebradt/2014/08/27/the-virgin-way-insights-into-richard-bransons-brave-leadership/#46b59d7655b5

Branson, R. (n.d.). Understanding the Richard Branson approach to leadership. Retrieved July 21, 2018 from: https://www.virgin.com/entrepreneur/understanding-richard-branson-approach-leadership

Brody (2018). Spanx Founder Sara Blakely Has 99 Pages of Business Ideas. Retrieved March 20, 2019 from: https://www.entrepreneur.com/article/322936

Briody (2018). Sara Blakely: Start Small, Think Big, Scale Fast. Retrieved March 20, 2019 from: https://www.gsb.stanford.edu/insights/sara-blakely-start-small-think-big-scale-fast

Brox, J. (2012). Words to Lead By: Thomas Edison. Retrieved February 12, 2018 from: http://www.refreshleadership.com/index.php/2012/12/words-lead-thomas-edison/

Bryce, S. (2005). Jack Welch and the 4 E's of Leadership. Retrieved August 4, 2018 from: http://www.refresher.com/jack-welch-and-the-4-es-of-leadership/

C., Vicki (2018). Leadership and Empathy – How to be an Effective Empathetic Leader. Retrieved August 22, 2019 from: https://leadershiphooligans.com/leadership-and-empathy/

Caldicott, S. (2013). Midnight Lunch. Hoboken, NJ: John Wiley and Sons.

Caldwell, S. (2017). A lesson in innovation from James Dyson the inventor. Retrieved June 8, 2018 from: http://businessadvice.co.uk/from-the-top/a-lesson-in-innovation-from-james-dyson-the-inventor/

Cassidy, S. (2016). 6 Reasons Leaders Must Develop Patience. Retrieved August 21, 2019 from: https://blog.bridgebetween.com/6-reasons-leaders-must-develop-patience/

Center for Servant Leadership (n.d.). What is Servant Leadership. Retrieved August 19, 2019 from: https://www.greenleaf.org/what-is-servant-leadership/

Center for Creative Leadership (2014). Innovation leadership: How to use innovation to lead effectively, work collaboratively, and drive results. Retrieved August 20, 2019 from: http://www.ccl.org/wp-content/uploads/2015/04/InnovationLeadership.pdf

Cesar Chávez Foundation (n.d.). Retrieved March 19, 2018 from: http://www.Chávezfoundation.org/_page.php?code=001001000000000&page_ttl=About+Cesar&kind=1

Champagne, J. (2016). The Grace Hopper Guide to Exceptional IT Leadership. Retrieved August 14, 2108 from: https://blog.capterra.com/the-grace-hopper-guide-to-exceptional-it-leadership/

Chan, J. (n.d.). Jack Ma: A leadership insight. Retrieved August 2, 2018 from: https://johnsonchan90.wordpress.com/jack-ma-a-leadership-insight/

Chief Executive Magazine (2012). 5 Lessons from Fedex CEO Fred Smith. Retrieved July 24, 2018 from: https://chiefexecutive.net/5-lessons-from-fedex-ceo-fred-smith__trashed/

Chris, J. (2015). 7 Bill Gates Leadership Style Lessons. Retrieved August 3, 2018 from: http://www.josephchris.com/7-bill-gates-leadership-style-lessons

Chris, J. (2015). 11 Indra Nooyi Leadership Style Rules. Retrieved August 4, 2018 from: http://www.josephchris.com/11-indra-nooyi-leadership-style-rules

Chernoff, R. (2005). Alexander Hamilton. New York: Penguin Books.

Citterman, T. (2016). Insights From Elie Wiesel: How Conviction Fuels The Best Leaders. Retrieved August 2, 2018 from: https://www.forbes.com/sites/forbescoachescouncil/2016/07/28/insights-from-elie-wiesel-how-conviction-fuels-the-best-leaders/#59b3b9e8643e

Clark, K. (2016). John Glenn Gave Me the Best Career Advice I Ever Got. Retrieved July 21, 2018 from: http://time.com/money/4596463/john-glenn-death-life-coach/

Clarke, S. (2015). The Leadership of Indira Gandhi. Retrieved August 8, 2018from:https://leaderonomics.com/life-inspired/leadership-indira-gandhi

Cocchi, R. (n.d.). Don't Be A Yertle! 5 Leadership Lessons From Dr. Seuss. Retrieved on February 19, 2018 from: https://www.resourcefulmanager.com/leadership-lessons-dr-seuss/

Colvin, G. (2016). Warren Buffett's leadership lessons. Retrieved July 23, 2018 from: http://fortune.com/2016/02/29/warren-buffett-leadership-lessons/

Coutu, D. (2009). Leadership Lessons from Abraham Lincoln. Harvard Business Review. April 2009 Issue.

Crowly. M. (n.d.). The leadership genius of Abraham Lincoln. Retrieved 1/4/18 from: https://www.fastcompany.com/3002803/leadership-genius-abraham-lincoln

Desko, J. (2019). Focus and Finish. Retrieved July 20, 2019 from https://www.centerconsulting.org/article/focus-and-finish-laser-leadership

Dhliwayo, M. (2018). 7 Reasons Why Nelson Mandela Was a Great Leader. Retrieved July 20, 21-8 from: http://africanleadership.co.uk/7-reasons-nelson-mandela-great-leader/

Dickson, G. (n.d.) 20 Surprising employee retention statistics you need to know. Retrieved August 5, 2019 from https://blog.bonus.ly/10-surprising-employee-retention-statistics-you-need-to-know

DiGirolamo, J. (n.d.) The Visionary leadership of Fred Smith. Retrieved July 24,2018 from: http://blog.turbochargedleadership.com/?p=237

Driscoll,S.(2018).Eightlessonsforasuccessfulcareer(andlife)fromJackMa at Alibaba's Gateway '17. Retrieved August 2, 2018 from: https://

www.scmp.com/tech/leaders-founders/article/2100302/eight-lessons-successful-career-and-life-jack-ma-alibabas

Duckworth, T. (2018). Duckworth Highlights Risk of War with North Korea, Calls on Congress to Reclaim Constitutional War Power Responsibilities. Retrieved June 24, 2018 from: https://www.duckworth.senate.gov/news/press-releases/duckworth-highlights-risk-of-war-with-north-korea-calls-on-congress-to-reclaim-constitutional-war-power-responsibilities

Duke, W. (n.d.). Is Leadership Complicated or Complex? What would Admiral Hopper think? Retrieved August 14, 2018 from: https://richtopia.com/women-leaders/leadership-grace-murray-hopper

Dumaine, B. (2012). FedEx CEO Fred Smith on…everything. Retrieved July 24, 2018 from: http://fortune.com/2012/05/11/fedex-ceo-fred-smith-on-everything/

Dyson, J. (2018). Organizational thinking: Why Dyson does it differently Retrieved June 8, 2018 from: https://www.theglobeandmail.com/report-on-business/careers/leadership-lab/organizational-thinking-why-dyson-does-it-differently/article26014150/

Edmonds, S. (2019). How to Beat Scrutiny During a Culture Change. Retrieved August 30, 2019 from: http://www.greatleadershipbydan.com/2019/08/how-to-beat-scrutiny-during-culture.html

Eikenberry, K. (n.d.). What Leading by Example Really Means. Retrieved August 24, 2019 from: https://blog.kevineikenberry.com/leadership-supervisory-skills/what-leading-by-example-really-means/

Eikenberry, K. (2014). Maya Angelou's Leadership Advice. Retrieved May 20, 2018 from: http://blog.kevineikenberry.com/

leadership-supervisory-skills/maya-angelous-leadership-advice/

Elberse, A. (2013). Ferguson's Formula. Retrieved August 17, 2018 from: https://hbr.org/2013/10/fergusons-formula

Elie Wiesel Foundation (n.d.). An Ethical Compass. Retrieved from: http://eliewieselfoundation.org/prize-ethics/ethical-compass-book/

Expedite (2019). How Important is Creativity as a Leadership Skill. Retrieved August 21, 2019 from: https://expedite-consulting.com/how-important-is-creativity-as-a-leadership-skill/

Family Business (2018). Family business lessons from Katharine Graham. Retrieved July 18, 2018 from: https://www.familybusinessmagazine.com/family-business-lessons-katharine-graham

Forsythe, G., Kuhla, K. & Rice, D. Understanding the challenges of a VUCA environment. Chief Executive. Retrieved June 22, 2019 from https://chiefexecutive.net/understanding-vuca-environment/

Fortune (2014). IBM CEO Ginny Rometty on leadership, challenges and reinvention. Retrieved July 20, 2018 from: http://fortune.com/2014/09/18/ibm-ceo-ginni-rometty-on-leadership-challenges-and-reinvention/

Freiberg, K. & Frieberg, J. (2018). Madiba Leadership: 5 Lessons Nelson Mandela Taught The World About Change. Retrieved July 20, 2018 from: https://www.forbes.com/sites/kevinandjackiefreiberg/2018/07/19/madiba-leadership-5-lessons-nelson-mandela-taught-the-world-about-change/#49a6a42241ba

Gates, B. (2016) Accelerating innovation with leadership. Retrieved August 9, 2019 from https://www.gatesnotes.com/About-Bill-Gates /Accelerating-Innovation

Gleeson, B. (n.d.). Why Complacency Kills Organizational Change Efforts. Retrieved August 29, 2019 from: https://www.inc.com/

brent-gleeson/why-complacency-kills-organizational-change-efforts.html

Goleman, D. (2013). The Focused Leader. Retrieved August 27, 2019 from: https://hbr.org/2013/12/the-focused-leader

Goforth, M. (2016). John Glenn embodied heroic leadership that's lacking today. Retrieved July 21, 2018 from: https://www.tcpalm.com/story/opinion/contributors/2016/12/13/guest-column-john-glenn-embodied-heroic-leadership-s-lacking-today/95370714/

Gordon, J. (2017). How Great Leaders Create and Share a Positive Vision. Retrieved August 23, 2019 from: https://medium.com/the-mission/how-great-leaders-create-and-share-a-positive-vision-322ce75ba79c

Gottlieb, M. (2004). Dyson: Conventional Wisdom Be Damned Retrieved June 8, 2018 from: http://www.industryweek.com/companies-amp-executives/conventional-wisdom-be-damnedGregersen, H. (2015). The one skill that made Amazon's CEO wildly successful. Retrieved 12/27/2017 from: http://fortune.com/2015/09/17/amazon-founder-ceo-jeff-bezos-skills/

Gourguechon, P. (2107). Empathy is an Essential Leadership Skill. Retrieved August 22, 2019 from: https://www.forbes.com/sites/prudygourguechon/2017/12/26/empathy-is-an-essential-leadership-skill-and-theres-nothing-soft-about-it/#786bf8a2b9da

Green, H. (2011). Leadership then and now. Forbes. Retrieved March 24, 2019 from: https://www.forbes.com/sites/work-in-progress/2011/08/30/leadership-then-and-now/#16f9cc46911f

Graham-Leviss, K. (2016). The 5 Skills that Innovative Leaders have in Common. Retrieved August 20, 2019 from: https://hbr.org/2016/12/the-5-skills-that-innovative-leaders-have-in-common

Gruwez, E. (2017). VUCA world – a quick summary. Retrieved June 20, 2019 from https://www.tothepointatwork.com/article/vuca-world/

Gupta, P. (2016). Remembering Indira Gandhi: The Leadership and the Pitfalls. Retrieved August 8, 2018 from: https://www.shethepeople.tv/news/remembering-indira-gandhi-the-leadership-and-the-pitfalls

Hamel, G. (1998). The challenge today: Changing the rules of the game. *Business Strategy Review, 9*(2), 19-27.

Harvard Business School (1998). Katharine Graham Offers Advice on Leadership. Retrieved 7/18/2018 from: https://www.alumni.hbs.edu/stories/Pages/story-bulletin.aspx?num=5522

Harvard Law School (2018). CEO tenure rates. Retrieved March 24, 2019 from https://corpgov.law.harvard.edu/2018/02/12/ceo-tenure-rates/Hedayati, F. (2014). Leadership Qualities of Indre Nooyi. Retrieved August 4, 2018 from: http://www.centerforworklife.com/leadership-qualities-indra-nooyi/

Hedayati, F. (2014). Leadership Qualities of Winston Churchill. Retrieved August 4, 2018 from: http://www.centerforworklife.com/3-leadership-qualities-winston-churchill/

Heemstra, M. (2018). Leaders and Focus. Retrieved August 29, 2019 from: https://cainellsworth.com/2018/11/12/leaders-focus/

Hino, S. (2006). Inside the Mind of Toyota: Management Principles for Enduring Growth. New York: Productivity Press.

Huang, L., Krasikova, D. V., & Liu, D. (2016). I can do it, so can you: The role of leader creative self-efficacy in facilitating follower creativity.*Organizational Behavior and Human Decision Processes, 132,* 49-62.

Husain, H. (2018). Leadership Qualities of Ginni Rometty that has Made IBM a Force to Reckon with. Retrieved July 21, 2018 from: https://blog.taskque.com/ibm-force-reckon/

Insights for Professionals (IFP) (2017). Jeff Bezos' Unconventional Steps to becoming a great leaders. Retrieved 12/27/2017 from: https://www.insightsforprofessionals.com/blog/jeff-bezos-unconventional-steps-to-becoming-a-great-leader

Jackson, R. (2014). Dr. Condoleezza Rice Shares Thoughts on Leadership, Norwich University. Retrieved August 14, 2018 from: https://online.norwich.edu/about-us/news-events/news/dr-condoleezza-rice-shares-personal-thoughts-leadership-norwich-university

Jacksonville University (n.d.). Leadership profile: IBM CEO Ginni Rometty. Retrieved July 21, 2018 from: https://www.jacksonvilleu.com/blog/business/leadership-profile-ibm-ceo-ginni-rometty/

Jacobson, D. (n.d.) One person at a time: The leadership genius of Mother Teresa.

Retrieved July 22, 2018 from: http://govleaders.org/one-person-at-a-time.htm

James, J. (2018). Leadership Lessons from Walt Disney – How to Inspire You Team. Retrieved August 19, 2018 from: https://www.disneyinstitute.com/blog/leadership-lessons-from-walt-disney--how-to/

Jarvie, J. (2018). Tammy Duckworth, senator and war hero, takes on President Trump, aka 'Cadet Bone Spurs.' Los Angeles Times. Retrieved June 24, 2018 from: http://www.latimes.com/nation/la-na-tammy-duckworth-20180207-story.html

Jobs, S. (n.d.). Steve Jobs Quotes. Retrieved August 6, 2019 from: https://www.goodreads.com/quotes/8586131-it-doesn-t-make-sense-to-hire-smart-people-and-then

John, J. (2013). Leadership Lessons from Jeff Bezos. Retrieved 12/27/2017 from: https://onlinemba.unc.edu/blog/leadership-lessons-from-jeff-bezos/

Kearns Goodwin, D. (2005). Team of rivals: The political genius of Abraham Lincoln. New York: Simon & Shuster Paperbacks.

Keller, S. & Meaney, M. (2017). Attracting and retaining the right talent. Retrieved August 6. 2019 from: https://www.mckinsey.com/business-functions/organization/our-insights/attracting-and-retaining-the-right-talent

Kelly, J. (2014). Vince Lombardi and Path-Goal Theory. Retrieved September 26, 2018 from https://sites.psu.edu/leadership/2014/11/09/vince-lombardi-and-path-goal-theory/

Khan, M. (2017). Powerful Women Leaders: Senator Tammy Duckworth. Retrieved July 20, 2018 from: https://www.collegemagazine.com/powerful-women-leaders-senator-tammy-duckworth/

Kiplinger (2017). Master the 7 Leadership Skills of Bill Gates. Retrieved August 3, 2018 from: https://store.kiplinger.com/gates.html

Klagsbrun, F. (2017). 4 Crucial Things Politicians Today Can Learn from Golda Meir. Retrieved May 21, 2018 from: http://www.signature-reads.com/2017/10/4-things-politicians-today-can-learn-from-golda-meir/

Kofman, F. (2108). The Meaning Revolution: The power of transcendent leadership. New York: Currency.

Kotler, P. & Casilone, J. (2009). Chaotics: The business of managing and marketing in the age of turbulence. New York: Amacon.

Krippendorff, K. (2012). Thomas Edison's Keys to Managing Team Collaboration. Retrieved January 18, 2018 from: https://www.fastcompany.com/3004139/thomas-edisons-keys-managing-team-collaboration

Lalonde, J. (2016). Leadership Lessons From The Life Of Astronaut John Glenn. Retrieved July 20, 2018 from http://www.jmlalonde.com/leadership-lessons-life-astronaut-john-glenn/

Landking (2010). Leadership — Chesty Puller Style. Retrieved July 19, 2018 from: https://iandking.wordpress.com/2010/07/24/leadership-chesty-puller-style/

Leadership Expert (n.d.). Great Leaders – Condoleezza Rice. Retrieved August 13, 2018 from: https://leadership.expert/leadership/great-leaders-condoleezza-rice/

LeaderhipGeeks (2016). Alex Ferguson Leadership Profile. Retrieved August 17, 2018 from: http://www.leadershipgeeks.com/alex-ferguson-leadership/

LeadershipGeeks (2016). Vince Lombardi Leadership Profile. Retrieved September 26, 2018 from: http://www.leadershipgeeks.com/vince-lombardi-leadership/

Leidner, G. (2017). The Leadership Secrets of Hamilton: 7 Steps to Revolutionary Leadership from Alexander Hamilton and the Founding Fathers. Sourcebooks, Naperville, IL.

Liker, J. & Convis, C. (2012). The Toyota Way to Lean Leaderhip. New York: McGraw-Hill.

Llopis, G. (2014) The Dangers of Complacent Leadership. Retrieved August 26, 2019 from: https://www.forbes.com/sites/glennllopis/2014/08/05/the-dangers-of-complacent-leadership/#1bf566643de5

Lohrenz, C.(n.d.). The FedEd School of Leadership. Retrieved July 24, 2018 from: https://careylohrenz.com/the-fedex-school-of-leadership/

Lombardi, D. (1996). Thriving in an age of change: Practical strategies for health care leaders. Chicago: American College of Healthcare Executives.

Lombardi, D. (1997). Reorganization and Renewal: Strategies for healthcare leaders. Chicago: American College of Healthcare Executives.

Lombardi Jr., V. (2001). What It Takes to be #1: Vince Lombardi on Leadership. New York: McGraw Hill

Lynch, P. (n.d.) Eight Lessons of leadership from Dr. Martin Luther King, Jr. Retrieved 12/27/2017 from https://oiglobalpartners.com/eight-lessons-of-leadership-from-martin-luther-king-jr/

Lynch, P. (2016). 13 Executive Coaching Lessons From Colin Powell.

Retrieved May 19, 2018 from: https://www.frontiergroupusa.com/blog/13-executive-coaching-insights-from-colin-powell/

McKay, B. & Mckay, K. (2019) How and why to become a lifelong learner. Retrieved June 21, 2019 from https://www.artofmanliness.com/articles/how-and-why-to-become-a-lifelong-learner/

Marcus, L. (2014). 10 Leadership Nuggets from Maya Angelou. Retrieved May 20, 2018 from: https://www.linkedin.com/pulse/20140528163854-60894986-10-leadership-nuggets-from-maya-angelou/

Masnick, M. (2011). Jeff Bezos on Innovation: Stubborn on vision; Flexible on Details. Retrieved May 25, 2019 from https:www.techdirt.com/articles/20110608/23514814631

McKinney, M. (2008). Golda Meir: A Study in Leadership. Retrieved May 21, 2018 from: https://www.leadershipnow.com/leading-blog/2008/05/golda_meir_a_study_in_leadersh.html

McLaughlin, C. (2001). Visionary Leadership. Retrieved August 28, 2019 from: http://www.visionarylead.org/visionary-leader-ship-article.html

Meacham, J. (2013). Meacham describes 'art of power' through leadership of America's presidents of the past. Retrieved May 17, 2018 from: http://www.csgmidwest.org/policyresearch/0813jonmeacham.aspx

Mikkelsen, K. & Jarche, H. (2015). The Best leaders are constant learners. Retrieved March 24, 2019 from: https://hbr.org/2015/10/the-best-leaders-are-constant-learners

Military Leaders in Transition (n.d.). Insights and Life Lessons from General Colin Powell. Retrieved May 19, 2018 from: http://seniormilitaryintransition.com/insights-and-life-lessons-from-general-colin-powell/

Mohamed, N. (2016). 5 Successful Traits that Business Leader can take from Sir Alex Ferguson. Retrieved August 17, 2018 from: https://www.gbnews.ch/5-successful-traits-that-business-leaders-can-take-from-sir-alex-ferguson/

Monk, K. (2017). 3 Important Leadership Lessons You Can Learn from Warren Buffett. Retrieved July 24, 2018 from: https://vintagevalueinvesting.com/3-important-leadership-lessons-can-learn-warren-buffett/

Montag, A. (2016). Warren Buffett and Mark Cuban agree on this one habit is key to success. Retrieved August 20, 2019 from: https://www.cnbc.com/2017/11/15/warren-buffett-and-mark-cuban-agree-reading-is-key-to-success.html

Moore, J. (2018). Leadership Lessons from Katharine Graham Retrieved 7-18-2018 from: http://www.talkativeman.com/katharine-graham-leadership/

Moran, W. D. (2002). Leading with Patience – The Will to Wait. Retrieved August 22, 2019 from: http://www.ifyouwilllead.com/leading-with-patience-the-will-to-wait

Murphy, C. (2016). Leadership Lessons from Colin Powell's "It Worked for Me." Retrieved May 19, 2018 from: http://cronkitehhh.jmc.asu.edu/blog/2016/11/leadership-lessons-colin-powells-worked/

Murphy, M. (2018). The Leadership Model Used by Steve Jobs, Henry Ford and Thomas Edison. Retrieved February 12, 2018 from: https://www.forbes.com/sites/markmurphy/2018/01/14/the-leadership-model-used-by-steve-jobs-henry-ford-and-thomas-edison/#508e534623f6

Navy Times Archives (n.d.) TAG Archives: Grace Hopper. Retrieved August 14, 2018 from: http://navylive.dodlive.mil/tag/grace-hopper/

NEA (n.d.) 11 Habits of Highly Effective Leaders. Retrieved July 19, 2018 from: https://www.nea.com/portfolio/resources/article/11-habits-of-highly-effective-leaders-a-u.s.-marine-corps-officer-shares-th

Newman, D.(2012). Leadership, Insanity And Change: Was Einstein Wrong? Retrieved on February 15, 2018 from: http://www.digitalistmag.com/innovation/2012/12/04/leadership-insanity-and-change-was-einstein-wrong-022555

Northhouse, P.G. (2016). *Leadership Theory and Practice Seventh Edition.* Thousand Oaks, CA: Sage Publications, Inc.

Ortiz, M. (n.d.) Cesar E. Chávez: The Man and the Servant Leader. Retrieved March 5, 2018 from: http://Chávez.cde.ca.gov/ModelCurriculum/Teachers/Lessons/Resources/Documents/The_Man_and_the_Servant-Leader_Essay.pdf

Pahl, J. (2015): Five Leadership Qualities We Learned from Walt Disney/ Retrieved August 19, 2018 from: https://blog.cetrain.isu.edu/blog/5-leadership-qualities-we-learned-from-walt-disney

PeopleTek (2017). MLK- A courageous leader. Retrieved 12/27/2017 from: https://www.peopletekcoaching.com/mlk-courageous-leader/

Phillips, D. (1992). Lincoln on Leadership: Executive Strategies for Tough Times. Illinois: DTP/Companion Books.

Popova, M. (n.d.). Elie Wiesel on the Loneliness of Leadership, How Our Questions Unite Us, and How Our Answers Divide Us. Retrieved August 2, 2018 from: https://www.brainpickings.org/2017/05/29/elie-wiesel-the-loneliness-of-moses/

Power, R. (2017). What Bill Gates and Steve Ballmer can teach you about running a better business. Retrieved August 3, 2018 from: https://www.cnbc.com/2017/08/24/what-you-can-learn-from-bill-gates-and-steve-ballmer.html

Predicative Success (n.d.) Top 10 In Leadership from Elon Musk. Retrieved June 10, 2018 from: https://www.predictivesuccess.com/blog/elon-musk-top-10-leadership-lessons/

Provizer (n.d.). Golda Meir, Duta and the Call to Power. Retrieved May 21, 2018 from: https://msudenver.edu/golda/goldameir/intheshadowofwashington/

Rajamani, R. (2009). Indira Gandhi: Fearlessness in the National Interest. Retrieved August 8, 2018 from: http://www.rediff.com/news/special/rrajamani-remembers-indira-gandhi-on-her-25th-death-anniversary/20091030.htm

Ramirez, L., Diaz, N., Anderson, J. & Covarrubias, A. (n.d.) Cesar E. Chávez. Retrieved on March 19, 2018 from https://cesardiazandgroup.weebly.com/leadership-qualities-and-legacy.html

Recruiting Daily Advisor (2019). What Efforts Are You Taking to Win the War for Talent? Retrieved July 20, 2019 from: https://recruitingdailyadvisor.blr.com/2019/03/what-efforts-are-you-taking-to-win-the-war-for-talent/

Redrup, Y. (2015). Malcolm Gladwell's three lessons in disruption. Retrieved August 3, 2018 from: https://www.afr.com/leadership/malcolm-gladwells-three-lessons-in-disruption-20150923-gjsyx4

Rick, T. (2015). Killed by a Corporate Culture of Complacency. Retrieved August 20, 2019 from: https://www.torbenrick.eu/blog/culture/killed-by-a-corporate-culture-of-complacency/

Rielly, M. (2017). Dr. Seuss on Leadership: 10 Lessons Plus 2. Retrieved February 19, 2018 from: https://www.linkedin.com/pulse/dr-seuss-leadership-10-lessons-plus-2-michael-rielly/

Ruggiero, V, (n.d.). Cesar Chávez. Retrieved on March 18, 2018 from: http://fa12phl301.providence.wikispaces.net/Cesar+Chávez

Russell, P. (2018) Reluctant leaders: Mother Teresa. Retrieved July 22, 2018 from: https://www.trainingjournal.com/articles/features/reluctant-leaders-mother-teresa

Schwantes (n.d.) Spanx Founder Sara Blakely Just Identified the No. 1 Reason Why People Don't Succeed (and It's Quite Brilliant). Retrieved March 20, 2019 from: https://www.inc.com/marcel-schwantes/spanx-founder-sara-blakely-just-identified-no-1-reason-why-people-dont-succeed-and-its-quite-brilliant.html

Schwantes (n.d.). Warren Buffett Says Look for this 1 Trait if You Want to Hire the Best People. Retrieved August, 29, 2019 from: https://www.inc.com/marcel-schwantes/warren-buffett-says-look-for-this-1-trait-if-you-want-to-hire-best-people.html?cid=sf01003

Schawbel, D. (2018). Condoleezza Rice shares 5 great ways to get ahead in your career. Retrieved August 14, 2018 from: https://www.cnbc.com/2018/05/08/condoleezza-rice-shares-5-ways-to-get-ahead-in-your-career.html

Schepici, K. (211). Lincoln's Leadership. Retrieved 1/4/2018 from: http://blog.linkageinc.com/blog/lincoln%E2%80%99s-leadership/

Schick, W. (2015). Three Principles for Leadership Success. Marine Corps Gazette, 99(9). Retrieved July 18,2018 from: https://

www.mca-marines.org/gazette/2015/09/three-principles-leadership-success

Schoemaker (n.d.). The 3 Decisions That Made Mandela a Truly Great Leader. Retrieved July 20, 2018 from: https://www.inc.com/paul-schoemaker/what-made-nelson-mandela-such-a-great-leader.html

Schnall, M. (2014). Things Maya Told Me: My Favorite Insights and Quotes From My Interviews With Maya Angelou. Retrieved May 20, 2018 from: https://www.huffingtonpost.com/marianne-schnall/maya-angelou-legacy_b_5418585.html

Schnall, M. (2018). 5 Lessons I Learned From My Interviews With Maya Angelou. Retrieved May 20, 2018 from: https://www.forbes.com/sites/marianneschnall/2018/02/13/5-lessons-i-learned-from-my-interviews-with-maya-angelou/#32b4e6804ce3

Schogol, J. (2017). Is it time to give Chesty Puller the Medal of Honor? MarineTimes. Retrieved July 19, 2018 from: https://www.marinecorpstimes.com/news/pentagon-congress/2017/02/19/is-it-time-to-give-chesty-puller-the-medal-of-honor/

Schrage. M.(2016). Like it or Not, You are Always Leading by Example: Retrieved August 29, 2019 from: https://hbr.org/2016/10/like-it-or-not-you-are-always-leading-by-example

Severson, D. (2017). The 8 Rules of Leadership by Jack Welch. Retrieved August 6, 2018 from: https://www.inc.com/dana-severson/these-8-simple-rules-of-leadership-from-jack-welch-are-more-important-now-than-ever-before.html

Shmula.com (2010): Shoulders of Giants: Sakichi Toyoda. Retrieved on February 12, 2018 from: http://www.shmula.com/sakichi-toyoda/7796/

Seijts, G. (2013). Good leaders never stop learning. Retrieved August 21, 2019 from: https://iveybusinessjournal.com/publication/good-leaders-never-stop-learning/

Severson, D. (n.d.). The 8 Rules of Leadership by Jack Welch. Retrieved August 19, 2019 from: https://www.inc.com/dana-severson/these-8-simple-rules-of-leadership-from-jack-welch-are-more-important-now-than-ever-before.html

Sinek, S. (2014). Leaders Eat Last. Penguin: New York.

Slaughter, D. (2014). Leadership lessons from Maya Angelou. Retrieved May 20, 2018 from: http://blog.linkageinc.com/blog/leadership-lessons-from-maya-angelou/

Smith, R. (2016). 7 Leadership insights from Martin Luther King, Jr. Retrieved 12/27/2017 from https://www.cuinsight.com/7-leadership-lessons-from-dr-king.html.

Snyder, B. (2015). Five Lessons in Leadership from Manchester United's Former Manager. Retrieved August 17, 2018 from: https://www.gsb.stanford.edu/insights/five-lessons-leadership-manchester-uniteds-former-manager

Snyder, B. (2015). 7 Quotes that prove what kind of leader Indra Nooyi really is. Retrieved August 4, 2018 from: http://fortune.com/2015/06/07/indra-nooyi/

Snyder, B. (2017). 7 Insights from legendary investor Warren Buffet. Retrieved July 24, 2018 from: https://www.cnbc.com/2017/05/01/7-insights-from-legendary-investor-warren-buffett.html

Spain, S. (2017). Five takeaways from Condoleezza Rice at the KPMG Women's Leadership Summitt. Retrieved August 14, 2018 from: http://www.espn.com/espnw/voices/espnw-columnists/article/19762601/five-takeaways-condoleezza-rice-keynote-address-kpmg-women-leadership-summit

Spungin, D. (2017). 3 Leadership Lessons from Dr. Seuss. Retrieved on February 19, 2018 from: https://www.linkedin.com/pulse/3-leadership-lessons-from-dr-seuss-david-spungin-msod-acc/

Stanford Business School (2018). Stanford Daily. IBM CEO Rometty talks technology and leadership. Retrieved July 22, 2018 from: https://www.stanforddaily.com/2018/02/07/ibm-ceo-ginni-rometty-talks-technology-leadership/

Stanford Business School (2005). Colin Powell: "Never Show Fear or Anger." Retrieved May 19, 2018 from: https://www.gsb.stanford.edu/insights/colin-powell-never-show-fear-or-anger

Stark, P. (2014). Great Leaders Have a Laser Focus. Retrieved June 20, 2019 from: https://peterstark.com/great-leaders-laser-focus/

Strock, J. (2003). Theodore Roosevelt on Leadership: Executive Lessons from the Bully Pulpit. New York: Three Rivers Press.

Strock, J. (2017). 10 Theodore Roosevelt Leadership Lessons. Retrieved August 3, 2018 from: https://servetolead.org/10-theodore-roosevelt-leadership-lessons/

Strock, J. (2018). 10 Winston Churchill Leadership Lessons. Retrieved August 4, 2018 from: https://servetolead.org/10-winston-churchill-leadership-lessons/

Sullivan, E. (2017). 7 Remarkable Leadership Qualities of Walt Disney the Entrepreneur. Retrieved August 19, 2018 from: https://projectfreedomgrowth.com/walt-disney-entrepreneur/

Syrkin, M. (1969). Golda Meir: Israel's Leader. New York: G.P. Putnam's Sons, p. 11.

The Guardian. (n.d.). Obama hails Elie Wiesel as 'conscience of the world' amid leaders' tributes. Retrieved August 2, 2018 from: https://www.theguardian.com/us-news/2016/jul/03/elie-wiesel-tributes-obama-clinton-netanyahu

Thiran, R. (2017). Leadership Lessons: Analyzing the Enduring Legacy of President Thomas Jefferson. Retrieved May 17, 2018 from https://leaderonomics.com/leadership/leadership-lessons-studying-thomas-jefferson

Thiran, R. (2018). The Unusual Lessons I Learnt Studying Albert Einstein. Retrieved February 15, 2018 from: https://leaderonomics.com/leadership/lessons-albert-einstein

Thiran, R. (2017). Mother Teresa: Petite in size, but big in heart and deep in impact. Retrieved July 23, 2018 from: https://leaderonomics.com/leadership/mother-teresa-deep-impact

Thomas, S. (2018). In the Age of Social Media, CEOs are Under Intense Scrutiny. Retrieved August 28, 2019 from: https://www.dmagazine.com/publications/d-ceo/2018/november/in-the-age-of-social-media-ceos-are-under-intense-scrutiny/

Thompson, M. (n.d.). 4 Insights from Richard Branson about discovering what matters most. Retrieved July 20, 2018 from: https://www.inc.com/mark-thompson/4-simple-game-changing-insights-from-richard-branson-about-how-to-get-done-what-.html

Toolshero (n.d.). Sakichi Toyoda. Retrieved February 12, 2018 from: https://www.toolshero.com/toolsheroes/sakichi-toyoda/

Tye, J. (2015). 10 Leadership Lessons from Florence Nightingale Retrieved June 8, 2018 from: http://connectionculture.com/post/10-leadership- lessons-from-florence-nightingale

Tye, J. (2018). Lessons on Leadership Loyalty from Florence Nightingale Retrieved June 8, 2018 from https://www.linkedin.com/pulse/lessons-leadership-loyalty-from-florence-nightingale-joe-tye/

Umoh, R. (2017). Steve Jobs and Albert Einstein both attributed their extraordinary success to this personality trait. Retrieved February 19, 2018 from https://www.cnbc.com/2017/06/29/

steve-jobs-and-albert-einstein-both-attributed-their-extraordinary-success-to-this-personality-trait.html

Umoh, R. (2018). Why Jeff Bezos wants Amazon employees to wake up every morning terrified. Retrieved May 26, 2019 from https// www.cnbc.com/2018/08/28/why-jeff-bezos-wants-amazon-employees-to-wake-up-terrified.html

Voepel, S. (2003). The mobile company, An advanced organizational model for mobilizing knowledge innovation and value creation. IFPM: St. Gallen.

Warrell, M. (2015). Five leadership lessons from a week with Richard Branson. Retrieved July 21, 2018 from: https://margiewarrell.com/ five-leadership-lessons-from-a-week-with-richard-branson/

Washington Post (n.d.). On Leadership. Transcript: Tammy Duckworth on leadership. Retrieved June 24, 2018 from: http:// views.washingtonpost.com/leadership/panelists/2010/04/ transcript-tammy-duckworth.html

Welch, J. & Welch, S. (n.d.). The 4 Es: Traits that get you hired and promoted. Retrieved August 6, 20178 from: https://www.askmen.com/money/career_150/150b_career.html

Wikihow (n.d.) How to lead like Thomas Jefferson. Retrieved May 17, 2018 from https://www.wikihow.com/Lead-Like-Thomas-Jefferson

Winder, John A. (Spring 2005). Book review: Alexander Hamilton: The trials and tribulations of leadership. *The Leadership Journey,* 2-5

Wintrip, S. (2017). How to Become a Visionary Talent Acquisition Leader. Retrieved July 20, 2019 from: https://www.ere.net/ how-to-become-a-visionary-talent-acquisition-leader/

Wroblewski, M. (2019). Characteristics of Visionary Leadership. Retrieved August 26, 2019 from: https://yourbusiness.azcentral.com/characteristics-visionary-leadership-9056.html

Yaeger, D. (2015). Leadership For The Long Haul: A Lesson From Thomas Jefferson. Retrieved May 17, 2018 from: https://www.forbes.com/sites/donyaeger/2015/11/03/leadership-for-the-long-haul-a-lesson-from-thomas-jefferson/#476264b24e7e

Bibliography References

King:

http://www.thekingcenter.org/about-dr-king
https://www.nobelprize.org/prizes/peace/1964/king/biographical/

Bezos:

[1]https://www.bloomberg.com/news/articles/2018-07-16/happy-prime-day-jeff-amazon-ceo-s-net-worth-tops-150-billion
[2]https://www.scoopwhoop.com/things-jeff-bezos-could-do-with-150-billion/#.6jw3hltef
[3]https://www.cnbc.com/2018/09/04/amazon-founder-jeff-bezos-from-son-of-teen-mom-to-the-worlds-richest.html
[4]https://www.nytimes.com/2015/08/16/technology/inside-amazon-wrestling-big-ideas-in-a-bruising-workplace.html
[5]https://www.theatlantic.com/business/archive/2015/08/amazon-jeff-bezos-response-times/401456/
[6]https://motherboard.vice.com/en_us/article/9k77vd/you-are-jeff-bezos-twine-game

Lincoln:

[1]https://www.britannica.com/biography/Abraham-Lincoln/Leadership-in-war
[2]https://www.infoplease.com/homework-help/poetry-and-poets/edwin-markham-lincoln-man-people

Edison:

[1]https://www.armyupress.army.mil/Portals/7/combat-studies-institute/csi-books/gabel4.pdf

[2]http://theconversation.com/thomas-edison-visionary-genius-or-fraud-99229
[3]https://www.atlasobscura.com/places/edisons-last-breath-henry-ford-museum
https://www.britannica.com/biography/Thomas-Edison

Toyoda:

[1]https://en.wikipedia.org/wiki/5_Whys
[2]https://www.metmuseum.org/toah/ht/10/eaj.html
[3]https://www.toyota-industries.com/company/history/toyoda_sakichi/

Blakely

[1]https://www.inc.com/video/1-trait-turned-sara-blakely-into-a-self-made-billionaire.html
https://en.wikipedia.org/wiki/Sara_Blakely
https://www.forbes.com/sites/clareoconnor/2012/03/07/under-cover-billionaire-sara-blakely-joins-the-rich-list-thanks-to-spanx/#1769325dd736
https://en.wikipedia.org/wiki/Spanx
https://www.famous-entrepreneurs.com/sara-blakely
https://www.floridainvents.org/sara-blakely/
https://www.glamour.com/story/sara-blakely-spanx
https://www.forbes.com/sites/clareoconnor/2012/03/12/how-spanx-became-a-billion-dollar-business-without-advertising/#68237b914d64

Einstein

https://www.britannica.com/biography/Albert-Einstein
https://www.britannica.com/biography/Albert-Einstein
https://www.biography.com/people/albert-einstein-9285408
https://www.history.com/news/9-things-you-may-not-know-about-albert-einstein
https://www.biography.com/people/albert-einstein-9285408

Dr. Suess:

[1]https://library.ucsd.edu/dc/object/bb5222708w
[2]https://www.newyorker.com/magazine/1960/12/17/childrens-friend
[3]http://www.drseussart.com/biopublishing/
https://www.biography.com/people/dr-seuss-9479638
https://www.britannica.com/biography/Dr-Seuss

Cesar Chávez

https://en.wikipedia.org/wiki/Cesar_Chávez
https://www.biography.com/people/cesar-Chávez-9245781
https://www.britannica.com/biography/Cesar-Chávez
https://en.wikipedia.org/wiki/United_Farm_Workers
https://aflcio.org/about/history/labor-history-people/cesar-Chávez
https://eu.thecalifornian.com/story/news/2018/12/04/cesar-Chávezs-stay-old-monterey-county-jail-commemorated/2202361002/
https://en.wikipedia.org/wiki/Salad_Bowl_strike
https://www.thoughtco.com/three-sisters-american-farming-173034

Tammy Duckworth

https://en.wikipedia.org/wiki/Tammy_Duckworth
https://www.duckworth.senate.gov/about-tammy/biography
http://mentalfloss.com/article/90692/16-things-you-might-not-know-about-tammy-duckworth
https://www.military.com/veteran-jobs/career-advice/military-transition/famous-veterans-congresswoman-tammy-duckworth.html
https://www.britannica.com/biography/Tammy-Duckworth

Thomas Jefferson

https://www.smithsonianmag.com/smithsonian-institution/paradox-of-liberty-tells-the-other-side-of-jeffersons-monticello-83738466/
https://www.monticello.org/site/jefferson/thomas-jefferson-brief-biography
https://www.biography.com/people/thomas-jefferson-9353715

https://www.britannica.com/biography/Thomas-Jefferson

Colin Powell

https://www.encyclopedia.com/people/history/us-history-biographies/colin-luther-powell
https://study.com/academy/lesson/general-colin-powell-biography-accomplishments.html
https://en.wikipedia.org/wiki/Colin_Powell
https://www.biography.com/people/colin-powell-9445708
https://www.britannica.com/biography/Colin-Powell

Maya Angelou

https://www.biography.com/people/maya-angelou-9185388
https://www.britannica.com/biography/Maya-Angelou
https://en.wikipedia.org/wiki/Maya_Angelou
https://www.history.com/this-day-in-history/maya-angelou-is-born

Florence Nightingale

https://www.florence-nightingale.co.uk/resources/biography/?v=79cba1185463
https://www.history.com/topics/womens-history/florence-nightingale-1
https://www.biography.com/people/florence-nightingale-9423539

Golda Meir

https://www.notablebiographies.com/Ma-Mo/Meir-Golda.html
https://www.britannica.com/biography/Golda-Meir
https://en.wikipedia.org/wiki/Golda_Meir
https://www.biography.com/people/golda-meir-9404859
http://mentalfloss.com/article/538467/facts-about-golda-meir
https://www.historytoday.com/richard-cavendish/golda-meir-becomes-israeli-prime-minister
https://en.wikipedia.org/wiki/Six-Day_War

James Dyson

[1]https://www.telegraph.co.uk/business/2017/03/27/sir-james-dyson-remain-controls-dyson-reports-record-results/

https://www.theguardian.com/technology/2016/nov/04/james-dyson-addresses-engineering-skills-gap-with-university-launch

https://en.wikipedia.org/wiki/James_Dyson

https://www.britannica.com/biography/James-Dyson

https://www.inc.com/magazine/201203/burt-helm/how-i-did-it-james-dyson.html

https://www.dyson.com.au/community/about-james-dyson.aspx

https://www.cbsnews.com/pictures/10-awesome-inventions-from-james-dyson/

https://www.bloomberg.com/news/videos/2019-01-24/james-dyson-becomes-richest-brit-video

Lewis Puller

https://www.encyclopediavirginia.org/Puller_Lewis_Burwell_Chesty_1898-1970

https://valor.militarytimes.com/hero/5665

https://en.wikipedia.org/wiki/Chesty_Puller

http://www.christchurchmiddlesex.com/Chesty-Puller/

https://www.raabcollection.com/chesty-puller-autograph/chesty-puller-signed-marine-marine-chesty-puller-wonders-how-he-got-his

https://www.marinecorpstimes.com/news/your-marine-corps/2018/03/19/meet-chesty-xv-the-new-marine-corps-mascot/

https://www.findagrave.com/memorial/55813157/samuel-duncan-puller

Elie Wiesel

https://www.huffingtonpost.com/entry/elie-wiesel-dead_us_57781653e4b0a629c1aa51bb

https://www.pbs.org/newshour/world/elie-wiesel-holocaust-survivor-and-nobel-peace-prize-winner-dies-at-87

https://www.britannica.com/biography/Elie-Wiesel
https://www.nobelprize.org/prizes/peace/1986/wiesel/facts/
https://www.chipublib.org/elie-wiesel-biography/
https://www.history.com/this-day-in-history/elie-wiesel-holocaust-survivor-and-best-selling-author-is-born
https://www.theguardian.com/childrens-books-site/2014/aug/25/elie-wiesel-night-jewish-identity-amnesty-teen-takeover-2014
https://www.biography.com/people/elie-wiesel-9530714
http://eliewieselfoundation.org
https://en.wikipedia.org/wiki/Elie_Wiesel

Malcolm Gladwell

https://www.telegraph.co.uk/culture/6416229/Malcolm-Gladwell-interview.html
https://www.history.co.uk/this-day-in-history/03-september/tipping-point-author-malcolm-gladwell-born
https://www.britannica.com/biography/Malcolm-Gladwell
https://www.telegraph.co.uk/culture/books/authorinterviews/10335491/Malcolm-Gladwell-interview.html
https://www.theguardian.com/books/2008/nov/16/malcolm-gladwell-interview-outliers
http://content.time.com/time/specials/packages/article/0,28804,1972656_1972712_1973774,00.html
https://en.wikipedia.org/wiki/Malcolm_Gladwell

Churchill

https://www.britannica.com/biography/Winston-Churchill

Grace Hopper

https://president.yale.edu/biography-grace-murray-hopper
http://archive.computerhistory.org/resources/text/Oral_History/Hopper_Grace/102702026.05.01.pdf
http://www.cs.yale.edu/homes/tap/Files/hopper-story.html

https://www.public.navy.mil/surfor/ddg70/Pages/namesake.aspx#.WNmCa2jys2w

Alex Ferguson

https://www.britannica.com/biography/Alex-Ferguson
Ferguson, Alex. *Alex Ferguson: My Autobiography*. Hodder, 2014.
http://news.bbc.co.uk/sport2/hi/football/teams/m/man_utd/8134301.stm
https://www.bbc.com/sport/football/14493263

Walt Disney

Barrier, J. M. *The Animated Man: A Life of Walt Disney*. Berkeley, CA: Univ. of California Press, 2008.

Gabler, Neal. *Walt Disney: The Triumph of the American Imagination*. Alfred A. Knopf, 2008.

https://www.britannica.com/biography/Walt-Disney

About the Author & Contributors

Dr. Richard Dool

Dr. Richard Dool is currently the Managing Director of Leaderocity™, LLC, a management consultancy offering solutions for change management, strategic development, leadership communication and organizational renewal.

Dr. Dool is on the faculty at the School of Communication and Information at Rutgers University, where he is also the Director of the Masters in Communication and Media program.

He has a MA in Strategic Communication and Leadership, a MS in Management and a Doctorate in Management/Organizational Processes. Dr. Dool is an active researcher and presenter in these areas and has published on the concepts of Change Fatigue™ and Leaderocity™. He is the author of "Enervative Change: The Impact of Persistent Change Initiatives on Job Satisfaction and "How Generation Z Wants To Be Led."

He has a comprehensive and diverse executive level leadership background including leading an $800M division of AT&T, global executive leadership roles (GE), and serving 12 years as CEO of both public and private companies. Background includes rescuing a company from near bankruptcy, leading the acquisition or divestiture of 11 companies and effectively managing companies in the US, UK, China, Brazil, Germany, France, India and Australia. He has been on the Board of Directors of five different companies as well as a member of several Boards of Advisors.

www.linkedin.com/in/richard-dool

Stephen M. Dool

Steve Dool is a writer and brand consultant from New York, currently living in London. Steve has contributed to *T: The New York Times Style Magazine*, CNN Style, *GQ*, *Esquire*, *Vanity Fair*, *Garage*, and *Out*. He is also the former Style Editor at *Complex Magazine* and is the author of *How to Shine a Shoe: A Gentleman's Guide to Choosing, Wearing, and Caring for Top-Shelf Styles* (2019, Clarkson/Potter). Steve has a Bachelor of the Arts in Communication from Boston College (2007) and a Master's of Science in Marketing from the London School of Economics (2018).

Gregory J. Dool

Gregory Dool is a New York-based writer and journalist currently serving as senior editor of *Folio:* magazine. Prior to that, he was an editor at Industry Publications, Inc., a reporter at the *News of Delaware County*, and has written for *Complex* and *Min: The Media Industry Newsletter*. He graduated from Villanova University in 2013, with a B.A. in English.

Rachel Beardsley

Rachel Beardsley is originally from the United States, but is currently based in London, where she works in the tech industry. She received her MA (Hons) degree in Art History and Modern History from the University of St. Andrews in 2013, before heading to University College London for her MA in European History, graduating in 2015.

Made in the USA
Middletown, DE
28 January 2020

83872824R00272